In Defense of
THE RELIGIOUS RIGHT

In Defense of
THE RELIGIOUS RIGHT

*Why Conservative Christians Are the
Lifeblood of the Republican Party
and Why That Terrifies the Democrats*

PATRICK HYNES

NELSON CURRENT

A Subsidiary of Thomas Nelson, Inc.

Copyright © 2006 by Patrick Hynes

All rights reserved. No portion of this book may be reproduced, stored in a retrieval system, or transmitted in any form or by any means—electronic, mechanical, photocopy, recording, scanning, or other—except for brief quotations in critical reviews or articles, without the prior written permission of the publisher.

Selections from *The Holy Bible, New King James Version* (NKJV) copyright © 1982 by Thomas Nelson, Inc. Used by permission. All rights reserved.

Scripture quotations marked (KJV) are taken from the *Holy Bible*, King James Version, Cambridge, 1769.

ISBN 1-59555-051-8
ISBN 978-1-59555-051-4

Printed in the United States of America

This book is dedicated to my wife, Michelle,
whose patience is much appreciated.

CONTENTS

Introduction   ix

1. The New Paranoid Style   1

2. In the Beginning   29

3. GOP—God's Own Party?   63

4. 1994   83

5. Janet vs. Mel   109

6. Thirty Million Jesus Freaks Can't Be Wrong   127

7. Mere Christians   157

8. I Scream, You Scream,
   but We Are the Mainstream   177

9. Onward, Secular Soldiers   201

10. The Fakers, the Secularlites,
    and the Leftwing Theocrats   215

    Notes   239

    Index   255

INTRODUCTION

This book is about decent people maligned by cultural and political elites. This book is about religious conviction under fire from powerful foes. This book is about the most powerful political force in America today; a force that, despite its political and cultural influence, is the victim of the most vicious, hateful, and bigoted smear campaign in history. This book is about the Religious Right.

In the subsequent chapters of this book, we will consider those people who make up the Religious Right, examine their beliefs, analyze their impact on politics and popular culture, and debunk a whole lot of myths and outdated stereotypes along the way. This book was written in an effort to save the political armchair-quarterbacking industry. In a very funny episode of *Seinfeld,* Jerry, sitting on a kneeler in a confessional, tells a Catholic priest that he fears his dentist has converted to Judaism for the jokes. The priest asks Jerry if this offends him as a Jewish person. To which Jerry exclaims: "No, it offends me as a comedian!"

Likewise, the recent whitewashing of the Religious Right's role in our democratic processes does not really offend me as a Christian. It offends me as a political hack! Through ignorance and rank prejudice, America's pundit class has denied the Religious Right of its rightful place as the nation's largest, most consequential voting bloc.

The conservative Christian voting bloc has experienced a remarkable transformation in the last decade. On the one hand, conservative Christians have become considerably more sophisticated when expressing their worldview with outsiders. The language they now use to talk about homosexuality, abortion, and other cultural issues is far less off-putting and not nearly as exclusionary as it was during the days of the Moral Majority or the Christian Coalition. On the other hand, interestingly, while conservative Christians have become far more politically savvy, they have paradoxically become less political. Today's big players in the culture wars—Focus on the Family, the National Association of Evangelicals, megachurch pastors—are not, in their essence, political operations, as the Moral Majority and the Christian Coalition overtly were. It is only when American politics encroaches on mainstream cultural values that we see these highly organized, highly motivated, Christian-based ministries, parachurch groups, or megachurch leaders inject themselves into the political process.

But when they do, they do it in huge numbers. Whereas the Christian Coalition numbered perhaps three million members in its prime (and Jerry Falwell's Moral Majority was never that large), Pastor Ted Haggard's National Association of Evangelicals represents forty-five thousand churched and thirty million worshipers. Dr. James Dobson's radio program reaches 7.5 million listeners every day. Some megachurches are more populous than the town I grew up in.

And yet there has hardly been a corresponding increase in respect for these folks around the public square. Pundits Left and

Right wrote off the impact of 2004's moral values voters as a "myth." And the Republican Party, the current venue for political expression among America's thirty million conservative Christians, often places the agendas of its corporate financiers and its neoconservative think tank allies above these, its most loyal and abundant voters. At the time of this writing, this attitude threatened the sustainability of the GOP's control of Congress.

In researching this book, I had the pleasure of interviewing a number of leaders of the Religious Right. Their friendliness and frankness underscored my preexisting notions of Christian conservatives as wholesome, kind, convivial folks; the complete opposite of the sweaty, angry, poor, and stupid creatures of left-wing mythology.

Together we will examine the enemies of the Religious Right—what motivates *them* to engage in such brutal demonizing; what *they* stand for (and against), and what they stand to gain from diminishing the role of the Religious Right in public life.

We will also look at the Religious Left and debunk a number of their absurd declarations of piety and their flagrant distortions of Scripture to suit political ends.

We'll look at the larger political Left's feeble and insulting efforts to manufacture common cause with conservative Christians by disguising their own antibiblical worldviews behind (often misquoted) Scripture passages. We will strip bare the phony olive branch offered by the very same people who only months, weeks, or days prior accused their new friends of trying to recreate the US government into a Islamic-style theocracy.

The Religious Right is an important subgroup of American society that exercises its God-given right to free expression and political activism in the face of monstrous insults from its enemies, a segment of the American populous with a clearly defined worldview that was present at our own nation's founding and currently stands as the vanguard of societal renewal and cultural sanity.

A word about words: some readers will object to the term *Religious Right.* My friend David Limbaugh has labeled it "pejorative." He almost always tosses in a "so-called" before he uses it. Peter Sprigg from the Family Research Council recoils at the phrase. In my conversations with Focus on the Family founder, James Dobson, he spoke of the "so-called Religious Right."

Pastor Ted Haggard of New Life Church in Colorado Springs, Colorado, and president of the National Association of Evangelicals rejects the phrase as well. According to Pastor Ted, "Religious Right" calls to mind an older variation of evangelicalism, one headed by what he terms "the Big Four"—Pat Robertson, Jerry Falwell, James Dobson, and Chuck Colson. Pastor Ted considers these guys his friends, but he also believes that the energy behind evangelicalism is transferring from "the Big Four" to local pastors. Pastor Ted has set about to revive the term *evangelical,* a term Kyle Fisk of the NAE told me was beginning to die out before Pastor Ted gave it a meaningful, useful definition. ("An evangelical is someone who believes the Bible is the Word of God, that Jesus is the Son of God, and who is born again.")

I understand these objections and have agonized over whether it is appropriate to use, especially in a book defending the Religious Right from its enemies, who brandish the phrase as a smear.

In the end, however, I have come to believe that rebranding commonly used words and phrases is an exercise of the Left. They are the ones who say "reproductive health" when they mean *abortion,* "user fees" when they mean *higher taxes,* "equal rights for all" when they mean *gay marriage.*

Whether we like it or not, *Religious Right* is here to stay. It will continue to be used by the mainstream media, liberal politicians and pundits, and many, many others. So I'll use it, too. Besides, it is a uniquely apt term. These people are indeed religious and they do reside on the Right side of the political spectrum.

Elsewhere in this book, I will use the terms *demographics* and *voting blocs*. I regard these to be distinct groupings of voters that are frequently confused through the din of punditry. A demographic is a cohort of voters defined externally, based on some quantifiable piece of datum or a characteristic. For example, ethnic or age groups are demographics. Demographics are by definition homogeneous. Every member of a Latino community is Latino; every member of the fifty-to-sixty-four-year-old age group is between the ages of fifty and sixty-four. Voting blocs, on the other hand, are heterogeneous. Voting blocs are chunks of voters who behave in a certain way because of some shared worldview or set of concerns.

If we look at the Religious Right as a voting bloc, as we should, and not as a demographic, it becomes easy to understand that the Religious Right can as easily house a twenty-five-year-old African American male from Cincinnati, Ohio, as it can a seventy-year-old white woman from the Atlanta suburbs. This distinction will become important when we discuss the electoral strength of the Religious Right.

I come to this subject as a bit of an outsider. I'm not an evangelical Christian, the dominant population group of the Religious Right. I don't worship at a megachurch. And I do not use the phrase "born-again" to describe my own faith journey. Nor do my personal political views jibe with the Religious Right in every way. But on the whole, my sympathy lies with the Religious Right.

This book does not provide theological or scriptural justification for the positions held by the Religious Right. I have neither the expertise nor the credibility to comment on such. Nevertheless, there are moments in this book when I have had to explore the Scriptures and peruse the scholarship of the leading theologians. When discussing key controversies over issues as varied as abortion, gay marriage, and poverty programs, I will occasionally quote from Scripture or cite someone more knowledgeable than I in these matters.

Finally, this book is neither a history of religion in public life nor a history of the Religious Right. However, I have had to rehash some of that history to provide context to the theme of this book. Whenever possible, I have relied heavily upon experts in church and American history.

So if I'm not a member of the Religious Right, I'm not a theologian, and I'm not a historian, what grants me the credibility to write a book on the Religious Right and its role in public life? Well, I earned my chops on the front lines of American democracy as a Republican campaign operative and consultant. I have befriended and acquainted myself with thousands of Christian conservatives over the years. I have organized with them, fought alongside and against them, argued, and, yes, prayed with them.

When the Terri Schiavo tragedy struck and Leftist (and even some conservative) pundits began to call those people who wanted that poor girl to live "theocrats," I'd had enough. I know these people. They are not "theocrats." They are wonderful, caring, passionate people who pray and work for public policy that will create the best possible outcome for God's children here on Earth.

With this faithful group of people under attack like never before, I felt that it was finally time to step up to the plate.

1

THE NEW PARANOID STYLE

In December of 2004, a small group of dispirited liberal activists in Northern Virginia began to gather regularly in the Falls Church home of Richard Lawrence to commiserate about the Democratic Party's declining fortunes. Pres. George W. Bush had recently been reelected with more votes than anyone had thought possible. The Republican Party had increased its majorities in the US House of Representatives and the US Senate. It was a dark time for these self-styled progressives.[1]

Some of the members of this group had held Kerry-Edwards signs at major traffic stops and intersections in the suburbs of Washington DC during the campaign, but they couldn't honestly be called "political junkies." Some of them had protested against America's involvement in Vietnam during the early 1970s, but had agitated for or against very little since. These folks seemed to become more politically active *after* the campaign than they had been *before* it. One of them, Mary Detweiler, admitted to the *Washington Post* that she had become "very depressed" since the election. The host of these gatherings, Richard Lawrence, confessed, "I fear for my country."

The fledgling organization wanted to take action. But first they needed a name. They settled on the name, the Message Group, an ambiguous label that granted them maximum flexibility, which was important because though they had lots of passion, they still had no mission and . . . no message. They discussed producing a "biting and pertinent" flyer to distribute at high traffic Metro stops in downtown Washington DC. They invited hundreds of fellow liberal activists to future meetings. They sought input from other disgruntled Democrat volunteers.

But nothing seemed to quite meet their need to make a difference. The Message Group needed to be for—or at least *against*—something to get noticed, to build momentum. Just being angry and liberal hardly made them unique or interesting.

Frustrated by the lack of groundswell support for their still undefined cause, the Message Group finally got around to formulating an agenda. Its members started kicking around hot-button issues. Social Security? The war in Iraq? The long-established, well-heeled, liberal special interest groups in Washington had those covered, they all agreed.

Finally sixty-one-year-old Irving Wainer suggested the Message Group focus on evolution—or rather on Intelligent Design, the movement that seeks to explain the gaps in Darwinian evolution. The Message Group would dedicate itself to thwarting the spread of Intelligent Design into Northern Virginia's public schools.

Intelligent Design adherents believe life on Earth is so diverse and complex, only an intelligent force, as opposed to the blind luck of Darwin's theory, could have created it and sustained its evolutionary advance. Opponents of Intelligent Design, mostly establishment scientists and public school teachers' unions, consider this theory nothing more than warmed-over Creationism.

Battles have begun to rage in all those little checkpoints along the invisible wall between church and state, known as public schools. For if Intelligent Design is indeed Creationism repackaged, an army of liberals would have to prevent it from ever being taught in government-run institutions of learning.

THE STATE TAKES SIDES

In Dover, Pennsylvania, for example, the local school board voted six to three in October of 2004 to become the first school district in America to require science teachers to instruct students that evolution is just a theory—not a fact—and that Intelligent Design is one alternative theory that might explain how we got here. The policy led to a tame addendum to the Dover Area School District's science curriculum, which required ninth-grade Biology teachers to read the following statement to their students:

> Because Darwin's Theory is a theory, it is still being tested as new evidence is discovered. The Theory is not a fact. Gaps in the Theory exist for which there is no evidence. A theory is defined as a well-tested explanation that unifies a broad range of observations.
>
> Intelligent Design is an explanation of the origin of life that differs from Darwin's view. The reference book, *Of Pandas and People* is available for students to see if they would like to explore this view in an effort to gain an understanding of what Intelligent Design actually involves. As is true with any theory, students are encouraged to keep an open mind.[2]

The school district decided to dedicate a single day of the curriculum's nineteen-day unit of ninth-grade Biology called "The Study of Life" to the discussion of Darwin's theory and its shortcomings, followed by open dialogue about other possible theories—Intelligent Design chief among them. The session was to last ninety minutes.

Inside a month, four school board members resigned in protest. Two weeks later, a fifth board member resigned. Teachers refused to read the required statement. Then two months after the school board's vote, eleven parents of Dover students joined the American Civil Liberties Union and Americans United for Separation of Church and State to file a federal lawsuit against the school board for violating the religious liberties of the students of Dover.

"Public schools are not Sunday schools, and we must resist any efforts to make them so. There is an evolving attack under way on sound science education, and the school board's action in Dover is part of that misguided crusade. 'Intelligent Design' has about as much to do with science as reality television has to do with reality," said the Reverend Barry W. Lynn of Americans United.[3]

At a news conference announcing the lawsuit at the Pennsylvania State House in Harrisburg, a Penn State professor of Developmental Genetics and Evolutionary Morphology characterized supporters of Intelligent Design as "mentally unbalanced" people who "don't understand the world and they're trying to get the world to slow down and accommodate their thinking." Brown University Biology Professor Kenneth R. Miller testified on September 26, 2005, the very first day of the trial, that Dover's ninety-minute "open discussion" about possible alternatives to Darwin's Theory was "terribly dangerous."[4]

The case—*Kitzmiller, et al. v. Dover Area School District*—soon came to overwhelm the small Pennsylvania town. No longer was this a parochial controversy between a school board and some putatively aggrieved students. Reporters and columnists from news outlets all over the world descended on the small town in Eastern Pennsylvania (population: 1,815) to capture the local color.

The Lynchburg, Virginia, chapter of Americans United for

Separation of Church and State marched—in Lynchburg, mind you—against teaching Intelligent Design in Dover. *Salon* staff writer Michelle Goldberg tried to explain the larger controversy, by calling the case "part of a renewed revolt against evolutionary science that's been gathering force in America for the past four years, a symptom of the same renascent fundamentalism that helped propel George Bush to victory."[5]

Indeed, the Intelligent Design vs. evolution controversy is not unique to Dover. In 1999 the Kansas Board of Education voted to extirpate any reference to evolution from the state's science curriculum. The antievolution majority was voted out of office in the next election. But in 2004, the year of the "moral values" voter, the anti-evolutionists won back their majority and have pledged to fight to give Intelligent Design a fair hearing in Kansas public schools. In Missouri, seven members of the state House of Representatives have pushed a legislative measure to require "equal treatment of science instruction regarding evolution and Intelligent Design" in public schools.[6] In Georgia, the Cobb County Board of Education voted to slap a sticker on their schools' science books that read:

> This textbook contains material on evolution. Evolution is a theory, not a fact, on the origin of living things. This material should be approached with an open mind, studied carefully, and critically considered. Approved by Cobb County Board of Education Thursday, March 28, 2002.

In January of 2005, US District Judge Clarence Cooper declared the stickers, which were placed on the inside cover of the textbooks, unconstitutional. "By denigrating evolution, the school board appears to be endorsing the well-known prevailing alternative theory, creationism or variations thereof, even though the sticker does not specifically reference any alternative theories," the judge wrote.[7]

A federal judge was friendly to the ACLU et al. in the Dover case, too. Judge John E. Jones ruled in later-2005 that the Dover Area School Board's policy violated the wall of separation between church and state.

Intelligent Design vs. evolution is a struggle being fought in disparate locales. The National Center for Science Education—an Oakland, California-based organization explicitly formed to thwart the teaching of Intelligent Design in public schools—claims that since 2001 they have conducted campaigns in forty-three states.

Curiously, though, the battle never raged in Fairfax County, Virginia, until Richard Lawrence and his Message Group declared war. That's right: no one had actually demanded or even suggested that public schools in Fairfax County give equal time to Intelligent Design. In fact, the exact opposite is true. Fairfax County School Board Chairman Phillip S. Niedzielski-Eichner—a supporter of teaching evolution only in public schools—was baffled by the aggressive activism shown by the Message Group. "There's no indication this is something we have to clarify for our community or those who teach science in our schools," he explained.

It was a spectacular misfiring of the liberal bumper-sticker slogan, "think globally, act locally." The Message Group had set its sights on a phantom menace. They may as well have picketed the local school board demanding that flat-Earth theories not be inserted into the curriculum.

Undaunted, armed now with members, a name, and, finally, a reason for being, the Message Group announced itself to the world as an organization dedicated to learning if "regular citizens could take effective action to counter the Culture War initiated by the leaders of the Religious Right."

RETURN OF THE PARANOID STYLE

Understanding why the members of the Northern Virginia's Message Group would see a Religious Right conspiracy where there is none would require an entirely new psychological discipline. If they were so inclined, the greatest headshrinkers in America could dedicate their lives to the science of unraveling what political historian Richard Hofstadter famously dubbed "the paranoid style in American politics."

Writing in 1964, Hofstadter observed that while American politics had "often been an arena for angry minds," recent years had seen an explosion of mental activity. He saw it at work in the Goldwater movement, in which the "animosities and passions of a small minority" managed to get the Republican nomination for the strident Arizona senator. Behind their movement, he detected a "style of mind that is far from new and that is not necessarily right-wing." That is, the paranoid style.[8]

Hofstadter used the highly charged phrase because he decided that "no other word adequately evokes the sense of heated exaggeration, suspiciousness, and conspiratorial fantasy that I have in mind." He didn't think that Goldwater supporters were all a bunch of nuts. Rather, it was the "use of paranoid modes of expression by more or less normal people that makes the phenomenon significant."

A contemporary rewriting of "The Paranoid Style" would have to include the modern political Left's irrational myth-making and demonizing of the Religious Right. By their own admissions, the Message Group's members were motivated by "fear" and "depression" when they started their local preemptive skirmish against the Religious Right. These were among the same symptoms of the paranoid style Hofstadter enumerated in 1964.

It mattered not to members of the Message Group that the so-called Religious Right wasn't actually trying to transform the Fairfax County public school science curriculum. "If we poke a stick at them, they'll come," explained Message Grouper Wainer.

And yet, despite the shear irrationality of the Message Group's "fear" and "depression"—to say nothing of the head nodding of the millions of aggrieved American liberals who see nothing peculiar about their behavior—one can understand how the frustrations from 2004 delivered them to a place where they blame the Religious Right for something it hadn't done, wasn't doing, and hadn't planned on doing.

As the British weekly opinion magazine the *Economist* posited in January of 2006, "Hofstadter argued that the politics of paranoia is fueled by a sense of dispossession—by fury at your loss of relative power to fringe groups. In the 1960s, the right was driven by a sense that it was being eclipsed by cosmopolitans and intellectuals. Now the left thinks it is losing power to businessmen and suburbanites. It cannot believe that the north-east—the vortex of civilized American—is losing influence to the South and the West, to people who believe in God and guns, to Mr. Bush."[9]

Worse still, the sparks of liberal paranoia are too often stoked by a liberal Washington-Hollywood nexus that bookends American civilization and has created a Frankenstein monster out of the Religious Right; a depiction so cartoonish, it's almost comical.

In Washington, where white-hot rhetoric too often rules the day, the Religious Right has long been the tackling dummy of liberal politicians and their mainstream media pep squad.

Consider the relatively uncontroversial nomination of Judge

John Roberts to serve as chief justice of the United States. The United States Senate ultimately confirmed Roberts by a 77-22 margin, with half the Senate's Democrats voting for Roberts.

But this broad-based support didn't prohibit extremists in the Democratic caucus from questioning Roberts "real" agenda: to tear down the alleged wall that separates church and state.

With nothing condemnatory in his record to stymie his ascendance to the high court, liberals formulated an illusion of Roberts out of shear stereotype. Senator Dianne Feinstein (D-CA), for example, openly implied during the committee hearings that Roberts, who is Catholic, was a theocrat. "At the time, he [Pres. John F. Kennedy] pledged to address the issues of conscience out of a focus on the national interests, not out of adherence to the dictates of one's religion. And he even said, 'I believe in an America where the separation of church and state is absolute.' My question is: Do you?" Feinstein asked.[10]

When Roberts tried to explain to the senator that it isn't as simple as all that; that the First Amendment contains an "establishment clause" as well as a "free exercise" clause, and the two are sometimes in conflict, Feinstein interrupted him, "You can't answer my question, yes or no?"

Americans United's Jeremy Leaming claimed that Roberts's judicial philosophy, as exposed in his exchange with Senator Feinstein, "would threaten a return to a time where the majority religion was celebrated by the government and religious minorities and non-believers were treated as outsiders and second-class citizens."[11] And of course the *New York Times* publicly worried about the fact that Roberts is a Roman Catholic and his wife was once a member of and legal advisor to Feminists for Life.

This irrational paranoia on the Left of phantasmal "theocrats" caused twenty-two liberal senators to vote against a man who the

American Bar Association gleefully deemed "Well Qualified."

Whether things go right for the political Left, as in 1992, or whether they go wrong, as in 2004, blaming the Religious Right has become a lazy crutch for the Monday-morning quarterbacks of political journalism.

In 1992, Arkansas Gov. Bill Clinton defeated Pres. George H.W. Bush. Despite a global recession that occurred under President Bush's watch, a massive tax increase he pledged never even to consider, and the presence of a right-of-center, third-party, billionaire populist candidate in that race, most pundits came to blame Patrick Buchanan for observing during his convention speech, "There is a religious war going on for the soul of America."[12] Twelve years later, pundits would paradoxically credit a huge Republican sweep to similar rhetoric.

As liberal author Kevin Mattson has written, "I have news for you: conservatives are winning the culture wars. Ok, that might not come as a shock, but here's the scary part: They have reason to be winning. The right has done a superb job at exploiting certain weaknesses on the left; liberals, in the meantime, have become gun shy."[13] What liberals counted as a net negative for conservative Republicans in 1992 has become a cynical exploitation to win votes today. The bottom line is that the Religious Right is a useful whipping boy for liberals in Washington looking to score political points.

This tactic of bashing the politically active faithful to buoy one's own political position is not a tactic exclusive to the Left. During the 2000 Republican presidential primary, Arizona Senator John McCain was in a hotly contested battle with then-Governor George W. Bush. McCain had recently defeated Bush in the New Hampshire and Michigan primaries, but had been trounced just as soundly by Bush in South Carolina. During an ill-conceived speech in Virginia Beach, McCain decided to let 'er rip and accused the

Religious Right of being naught more than a special interest group, akin to the very fat cats he was crusading to disarm through his campaign finance reform proposal.

"We are the party of Ronald Reagan, not Pat Robertson. We are the party of Theodore Roosevelt, not the party of special interest. We are the party of Abraham Lincoln, not Bob Jones," McCain said. "They are corrupting influences on religion and politics. And those who practice them in the name of religion or in the name of the Republican Party or in the name of America shame our faith, our party, and our country."[14]

McCain went on to liken the Reverend Jerry Falwell to "Louis Farrakhan and Al Sharpton on the left." Of the Reverend Pat Robertson, McCain said, "The union bosses who have subordinated the interests of working families to their own ambitions—to their desire to preserve their own political power at all costs—are mirror images of Pat Robertson." (Incidentally, union bosses were and are exempt from McCain's onerous limitations on campaign activity.)

It was either the most courageous or the stupidest political speech of all time. But considering McCain had no record of Religious Right baiting prior to giving the speech, one suspects that the senator was searching for a target to attack, upon whom the famously pro-McCain mainstream press would gladly pig pile. And it worked. Writing about the matter for *Slate*, William Saletan stated, "In New Hampshire, South Carolina, and Michigan, McCain's enemies in the religious right—particularly Robertson and the National Right to Life Committee—tried to bludgeon him to death. . . . The cardinal rule of regicide is that if you go after the king, you had better kill him. John McCain is still alive."[15]

Tried to "bludgeon him to death"? What exactly was this controversy about? Well, not much, really. In an automated telephone message delivered to thousands of voters in Michigan, Pat Robertson said

McCain "wanted to take First Amendment freedoms from citizen groups while he gives unrestricted power to labor unions." In another phone call, Robertson urged Michiganders to call on McCain to disavow his campaign chairman Warren Rudman's sharp attack on Christian conservatives, who Rudman characterized as "antiabortion zealots, would-be censors, homophobes, bigots and latter-day Elmer Gantrys" in his autobiography.[16]

For this, Senator McCain declared leaders of the Religious Right, "agents of ignorance."

That was it: a few unflattering words about a political opponent. Again, I ask: tried to bludgeon him to death?

THE KILLER INSTINCT

Suspecting the Religious Right of a murderous impulse is a consistent theme in liberal media circles. Paul Krugman of the *New York Times* hypothesized—no *averred; averred* would be a better word—that conservative Christians were only one or two outrages away from assassinating Democrats.

During the Terri Schiavo controversy of March 2005, Krugman wrote in his column that he would go where few would dare by talking about "the threat posed by those whose beliefs include contempt for democracy itself." He likened American evangelicals to murderous Muslims in the Netherlands.

Krugman allowed that "America isn't yet a place where liberal politicians, and even conservatives who aren't sufficiently hard-line, fear assassination." However, he warned, "unless moderates take a stand against the growing power of domestic extremists, it can happen here."[17]

Yet?

That, of course, wasn't Krugman's first attack on Christians. Shortly after the 2004 election, Krugman wrote, "President Bush isn't a conservative. He's a radical—the leader of a coalition that deeply dislikes America as it is . . . thanks to a heavy turnout by evangelical Christians Mr. Bush has four more years to advance that radical agenda. . . ."[18]

Of course, the standard in Religious Right baiting was set by Michael Weisskopf in a *Washington Post* article on 1 February 1993, when he wrote, the "gospel lobby . . . does not lavish campaign funds on candidates for Congress, nor does it entertain them. The strength of fundamental leaders lies in their flocks. Corporations pay public relations firms millions of dollars to contrive the kind of grass-roots response that Falwell or Pat Robertson can galvanize in a televised sermon. Their followers are largely poor, uneducated, and easy to command."

60 Minutes pundit Andy Rooney agrees. He charged on the air that conservative Christianity resulted from "a lack of education. They [conservative Christians] haven't been exposed to what the world has to offer."[19]

Comedian Bill Maher called religion "a neurological disorder."[20]

And, apparently lacking any other explanation for America's deep sense of faith, the *Atlantic* ran a story in late 2005 suggesting religious conviction simply has to be an accident of evolution.[21]

A decade after Weisskopf offered his offensive caricature of Christians, Thomas Frank would use the word "derangement" on page one of his best-selling book, *What's the Matter with Kansas?*, to describe the tendency of some Americans (read: socially conservative Christians) to vote against their "economic self-interest" and in favor of moral values.

Frank was fairly obviously writing about poor, stupid Christians whom he alleges Republicans have duped into voting to make the rich richer and themselves poorer in return for fiery culture war rhetoric.

WHAT WOULD JIHADIS DO?

The most obnoxious fear-mongering comes in the pairing of conservative Christians and Islamic radicals, a rhetorical device that has seen an escalation in use among liberals since the dreadful terror attacks on 11 September 2001.

In the minds of a great many liberal pundits and opinion leaders, politically active evangelicals and Mohammed Atta are two peas in a pod. The story these folks have concocted—and apparently believe—is that radical Islam is not the enemy in this nation's War Against Terror. The real enemy is conservative or orthodox religious belief itself. It matters not if you wear ashes on your forehead, glue a fish symbol to your car, pray five times a day while facing east, or strap a bandolier full of deadly explosives and walk into a crowded mall. It's all the same to them.

Comparing Republicans or conservative Christians to the Taliban, the failed tin-pot dictatorship in Afghanistan, which harbored Osama bin Laden before the US-led coalition demolished it in 2001, became a cute trick of the political Left after—and even before—9/11. Kathy Sullivan, for example, the chairwoman of the New Hampshire Democratic Party, said the Republican Party was "our very own version of the Taliban" because the Republican Speaker of the New Hampshire House of Representatives and the GOP leader in the state Senate were both men.[22]

Speaking at a rally in support of the Democratic candidate for the US House of Representatives in a 2004 special election, South Dakota Democrat Senator Tim Johnson exclaimed to a cheering crowd, "How sweet it's going to be on June 2 when the Taliban wing of the Republican Party finds out what's happened in South Dakota." Senator Johnson later apologized for the hateful smear, but only after negative reaction to his remarks snowballed and threatened Democrat chances in the special election.[23]

The Interfaith Alliance, an ecumenical leftwing coalition based out of Washington DC, distributed a fundraising flyer in late 2005 that claimed the Religious Right "believes adhering to their narrow interpretation of biblical law is more important than protecting individuals from hate, violence and discrimination."

Fringe elements of the Left do not act out on this fetish alone. Indeed, according to Howard Fineman of *Newsweek*, the Democratic Party actually made a strategic decision to liken the Religious Right in America to oppressive, terror-sponsoring theocrats in the greater Middle East. Fineman wrote, "The theory goes like this. Our enemy in Afghanistan is religious extremism and intolerance. It's therefore more important than ever to honor the ideals of tolerance—religious, sexual, racial, reproductive—at home. The GOP is out of the mainstream, some Democrats will argue [this] year, because it's too dependent upon an intolerant religious right."[24]

Occasionally, the paranoid Left will alter the story a little bit. After all, there are other devious villains of history for them to compare Christians to. Like Hitler. Former *New York Times* correspondent Chris Hedges wrote, "But fascism, warned [Dr. James Luther] Adams, . . . would not return wearing swastikas and brown shirts. Its ideological inheritors would cloak themselves in the language of the Bible; they would come carrying crosses and chanting the Pledge of Allegiance."[25]

Or white supremacist. *Washington Post* columnist Colbert I. King wrote that the Religious Right "warrant as much deference as religious leaders, as do members of the Ku Klux Klan, who also marched under the cross."[26] And *New York Times* slap-fight artist

Frank Rich has likened religious conservatives to Joseph McCarthy and George Wallace.

When all the hyperbolic rhetoric becomes too much, some have attempted to prove *scientifically* that religion in general and Christianity in particular is dangerous for society. The *Journal of Religion and Society*, for example, published an article by Gregory S. Paul in which Paul asserts that the United States has a disproportionately high level of social ills, such as murders, abortions, out-of-wedlock births, suicide, etc., *because* it has such a high level of religiosity.[27]

The article was a synopsis of Paul's larger study, obtusely titled, "Cross-National Correlations of Quantifiable Societal Health with Popular Religiosity and Secularism in the Prosperous Democracies," for which he compiled data from eighteen Western democracies and concluded that Christianity is the root of all evil in America.

Legendary pollster George H. Gallup Jr. utterly eviscerated Paul's methodology and unsubstantiated conclusions,[28] but Paul's "study" and article had the desired effect. "The message to those who claim in any sense to be pro-life is unequivocal. If you want people to behave as Christians advocate, you should tell them that God does not exist," opined a columnist in the *Guardian*.[29]

When folks like Senator Gary Hart warn of the "dangers" posed by the Religious Right, when *Harper's* casts hysterical headlines, such as, "The Christian Right's War on America," this is what they are talking about. Their paranoia has convinced them that they are in personal danger, not merely of losing their freedoms, but of losing their *lives*. They have convinced themselves that America's conservative Christians pose at least as great a danger—if not a greater danger—to America than our terrorist enemies, that their ancestors are some of the most objectionable figures in history and that they are the cause of social ills.

How can one have a reasonable conversation with adherents to such unhealthy fantasies?

POP ICONOCLASTS

Popular culture has also made a whipping boy of the Religious Right. It sometimes seems that no Hollywood formula would be complete without a villainous corporate CEO, a power-hungry rogue military leader, and/or a deranged Christian.

During the 2004 election cycle, singer Linda Ronstadt said, "I think we're in desperate trouble and it's time for people to speak up and not pipe down. It's a real conflict for me when I go to a concert and find out somebody in the audience is a Republican or fundamental Christian. It can cloud my enjoyment. I'd rather not know."[30] I believe Ms. Ronstadt's remarks reflect the prevailing point of view toward conservative Christianity among those in the entertainment business.

Without question, the Nero Award for Christian Demonizing in a Comedy or Drama goes to the long running NBC hit show *Law & Order*. Virtually every season of the show's run has included a storyline in which a religious extremist kills in the name of God. The formula is almost always the same: a demur person of faith is ruled out as a murder suspect until new evidence reveals him or her as a deranged servant of God. These episodes climax in the bleary-eyed sinner-killer confessing to the brutal crime, but also claiming religious or biblical authorization. So-and-so had to die because God commanded it/he violated God's law/she was a flagrant sinner. Take your pick.

The anecdotes are legion. From a recent issue of *National Review*, I read about the Elizabethtown College theater department's dramatic interpretation of *Jesus Christ Superstar*, in which "Jesus was played by an actress and 'his' disciples were portrayed as NOW-style abortion advocates. Christ's accusers wore Pat Robertson masks. During the flogging of Jesus, images of prominent conservatives, such as Rush Limbaugh, were projected onto an overhead screen."

ABC's *Prime Time Live* with Diane Sawyer ran a special in early 2006 in search for the truth of the legend of Pope Joan. *Who?* Well, Pope Joan is a mythical character who lives in the minds of anti-Catholic bigots. They posit that Pope John VIII, who served as pontiff briefly in the ninth century, was actually a woman and that she once gave birth in the street while shuttling between the Vatican and the Laterin. Only the legend of Pope Joan did not appear in literature until 350 years after s/he was supposed to have lived and was discredited long ago as an anti-Catholic smear. (That's why you've never heard of her.) Nevertheless, ABC dedicated a full two hours of "investigative journalism," complete with interviews with feminists. Sawyer's story teased viewers with a "we may never know the truth" ending.

NBC took it down another notch by broadcasting *The Book of Daniel* about a pain-killer-addicted Episcopal priest who had a gay, Republican son, a drug-dealing daughter, and an adopted son who was sleeping with the daughter of the bishop. Jesus appeared on the show as a toked-up hipster, dispensing church-of-what's-happening-now advice and devil-may-care libertinism. The network pulled the plug after three weeks.

In January of 2006, an organization calling itself World Can't Wait ran an ad in the *New York Times* in order to inspire yet more protests marches on Washington DC. The ad accused President Bush of, among other things, attempting to establish a theocracy. Just a bunch of aggrieved leftist quacks, you say? Among the organization's members are actress Jane Fonda, novelist Kurt Vonnegut, and essayist Alice Walker.

This hostility is like a steady drumbeat. On a single day in mid-December 2005 you could read positive previews of NBC's *The Book of Daniel*. On that day you could also read in the *Economist* about the California State University system not granting course credit to children who graduate from certain Christian high schools that use a certain biology textbook because the textbook mentions Intelligent Design. Pick up your morning *Washington Times* on that day and you could read about Lt. Gordon Klingenschmitt, a navy chaplain who was fired for praying in the name of Jesus. And then you could pick up the current issue of *Newsweek*, which featured a fawning profile of Ron Howard's film adaptation of Dan Brown's *The Da Vinci Code*, a book that posits Jesus had a daughter with His wife, Mary Magdalene, and a secret order of the Catholic Church has covered it up for centuries.

Just one day's news in the ongoing battle against Americans of faith.

THE THEOCRACY LIBEL

Another curious thing worth commenting on is the way in which our old friends from the Message Group framed the culture debate in their minds: regular citizens versus the Religious Right. This frame descends directly from what I believe to be an orchestrated effort to depict members of the Religious Right—who are your next-door neighbors and workmates—as abnormal or irregular.

According to this frame, which is hardly unique to or the creation of the Message Group in Northern Virginia, the Religious Right is some kind of mysterious and maniacal population of "others" bent on taking over our schools, killing nonbelievers, and hastening the apocalypse through environmental degradation, not to mention the balance of extraordinary claims and hyperbolic characterizations once reserved for Martians, Commies, and the Tri-Lateral Commission.

The most extreme variant of this attack holds that these religious zealots are trying to remake American democracy into a theocracy.

In a truly bizarre essay in the *New York Review of Books* on October of 2005, Garry Wills revealed a level of religious paranoia not seen in American politics for decades.[31] Wills, an academic and popular historian, lashed out at what he called a Catholic "gang of four," who, he implied, has a disproportionate and secretive influence on American domestic policy. Wills named names: Fr. Richard John Neuhaus, Michael Novak, George Weigel, and Joseph Fessio, to whom Wills ominously refers as "the present pope's men in America."

These four Catholics head up a "fringe government" that has co-opted the electoral enthusiasm of evangelical Christians under the principle that "a collection of aggrieved minorities must seize the levers of power in every way possible."

Because the president of the United States often calls on these men for advice (the essay even features a damning photo of President Bush shaking hands with Mr. Weigel), Wills—who is himself Catholic—leads the reader to believe that these four are secretly running America's domestic policy.

But who do they really work for? In a Kennedy-era-sounding conclusion, Wills implies that the "gang of four" pulls the strings for the Vatican, making the American president dance: "Given the resemblance between the strategies for governing from the margins, it is easy to see how well placed is the Catholic gang of four I began with. Its members are perfectly able to serve as both the Pope's men and [Karl] Rove's men, for reciprocally strengthening reasons. They are at the interface between two systems of power exercised from the fringes."

I asked Fr. Richard John Neuhaus about this charge. His answer betrayed a bewildered exasperation and a resignation that this kind of hysteria would remain a permanent blemish on our public dialogue.

"There is much hysteria and evidence of 'the paranoid style in American politics' on the Left today," he told me. "See the full page ad in the *New York Times* this week comparing President Bush with Hitler and warning against the threat of 'theocracy.' There have always been hysterics on both the Left and the Right. One hopes the paranoia on the Left is not a permanent feature and will be marginalized in due course, but I expect it will be a major feature of our political life for the next several years. It is an understandably panicked reaction to the demise of belief systems passionately held, ranging from socialism to dogmatic secularism."

The theocracy libel has become a stock talking point of the paranoid Left. "Jesus is not a theocrat," Clint Willis writes. "Theocrats among us back up their agendas with Gospel passages that portray a self-important and intolerant Jesus. Their Jesus is an invention of the early Christians, who had their own emotional and political agendas."[32]

"Where else [but in America] do we find fundamentalists zeal, a rage at secularity, religious intolerance, fear of and hatred for modernity?" asks Willis. "We find it in the Muslim world, in al Qaeda and in Saddam Hussein's Sunni loyalists."

Gary Hart calls conservative Christians the "New American Theocrats." And then he (again) goes off the deep end:

If twenty-first-century Americans try to join the church to politics they will do nothing but restore the frightful age of

medieval Europe. Popes will be selecting kings and kings will
be dethroning popes. Only murderous mayhem can ensue,
and only some future Machiavelli will know how to advise
the prince to manipulate the church to ensure his own
power.[33]

The paranoid style is strong. It can even cause smart people to
write really dumb things. In an otherwise thoughtful and considered
article on the "under God" controversy then before the US Supreme
Court, Leon Wieseltier wrote this little cutie in the 12 April 2004
edition of the *New Republic*: "Why do the God-inebriated opponents of the separation of church and state in America, the righteous
citizens who see God's hand in everything that Fox News reports,
insult the Founders by revising and even rejecting their God?"

Another common slur against conservative Christians posits
that these repressed holy rollers are obsessed with sex. "In our midst,
there is a collection of individuals who—politically incorrect as it
may be to say it—have an unhealthy obsession with gay sex. This
group, of course, is the religious right," opines Hans Bjordahl in the
Boulder Weekly.[34]

William Fischer of the InterPress News Service couldn't agree
more: "So the issues most trumpeted by the so-called religious right
are about how we got here, how we reproduce ourselves, how we
should die, the kinds of intimate relationships we should and
shouldn't have, who should judge the appropriateness of those relationships—and how our Constitution should be protecting us
against the 'devil' in our midst. In other words, by an obsession with
reproduction. SEX!"[35]

In our irony-obsessed culture, I suppose it makes some sense for
nitwits to conclude that the most sexually modest members of society are secret, night-stalking lechers. But to any normal-thinking

individual, this argument is pure drivel and hardly worth engaging.

Nevertheless, it is fun to point out that in our coastally divided, red-blue nation, one color-coded cluster of states is indeed obsessed with sex. After the 2000 election, the *Wall Street Journal* reported that "Mr. Gore carried the areas with the highest percentages [of pornographic video stores] (40% on the West Coast and 37% in New England and the Middle Atlantic states); Mr. Bush carried the area with the lowest percentage (14% in the South), and they split the rest of the country that had middling sex movie percentages."[36]

CODEBREAKERS

No self-respecting paranoid conspiracy theory can survive for long without working an unreasonable suspicion of secret communications into the fantasy. In the case of the Left's anti-Christian paranoia, the secret language is available for all to hear and interpret. Liberals believe that Republican politicians and conservative Christians have embedded their secret code into their everyday conversation.

I'm not making this up. Former US Senator Gary Hart comes off as positively off-his-rocker when trying to explain the "secret code" that Republicans and Christians ping back and forth to one another:

> Whatever the reason for remaining purposely obscure about 'faith' in what—and the creators of this new language are not saying—the early twenty-first-century religious revival as imposed upon politics relies strongly on the language of "faith" and "values.". . . They represent a kind of code, what today's pundits call "buzzwords," to those who speak the language.

Indeed, coded political communications require rather cynical use of special language, including "dog whistle" messages. *As the phrase suggests, these are communications on a frequency only the select can hear. If your ears are not keen enough to be tuned to the secret frequency, you will not be able to get the message.* These kinds of communications are meant to shut out those who are not among the elect. The need for this kind of code language in a democracy raises all kinds of questions and suspicions.[37] (Emphasis added for comical effect.)

Living life out of the public eye has undoubtedly been a difficult shock to Senator Hart's system. But these kinds of inane ramblings go beyond just one dejected former celebrity politician's discomfort in retirement. They are part-and-parcel with the paranoid style manifest in the Message Group and the mainstream media's anti-Christian crusade against their invisible nemesis.

For the record, Christians and conservative politicians don't use a special code. As Bush advisor and evangelical Christian Michael Gerson explains, "They're not code words. They're our culture."

These anecdotes are not obscure, out-of-context extractions from otherwise rational and fair speeches, columns, and public utterances. Instead, they represent the dominant and pervasive thinking of political and cultural elites.

LESS WINNED AGAINST THAN WINNING

The Religious Right is simply the most maligned group of Americans in the country. They have been blamed, mocked, ridiculed, chastised, libeled, slandered, demonized, scapegoated, belittled, decried, scorned, insulted, smeared, disparaged, and mythologized by opinion leaders and activists who do not know what the Religious Right is, do not understand what it believes, and have personal and political stakes in seeing it marginalized.

Amidst this pervasive shroud of hyperbole and fear-mongering from our nation's "leaders" and the fabulists of the Left Coast, is it any real surprise that the hypersensitive liberals of Northern Virginia would conclude in their hour of grief that the Religious Right is out to get them? As Rice University professor William Martin has explained, "To many, the Religious Right is an obstreperous demon that threatens to upset the valuable balance of religious and secular interests and to create a repressive theocracy that will trample on the freedoms of all those who do not share its theological and political beliefs."[38]

It is axiomatic that political organizations and parties Left and Right demonize their opponents as a matter of course. But it is a foundational premise of this book that the demonization of the Religious Right is the most successful and thorough demonization in American political history, having enrolled respected politicians, the news media, the entertainment industry, Internet pundits, academia, and even rank-and-file leftwing activists like the members of the Message Group in Northern Virginia in a crusade of ignorance and hatred.

Or perhaps it has been the *least* successful exercise in demonization—for the Left's crusade against the Religious Right has come at an extraordinary price for the Democratic Party.

Religious voters have an almost complete and irreparable distrust of the Democratic Party today. This has resulted in the Democrats' structural minority in the US House of Representatives, its persistent minority in the US Senate, and a political realignment that very nearly gives the Republican Party the requisite number of presidential electors right out of the gate.

As with all crises, this one has opened a rift in the Democratic Party, one barely visible through the mainstream media's soft lens, but a very real one nonetheless. Three factions have responded to this crisis in three incompatible ways. The first group, the secular humanists, seeks to write off religious voters altogether and proceed in the Democratic Party's campaign of demonization. The second group, the Religious Left, seeks an end to the campaign of demonization and to find "common ground" with rank-and-file Religious Rightists on issues such as poverty and the environment. This group nevertheless remains hostile to the "leaders" of the Religious Right.

The last group—let's call them the Fakers—wants to use all the imagery and language of the Religious Left to trick conservative Christians into believing there is common ground to be found. The two most prominent members of this group, Senator Hillary Clinton and Democrat National Chairman Howard Dean, sit by while the campaign of demonization rages on.

However, as difficult as it is for Democrats to overcome the electoral obstacles that stand between them and conservative Christians, it is the Republican Party that has the most to lose by mistreating this important voting bloc. Worse, the Republicans in Washington have sometimes behaved as though mistreating them was their goal.

In March of 2006, the Family Research Council released a poll that ought to have been troubling for Republican strategists. At the time, the Republicans in Congress were struggling mightily; they had the worst favorability ratings in the history of congressional public opinion, and some Republicans in Congress had become enveloped in the shadow of various ethics scandals that certainly did not seem to impart the kinds of moral values some political analysts credited with the Republican majority.

Some pundits blamed President Bush's tumbling popularity as

the reason for congressional GOP decline. Still others blamed the ethics scandal, or disunity in the House and Senate Republican caucuses. Or the war in Iraq. Or the massive increases in government spending.

But the Family Research Council survey revealed that 63 percent of voters felt that "the Republican Party has not kept its promises to moral values voters." Now, some conservative pundits consider moral values a "myth" and would therefore fluff off such an eye-popping statistic. Some Republican bigwigs regard Christian conservatives to be a useful part-time ally, good for churning out votes, but hardly worth placating. Indeed, something of that old ghost who whispers the Religious Right hurts, rather than helps, Republicans still haunts the halls of power in Washington. But as we will examine in subsequent chapters, the Religious Right is the Republican Party's indispensable voting bloc, representing thirty million conservative evangelicals and Roman Catholics. Without the Religious Right, the GOP would never have obtained power in Congress in 1994, and they never would have reasserted their control over Washington in 2004. And yet GOP congressional leaders appear to have forgotten who put them into power. And this obstinately dismissive attitude might cost them that power.

2

IN THE BEGINNING

Is America a Christian nation?

Hold on. Don't answer that. Your immediate response is probably: Of course it is. Don't be ridiculous. What a stupid question.

You might point to the fact that over 84 percent of Americans consider themselves Christians.[1] That God plays a starring role in most of our nation's founding documents. That Congress and the Supreme Court open their respective sessions with tributes to His divine inspiration and appeals that He grant them wisdom and discernment. That the president of the United States takes the oath of his high office with one hand on the Holy Bible and concludes the oath with an appeal to God for help. You could hold out your palm with various coins that read "In God We Trust." You could point out that the Pledge of Allegiance—our nation's creed, in a sense—asserts ours is "one nation under God."

And you would, of course, be right. Unfortunately, it isn't that simple. You see, a vocal minority of the American public refuses to acknowledge our Christian heritage. These heritage-deniers are powerful people. They run universities and public schools; they hold high public office; they wear black robes; they decide what is broadcast on the news and printed in your newspaper. This elite is not merely ignorant of what contemporary Americans of faith believe and how they live their lives, but they are openly hostile to those beliefs—and paranoid. They can't possibly imagine that the Founding Fathers, those brilliant architects of our democracy, were themselves Americans of faith.

And yet, no debate defines the controversy over the Religious Right and its role in American politics in quite the same way as this one. It is on this specific point that the demonization campaign, fueled by paranoia and waged against the Religious Right, rises or falls. For if America is a Christian nation, then the Religious Right has a legitimate claim as defenders of our cultural and political heritage. But if we are not, in fact, a Christian nation, if we are a secular state, officially and in spirit, then the leaders and members of the Religious Right are political heretics.

A lot is at stake in how we answer the question, "Is the United States a Christian nation?" Some powerful people desperately want that answer to be no.

HATE THE SAINT, LOVE THE SILENCE

When Lieutenant General Boykin, deputy undersecretary of Defense for intelligence, told a reporter in October of 2003 that radical Muslims hate America "because we're a Christian nation," he had no idea his words would ignite a firestorm of controversy. Boykin thought he was merely stating a fact; a fact, by the way, that Osama bin Laden, America's archenemy, would probably endorse.

Nevertheless, Senator Joseph Lieberman (D-CT) called Boykin's remarks "hateful."[2] Democrat Congressman John Conyers (D-MI) responded by saying, "It is outrageous that someone who holds such extreme, close-minded, zealous views would be allowed such a prominent position in our military."[3]

Boykin eventually apologized. And the message went out across the nation: say what you know to be true about our Christian heritage, and some very powerful people will humiliate you in public.

Another favorite technique is to assert that the very phrase "Christian nation" is anti-Semitic. Author Marty Jezer wrote, "Anti-Semitism in America, except on the margins of society, rarely includes overt acts of violence and discrimination. It is usually more subtle, expressed politically in the belief that the United States is a Christian nation or, among evangelical and some other fundamentalist Christians, that Jews cannot find salvation unless they accept Christian dogma."[4]

Former *Crossfire* cohost Michael Kinsley grilled former Mississippi Gov. Kirk Fordice years ago for declaring the United States a Christian nation. "The less we emphasize the Christian religion the further we fall into the abyss of poor character and chaos in the United States of America," Fordice had said. Kinsley likened this remark to white supremacy, asking if Fordice would consider the United States a "white nation" because like Christians, whites were a majority.[5] Get it? Fordice was the governor of Mississippi (wink, wink).

But charges of anti-Semitism and racism have long been the rhetorical refuge of liberals desperately trying to avoid a serious conversation. Whenever they creep into the public dialogue, you can be sure there is something more to the story. And on this matter, there is quite a bit more. As with many contemporary controversies, this story finds its roots at the founding of this nation.

SOFT-HEADED RIGHTWING JESUS FREAKS

There are two ways of looking at our nation's founding in the contexts of Christianity. The first way is what we'll call the *traditional view*, the view that adheres to the proposition that the United States of America is a Christian nation and has been since its infancy. The second view is precisely the opposite. This view holds that the United

States is a grand historical experiment in cleaving religion from public life. We will refer to this view as the *theophobic view* and we will call those who promote this view *theophobes*.

Traditionalists believe that from the first settlements in Plymouth Bay Colony to the reelection of George W. Bush, the story of American politics is incomplete without first understanding the Christian worldview of her body politic. This nation was founded by Christians, settled and populated by Christians, and run (for the most part) by men of Christian virtue and Christian ideals. Until recently, America exercised a decidedly Christian brand of morality between her left and right coasts.

On legal matters, traditionalists are often called "accommodationists" or "nonpreferentialists" because they hold that the Constitution respects religion and each individual's right to express his religion freely. Traditionalists argue the Founders sought merely to prohibit the federal government from endorsing one sect over another and forcing all citizens to worship in that approved manner.

The evidence traditionalists present is stout: stacks of founding documents from the Declaration of Independence to the Bill of Rights to virtually all state constitutions, which, in general, express an even more strident Christian reflection of the American people. Traditionalists also have the lives and personal views of most of the Founders in their corner. John Adams once said, "Our constitution was made only for a moral and religious people. It is wholly inadequate for any other."

Theophobes, on the other hand, believe the United States is a child of the Enlightenment, that the Founding Fathers deliberately set about to construct a distinctively secular state bound together with new-fangled ideas of radical personal autonomy rather than Christian virtue and morality.

In legal circles, theophobes are known as "separationists" for their ardent commitment to the "wall of separation between church and state," which they regard as a foundational principle of our nation. Theophobes reject the Founders' religiosity as relics of a bygone era and focus their attention on the secularist ramblings of Thomas Jefferson, the principle drafter of the Declaration of Independence, and James Madison, the Father of the Constitution. Theophobes, too, present mountains of evidence. Except their evidence is a bit tainted, for it lies not in the founding documents of our country, but in judicial interpretations of those documents by academics and jurists who brought an agenda-driven worldview to the debate.

Like the liberal dad and conservative son sitting at the breakfast table in the cereal commercial, traditionalists view theophobes as hard-hearted, liberal ignoramuses with sinister motives, while theophobes think the traditionalists are soft-headed, rightwing Jesus freaks living in the past.

Who is right?

The soft-headed, rightwing Jesus freaks living in the past, of course.

TEAR DOWN THIS WALL

To settle the question, we need first to knock down the wall of separation between church and state. This wall has become an object of liberal veneration. Liberal theophobes bow down before the wall, morning, noon, and night. Theophobes insist the Founding Fathers always intended for the wall to be "high" and even "impregnable," and they think they find its bricks and mortar in the US Constitution.

Here is how the Reverend Barry Lynn of Americans United for Separation of Church and State describes Pres. George W. Bush's faith-based initiative: "The goal here is to erode the vitality of the church-state separation principle, to get a lot of judges in place who have trouble distinguishing that which is illegal and that which is sinful, and to put in place regulations—and perhaps later statutes—that make it easier to require Americans to pay for the Christianizing of the country."[6]

Bill Press writes in *How the Republicans Stole Christmas* that "tearing down the First Amendment's historic wall of separation between church and state is the express aim of religious conservatives today and they make no bones about it."[7]

Theophobes rely on ill-thought public comments by political conservatives and leaders of the Religious Right to prove a conspiracy exists to tear down that wall. Chief among these comments is Pat Robertson's 1995 quote about church-state separation: "That was never in the Constitution. However much the liberals laugh at me for saying it, they know good and well it was never in the Constitution. Such language only appeared in the constitution of the communist Soviet Union."[8]

America's children are taught to worship the "wall of separation between church and state" as the theophobes do from their very first civics lesson in grade school to their bar exam. Merely denying the concept will not cut it. Traditionalists need to engage the American public in a dialogue about the origins of that dubious principle and allow Americans to decide for themselves the merits of the idea.

This is a debate the Religious Right should want to have and one they will ultimately win. For example, by taking the above position, Reverend Lynn is operating far outside the mainstream of American opinion. Despite decades of indoctrination in our public schools, the vast majority of Americans—66 percent, in fact— "favor allowing churches and other houses of worship to apply, along with other organizations, for government funding to provide social services, such as drug counseling."[9]

As Dr. James Dobson told me, "It sounds overly simplified, but those who say that our Constitution guarantees 'freedom *of* religion, not freedom *from* religion,' have it right. Liberals only want the latter."

Hear, hear, said Father Neuhaus: "The two provisions of the one religious clause of the First Amendment are clearly aimed at protecting the free exercise of religion. For a long time the two provisions have been turned upside down, making the free exercise 'clause' subordinate to the no establishment 'clause.'"

He added, "With changes in the Supreme Court, it is reasonable to believe that is being remedied."

ANOTHER BRICK IN THE WALL

In order to adhere to the separation argument and therefore to believe the United States is a secular nation, you would have to elevate a letter written by Thomas Jefferson in 1802 to a Baptist congregation in Connecticut to the level of a founding document. Then you would have to elevate Supreme Court Justice Hugo Black (who served from 1937 to 1971) to the level of Founding Father.

During our interview, Dr. Dobson was emphatic: "[T]hat phrase [wall of separation] is not even part of our Constitution. It appeared in a personal letter written by Thomas Jefferson fifteen years after the Constitution was ratified, and the original context clearly shows Jefferson was referring to structures and institutions, not to the deeply held religious conviction of the American people."

The letter he refers to came in 1802 when Pres. Thomas Jefferson finally got around to returning a constituent letter from three elders of the Danbury Baptist Association.

Writing for the Baptist association, Nehemiah Dodge, Ephraim Robbins, and Stephen S. Nelson appealed to President Jefferson on the grounds that the Connecticut Constitution—which predated the US Constitution—recognized an established religion and this, they argued, offended the very nature of religious liberty:

> Our sentiments are uniformly on the side of religious liberty—that religion is at all times and places a matter between God and individuals—that no man ought to suffer in name, person, or effects on account of his religious opinions—that the legitimate power of civil government extends no further than to punish the man who works ill to his neighbors; But, sir, our constitution of government is not specific. Our ancient charter together with the law made coincident therewith, were adopted as the basis of our government, at the time of our revolution; and such had been our laws and usages, and such still are; that religion is considered as the first object of legislation; and therefore what religious privileges we enjoy (as a minor part of the state) we enjoy as favors granted, and not as inalienable rights; and these favors we receive at the expense of such degrading acknowledgements as are inconsistent with the rights of freemen.
>
> Sir, we are sensible that the President of the United States is not the National Legislator and also sensible that the national government cannot destroy the laws of each State, but our hopes are strong that the sentiment of our beloved president, which have had such genial effect already, like the radiant beams of the sun, will shine and prevail through all these States—and all the world—until hierarchy and tyranny be destroyed from the earth. Sir, when we reflect on your past services, and see a glow of philanthropy and goodwill shining forth in a course of more than thirty

years, we have reason to believe that America's God has raised you up to fill the Chair of State out of that goodwill which he bears to the millions which you preside over. May God strengthen you for the arduous task which providence and the voice of the people have called you—to sustain and support you and your Administration against all the pre-determined opposition of those who wish to rise to wealth and importance on the poverty and subjection of the people.[10]

The language is a bit antiquated, and it is somewhat difficult to comprehend in our bottom-line-it-for-me world what exactly the gentlemen from Connecticut were asking of the president. Essentially, they asked the president of the United States to adopt their separationist cause and to use the bully pulpit of his office to end the state of Connecticut's official relationship with the Episcopal Church. While recognizing that the president could not unilaterally overturn state laws, Messrs. Dodge, Robbins, and Nelson asked President Jefferson to broaden the establishment clause in the US Constitution—which was universally understood to prevent the establishment of a state religion at the *federal* level—to also prohibit established religions at the state level.

And President Jefferson, putatively the great separationist of history, blew them off. Here is Jefferson's reply in full:

Gentlemen,—The affectionate sentiment of esteem and approbation which you are so good as to express towards me, on behalf of the Danbury Baptist Association, give me the highest satisfaction. My duties dictate a faithful and zealous pursuit of the interests of my constituents, and in proportion as they are persuaded of my fidelity to those duties, the discharge of them becomes more and more pleasing.

Believing with you that religion is a matter which lies solely between man and his God, that he owes account to none other for his faith or his worship, that the legislative powers of government reach actions only, and not opinions, I contemplate with sovereign reverence that act of the whole American people which declared that their legislature would "make no law respecting an establishment of religion, or prohibiting the free exercise thereof," thus building a wall of separation between Church and State. Adhering to this expression of the supreme will of the nation in behalf of the rights of conscience, I shall see with sincere satisfaction the progress of those sentiments which tend to restore to man all his natural rights, convinced he has no natural right in opposition to his social duties.

I reciprocate your kind prayers for the protection and blessing of the common Father and Creator of man, and tender you for yourselves and your religious association, assurances of my high respect and esteem.

Th Jefferson
Jan. 1. 1802[11]

When Jefferson wrote, "I contemplate with sovereign reverence that act of *the whole American people* which declared that *their* legislature would 'make no law respecting an establishment of religion, or prohibiting the free exercise thereof,' thus building a wall of separation between Church and State," he punted on the issue, refusing to take up the cause of eradicating established religions in the states. "The whole American people" is a clever, Jeffersonian way of saying I'm not interested in your parochial problem. Instead, Jefferson stated that it was the constitutional policy of the *federal* government never to establish a religion, exactly as other Founders (and modern-day Religious Rightists) contended.

The real importance of this mythical letter lay in President Jefferson's reaffirmation of states' rights. But that's not what liberals have gotten out of it. The gravity of this letter has been debated almost as much those fateful words "wall of separation between church and state," themselves. What exactly was Jefferson trying to accomplish with this letter? Was it merely, as former Chief Justice of the United States William Rehnquist called it, "a short note of courtesy"?[12] Or was it a profound proclamation designed to clear the air over the confusing First Amendment: "Congress shall make no law respecting an establishment of religion, nor prohibit the free exercise thereof"? And by the way, what the heck does *that* mean?

MY BABY, SHE WROTE ME A LETTER

Rice University Sociology professor William Martin has written that Jefferson was up to something much grander than polite correspondence with his constituents: "On close inspection, it appears the separationists have the correct interpretation of Jefferson's letter. Far from dashing off a perfunctory mollifying letter to a disgruntled group of sectarians, the president regarded his response to their appeal as a signal opportunity to reiterate his long-standing convictions. So concerned was he to strike the right tone that he asked Attorney General Levi Lincoln to review what he had written."[13]

At least Professor Martin went to the effort of weighing the evidence. Liberal commentator Bill Press gave the Constitution no such courtesy. "Was this . . . just some private, personal letter Jefferson dashed off before powdering his wig?" Press writes. "Hardly. Before posting it, he first sought the advice of Attorney General Levi

Lincoln and Postmaster General Gideon Granger because, Jefferson wrote, he wanted his message to serve the purpose of 'sowing useful truths and principles among the people, which might germinate and become rooted among their political tenants.'"[14]

But the theophobes have it wrong.

Jefferson didn't ask Lincoln for his advice on the letter because Lincoln was his attorney general. The letter was not a legal document. In fact, this constituent letter had no bearing on public policy whatsoever. Jefferson sought the advice of Lincoln because Lincoln was a *New Englander* (so was Gideon Granger, by the way), and Jefferson was afraid the New England gentlemen in Connecticut would find his letter insulting.

As James Hutson, chief of the Manuscript Division of the Library of Congress, has written, "That Jefferson consulted two New England politicians about his messages indicated that he regarded his reply to the Danbury Baptists as a political letter, not as a dispassionate theoretical pronouncement on the relations between government and religion. His letter, he told Lincoln in his New Year's Day note, was meant to gratify public opinion in Republican strongholds like Virginia, 'being seasoned to the Southern taste only.'"[15]

Jefferson had written a letter he knew would get circulated publicly (it appeared in a Massachusetts newspaper shortly after it arrived in Connecticut), and he sought political advice about its contents from his underlings more intoned to New England sensibilities, a nineteenth-century variation of "how's this gonna play in Peoria?"

Liberals have made altogether too much of the Jefferson letter. In fact, there is no evidence the letter caused a political splash at the time. Rather, it languished in relative obscurity for the better part of 150 years until 1947 when Justice Hugo Black, writing for the majority of the Supreme Court in *McCollum v. Board of Education*, treated it as though it were the Constitution itself.

In *McCollum v. Board of Education*, the Court decided that taxpayer-funded property could not be used for religious education purposes, which was uncontroversial enough. But in his opinion, Black badly distorted the First Amendment and Jefferson's letter.

"Neither a state nor the Federal Government can, openly or secretly, participate in the affairs of any religious organizations or groups, and vice versa. In the words of Jefferson, the clause against establishment of religion by law was intended to erect 'a wall of separation between Church and State,'" wrote Black.[16]

Obviously, the First Amendment is quite clear that "*Congress* shall make no law respecting an establishment of religion," while it is silent on state governments doing so. But even more curious is the fact that Black references Jefferson's letter despite Jefferson's explicit refusal to denounce the establishment of religion by the several states. The very purpose of the original letter from the Danbury Baptist Association was to recruit Jefferson into their cause, something President Jefferson refused to do at the time, but which Justice Black enthusiastically did almost a century-and-a-half later.

What's more, what the hell was Hugo Black thinking basing the Court's decision in a major First Amendment case on a constituent letter meant to score political points in Virginia? Present-day conservatives anxious about Justice Anthony Kennedy's use of European public opinion to decide cases of American jurisprudence should take note.

Imagine a piece of constituent mail being taken so seriously today. The very idea is absurd!

Nevertheless, while it's clear liberals—Hugo Black chief among them—made a mountain out of Jefferson's molehill, it is equally clear that among the Founding Fathers, Thomas Jefferson was especially skeptical of orthodox Christianity. Jefferson was a self-professed Deist.

While we can assume that his letter doesn't rise to the level of serious theology, serious philosophy, or serious governance, Jefferson was sincere in his desire to build up some hearty distance between church and state. . . . He just had this thing called the Constitution that prevented him from doing so.

JEFFERSON'S HAND

The words and public deeds of Thomas Jefferson are often appropriated by both sides of the debate over our Christian heritage. Jefferson was a sometimes-harsh critic of organized religion, did not believe in the divinity of Christ, and certainly did not buy into the Trinity. Moreover, for a period of time in his life, Jefferson did not think much of Jesus of Nazareth, once calling him "a man of illegitimate birth, of a benevolent heart, enthusiastic mind, who set out without pretensions to divinity, ended in believing them [his followers], and was punished capitally for sedition."[17] Jefferson later altered his view of Jesus, however. After years of studying Scripture, he came to see Jesus as history's foremost ethicist.

That's one reason why it is so hard to use Thomas Jefferson as an example of colonial or revolutionary thinking on religion in public life. His views on religion, in general, and Christianity, in particular, were complex, often contradictory, and as is the case with most people, evolved over time.

Consider, for example, the historical conundrum of this high-profile fellow who refuses to accept the divinity of Jesus Christ still attending church throughout his entire public career, donating handsome sums of money to various Christian churches, and even establishing the first National Day of Prayer. What was Jefferson up to?

The answer is simple. Both theophobes and traditionalists can use words and examples from Jefferson's life in pursuit of their adversarial causes because Thomas Jefferson was first and foremost a shrewd national politician, and he had to keep up appearances, no matter what he believed privately.

Throughout most of his life as a public figure, Jefferson was brutally attacked by his political opponents for being an atheist. The charge dogged him for years and, judging from his private notes, clearly got under his skin. Federalist politicians claimed in the 1800 campaign for the presidency, for example, that Jefferson was an atheist in league with French revolutionaries in a plot to destroy Christianity.

The *Gazette of the United States* wrote of that campaign, "At the present solemn moment the only question to be asked by every American laying his hand on his heart, is Shall I continue in allegiance to God—and a religious president; or impiously declare for Jefferson—and no God!!!"

But why would an "atheist" attend church so frequently, as Jefferson did? Why would an atheist donate to churches across Virginia? Why would an atheist make public displays of piety, especially during election time?

First, Jefferson was *not* an atheist. Second, America *is* a Christian nation, and Jefferson knew it. While he wasn't personally concerned about getting right with God, he was concerned about *appearing* to be getting right with God in order to get elected. Jefferson knew an atheist could not become a significant national figure—let alone president of the United States—in Christian America, so he carefully groomed his public image as someone who respected the gods.

Think of Bill Clinton exiting church, Bible in hand, as he admits to having lied about having "sex with that woman." As Kevin Seamus Hasson of the Becket Fund for Religious Liberty has written, "So in much the same way that Bill Clinton campaigned for governor of Arkansas by singing in the choir at televised church services, Jefferson said he was, too, religious."[18]

The Federalists' vicious attacks against Jefferson presuppose a society that expects their leaders to be men of faith. And Jefferson's clever political reaction underscores that presupposition.

MADISON HAS THE FLOOR

The only other Founding Father worth his salt according to the theophobes was James Madison, the Father of the Constitution. As Bill Press has written, "James Madison was perhaps the only man in America more dedicated than Thomas Jefferson to building a healthy distance between church and state. He was, in fact, fanatical about it."[19]

Madison was the "floor leader" for Thomas Jefferson's Virginia Bill on Religious Freedom, a measure to separate permanently and inalterably the government of Virginia from any established religion. The measure was popular among religious minorities, such as Jews, Presbyterians, and Baptists, because it directly challenged the political strength of the Church of England in Virginia.

Principally a law to prohibit tax dollars from being used to pay clergy, the bill nevertheless expounded on some broader concepts:

> Be it enacted by the General Assembly, That no man shall be compelled to frequent or support any religious worship, place or ministry whatsoever, nor shall be enforced, restrained, molested or burdened in his body or goods, nor shall otherwise suffer on account of his religious opinions or belief; but that all men shall be free to profess, and by argument to maintain, their opinion in matters of religion, and that the same shall in no wise diminish, enlarge, or affect their civil capacities.

Incidentally, elsewhere in the text comes some very strong language that modern-day pro-abortion extremists might not appreciate: "To compel a man to furnish contributions of money for the propagation of opinions which he disbelieves and abhors, is sinful and tyrannical. . . ." But I digress . . .

During debate on the Virginia Bill on Religious Freedom and focusing on an alternate piece of legislation floated by Patrick Henry, who supported the Commonwealth's continued establishment of Anglicanism, Madison delivered an impassioned speech titled "A Memorial and Remonstrance *Against Religious Assessments* [i.e., involuntary church taxes]."

It bears noting at this point that if James Madison were to regenerate and take the floor in some public setting today and declare that under no circumstances should the Commonwealth of Virginia compel people to attend church or use taxpayer funds to pay priests' salaries, members of the Religious Right would look at one another quizzically, shrug their shoulders, and say, "Um . . . okay."

Theophobes have extracted a whole lot of meaning from some very narrow and specific language; language modern-day "theocrats" in the Religious Right would hardly find objectionable. "The activities of the so-called Religious Right in no way violate the principle of the separation of church and state," says Dr. Dobson.

Moreover, some historians posit Madison was attempting to fan the public flames of bitterness against the Church of England in order to recruit religious minorities into the revolutionary cause.

It is clear that the controversies that led to the drafting and lobbying of the Virginia Bill on Religious Freedom involved an English entity levying a tax on Virginia shop owners and farmers, nothing more, however far Jefferson and Madison decided to take it. In addition, the fact that similar laws were not enacted in the other colonies—eight others of which had established churches—

indicates that Jefferson and Madison's drive to marry their revolutionary campaign with antiestablishmentarianism was uniquely their own.

Ironically, James Madison's motives in promoting the Bill on Religious Freedom placed the Religious Right forever in his debt. Until then, most of early America had come to accept the freedom of conscience as axiomatic. It was hardly a revolutionary tocsin to say you can think what you want to think. Madison was concerned, rather, about the freedom of religious expression, not merely religious conscience. This is important because, as we will examine in subsequent chapters, the prevailing view of many on the political Left holds that Americans have a right to think and believe what they want about religion, they just need to keep it to themselves.

Madison said, "Nuts to that!" The right to free expression of one's religion was inalienable because, Madison believed, our duty to our Creator was paramount to our duty to the state. So, said Madison, "We maintain therefore that in matters of Religion, no man's right is abridged by the institution of Civil Society and that Religion is wholly exempt from its cognizance."

By making free *expression* the essence of religious liberty in America, rather than free *thoughts* about religion, Madison—a putative opponent, if liberals are to be believed, of the Religious Right—helped to codify our nation's most powerful freedom of all.

SO WHAT HAPPENED?

When Madison tried to expand his ideal of a proper church-state relationship (one that keeps them eternally distinct) from Virginia to the whole United States of America during the Constitutional Convention of 1789, his efforts fell flat. If there is a singular failure on the part of the Father of our Constitution, it was his inability to inspire the same strict separationist worldview in his fellow statesmen.

Madison stood on the floor of the hall in Philadelphia in the spring of 1778 to propose the following language for what would eventually become the religious language of the First Amendment to the Constitution:

> The civil rights of none shall be abridged on account of religious belief or worship, nor shall any national religion be established, nor shall the full and equal rights of conscience be in any manner, or on any pretext, infringed.

And . . .

> No State shall violate the equal rights of conscience, or the freedom of the press, or the trial by jury in criminal cases.

Madison was attempting to do three things with these words: (1) to protect individual religious conscience from the federal government; (2) to prohibit the establishment of a national religion; and (3) to prohibit the states from violating "the equal rights of conscience."

The other framers adopted Madison's approach to the federal prohibition on religious establishment, though they watered it down somewhat from Madison's original and added "free exercise thereof" language.

But they specifically rejected Madison's idea that the Constitution should prohibit states from "violating the equal right of conscience." That is to say, the US Constitution deliberately protects the rights of states to decide matters of conscience on their own. Again, it was not until Justice Hugo Black misappropriated the Fourteenth Amendment and applied it to the First Amendment (along with Jefferson's notorious letter) that the idea that states had no right to establish a religion took hold.

Now, I don't write this to suggest that Michigan or Illinois or New Hampshire ought to go out and establish a state religion. But I do write it to impart to the reader the fundamental truth that the framers of the Constitution believed states *could* establish a religion if they wanted to. Several of the original states did, in fact, have established religions that predated the ratification of the US Constitution and did not disestablish their respective state religions until, in many cases, decades later.

Nevertheless, even after these states disestablished their official religions, forty-nine states of the Union drafted, ratified, and amended their Constitutions to pay explicit tribute to God, the source of our freedoms, and to the Christian founding of our representative democracy. "Over the next 175 years or so [since the ratification of the US Constitution]," write Michael Novak and Ashley Morrow, "as new states entered the Union, the people of all but one of the states (Oregon) took care to give their belief in God prominence of place in the preambles of their state constitutions."

Novak and Morrow itemized the explicitly Christian tones of each state's constitution. Among them were the following:

Arizona, 1911: "We the people of Arizona, grateful to Almighty God for our liberties, do ordain this Constitution."

Illinois, 1870: "We the people of the State of Illinois, grateful to Almighty God for the civil, political and religious liberty which he hath so long permitted us to enjoy and looking to Him for a blessing on our endeavors . . . do ordain and establish this Constitution for the State of Illinois."

Maryland, 1867: "We the people of the State of Maryland, grateful to Almighty God for our civil and religious liberty, and taking into our serious consideration the best means of establishing a good Constitution in this State for the sure foundation and more permanent security thereof, declare . . ."

North Carolina, 1868: "We, the people of the State of North Carolina, grateful to Almighty God the Sovereign Ruler of Nations, for the preservation of the American Union and the existence of our civil, political and religious liberties, and acknowledging our dependence on Him for the continuance of those blessings to us and our posterity, do, for the more certain securities thereof and for the better government of this State, ordain and establish this Constitution."[20]

Shall I go on?

UNLIKELY HEROES

Theophobes are correct about Jefferson and Madison insofar as these two Founders envisioned a relatively bright line between church and state (though hardly as bright as the line modern-day theophobes envision). But they are wrong in applying their own antipathy to religion to those two Founders.

James Madison—generally viewed as the more hard-core separationist of the two—fought throughout his life for the principle of religious freedom, not the squelching of religious expression. As Joseph Loconte has written:

A wide-eyed and youthful James Madison, traveling in Culpeper County in Virginia, came upon a jail that housed half a dozen Baptist preachers, held simply for publishing their religious views. Madison bristled with indignation at the "diabolical Hell conceived principle of persecution." Writing to his friend William Bradford, he ended with a lament: "So I leave you to pity me and pray for Liberty and Conscience to revive among us."[21]

This anecdote clearly puts Madison at odds with theophobes who aggressively encouraged government investigations into the "rights of conscience" of modern-day Religious Rightists. For example, during the 2004 campaign for president, both the *New York Times* and National Public Radio ran stories which all but begged the federal government to launch investigations against (and potentially revoke the tax exempt status of) religious institutions because these institutions had encouraged their members to vote. They hadn't endorsed any candidate; they had simply encouraged civic participation.

Madison and Jefferson would have gagged at such overbearing attempts by the federal government to regulate the "free exercise" of religion.

Jefferson and Madison were above all else republicans. These two fellows thought they were founding a nation based on principles of federalism, individual liberties, and freedom. No one with a right mind (or without a political agenda) would ever argue that Jefferson and Madison thought they were constructing a behemoth of a federal government, complete with thousands of departments, a three-trillion-dollar budget, and a federal income tax.

If these two Founders were to mosey through downtown Washington DC today, they wouldn't get bent out of shape over the fact that Moses and the Ten Commandments are on display in the Supreme Court or that our coins say, "In God We Trust." They would be driven to drink over the sad fact that the nation they helped found and the federalist system they helped construct has become so unrecognizable. They would be less upset about prayer in public schools than they would be to find out that federal tax dollars are used to finance local schools at all.

Jefferson and Madison therefore make for strange bedfellows with the modern political Left. And yet, they are the only two Founders the theophobes can legitimately cling to. As we have seen, the views of these two Founders are not exactly in concert with those of the theophobes, but they're as close as we are likely ever to find in a country in which the third president of the United States had to pretend to worship a do-gooder of "illegitimate birth" just to maintain his political viability.

THE THING WITH THE GUYS IN THE PLACE

By conscripting Jefferson and Madison on to their "team," liberal theophobes have created the impression that "the guy" who wrote the Declaration of Independence and "the guy" who wrote the Constitution were strict separationists.

But in addition to those premises being untrue in the first place, theophobes face the unhelpful fact that neither of those documents was a solo project. Both the Declaration and the Constitution were collaborative efforts among men of disparate backgrounds and various levels of personal piety.

So what about those *other* Founding Fathers—you know, the fifty-six men who signed the Declaration of Independence and the fifty-five who crafted the US Constitution?

Father Neuhaus held forth on this subject: "The Founders were a mixed company. A very few were of the Jeffersonian Deist persuasion while most understood themselves to be committed Christians in the Puritan, Congregationalist, Calvinist streams of thought. The portrayal of the Founders as radical secularists is increasingly debunked by contemporary scholarship."

So, did *those other guys* have anything to say about our national Christian heritage?

Charles Pinckney of South Carolina and John Langdon of New Hampshire, both signers of the US Constitution, were founders of the American Bible Society. James McHenry, who represented Maryland at the Constitutional Convention, was the founder of the Baltimore Bible Society. Rufus King of Massachusetts helped found a Bible society for Anglicans and once stated, "The law established by the Creator extends over the whole globe, is everywhere and at all times binding upon mankind. . . . [This] is the law of God by which he makes his way known to man and is paramount to all human control."

Abraham Baldwin of Georgia signed the Constitution. He was a chaplain in the Revolution and considered the youngest theologian in America at the time.

When debate over the Constitution got testy, Ben Franklin—who is sometimes conscripted by the theophobes along with Jefferson and Madison—urged the delegates to appeal to God's guidance to see the struggle through:

> All of us, who were engaged in the struggle, must have observed frequent instances of a superintending Providence in our favor. And have we now forgotten that powerful friend? Or do we imagine we no longer need its assistance? I have lived, sir, a long time; and the longer I live, the more convincing proofs I see of this Truth, that God governs in the affairs of men. And if a sparrow cannot fall to the ground without his notice, is it probable that an empire can rise without his aid?

The old man then called for a formal prayer at the beginning of each morning's sessions.

William Few from Georgia made his motives clear when he said, "I can safely promise that neither my tongue, nor my pen, nor purse shall be wanting to promote what appears so inconsistent with humanity and Christianity."

We could go on.

Of the fifty-five delegates to the Constitutional Convention, thirty-nine of whom signed the Constitution itself, not one was a non-Christian religious dissenter. Not one atheist. Not one Muslim. Not a Wiccan, a Satanist, nor a Buddhist. There were thirty-one Episcopalians, sixteen Presbyterians, eight Congregationalists, three Quakers, and two each of Catholics, Methodists, Lutherans, and Dutch Reform.

The document's draftsman, Gouverneur Morris of Pennsylvania, had this to say about the importance of religion in public life: "There must be religion. When that ligament is torn, society is disjointed and its members perish. The nation is exposed to foreign violence and domestic convulsion. Vicious rulers, chosen by vicious people, turn back the current of corruption to its source. They take bribes. They sell statutes and decrees. They sell honor and office. They sell their conscience. They sell their country. By this vile traffic they become odious and contemptible. . . . But the most important of all lessons is the denunciation of ruin to every state that rejects the precepts of religion."

What about the Father of our country, George Washington? Here is another figure from our history that theophobes like to conscript into their cause. James Thomas Flexner, who wrote a four volume biography of Washington, for example, wrote: "Like Franklin and Jefferson, he was a Deist."

No, he wasn't. Washington was baptized a member of the Church of England and regularly attended church in Alexandria, Virginia. And even though he was the closest thing to a political Messiah our nation ever conceived, he understood his proper role in his relationship with the Creator. "It would be improper to omit, in this first official act, my fervent supplications to that Almighty Being who rules over the universe, who presides in the councils of nations and whose providential aid can supply every human defect. . . . No people can be bound to acknowledge and adore the Invisible Hand which conducts the affairs of men more than the people of the United States," stated Washington during his first inaugural address.

In a letter to William Gordon on 13 May 1776, Washington wrote, "No Man has a more perfect Reliance on the alwise, and powerful dispensations of the Supreme Being than I have nor thinks his aid more necessary."

Deism is the belief in a blind watchmaker god, an impersonal deity who plays no role in our lives. Why would Washington rely on God and think His aid necessary if he were a Deist?

As for Ben Franklin, as we noted above, he had a strange way of reaching out to the dead, detached god of Deism. Moreover, in his "Information to those who would remove to America," sort of an eighteenth-century tourist brochure, Franklin wrote of America, "Atheism is unknown there; Infidelity rare and secret so that persons may live to a great Age in that Country, without having their Piety shocked by meeting with either an Atheist or an Infidel."

We have barely scratched the surface of the empirical and anecdotal evidence supporting the proposition that the Founders intended for the United States of America to be a Christian nation, populated by Christian people and governed by Christian principles. And yet, the evidence has already become too overwhelming for theophobic separationists to counter.

Efforts to conscript Thomas Jefferson and James Madison to the cause of modern-day secularism are insincere, and the case that they were theophobes is wrong. While these two Founders did not share the same hard-line vision of state-supported religion that the vast majority of their fellow Founders and fellow Americans did, they hardly advocated for an irreligious America. Attempts to claim George Washington and Ben Franklin as honorary founding members of Americans United for Separation of Church and State are equally absurd.

It is a supreme irony that the present-day Religious Right is closer to the Jefferson/Madison vision—to protect religion from the state—than they are with the other Founders who literally supported established religions in the states. Had most of today's politically active evangelicals and conservative Catholics lived in the late-eighteenth century, theirs would be a *moderate* position, far closer to what we would call "the center" than, say, Patrick Henry, who wanted the Church of England to be the official religion of the Commonwealth of Virginia.

WHAT REALLY HAPPENED

Have you ever considered the peculiar language of the First Amendment? I have. "Congress shall make no law *respecting* the establishment of religion." *Respecting* the establishment of religion? What does that *mean*?

It means that the United States of America already had established religions. At the time of the Constitutional Convention, most states had established religions and wanted to keep them.

This view was not unanimous among our nation's early political leaders. Madison's first crack at what would become the First Amendment to the Constitution would have prohibited states from establishing religions. But Madison's draft was quickly scrapped because Peter Silvester of New York feared "it might be thought to have a tendency to abolish religion altogether," and as Thomas Tudor Tucker of South Carolina argued, "It will be much better, I apprehend, to leave the State Governments to themselves, and not to interfere with them more than we already do; and that is thought by many to be rather too much."

As Kevin Seamus Hasson has observed, "America under the Articles of Confederation had been a patchwork of state-supported religions. What did it look like after the new Constitution was ratified? A patchwork of state-supported religions. And after the First Amendment was added, what did it look like then? Well, actually, it looked like a patchwork of state-supported religions."[22]

The First Amendment to the US Constitution deliberately protects the rights of states to establish religions. Virginia, the home of Jefferson and Madison, chose to have none. Massachusetts, Connecticut, and many other states, particularly in New England, but also New York, Pennsylvania, and Delaware, chose to establish and support religions consistent with the Christian heritage of those respective states.

Jefferson's idea of an impregnable wall between church and state was an innovation, one that had little historical precedent in the short but substantial history of America and one that does not appear to have been overwhelmingly popular among most Americans. The Declaration of Independence, Jefferson's bold thumb in the eye to the king of England, lists a host of grievances; not one relates to the establishment of the Church of England in the United States. The only reasonable conclusion to draw is that the state establishment of religion did not stir thoughts of war in most of Jefferson's contemporaries.

Tradition, instead, was on the side of religious establishment. Article III of the Articles of Confederation took as a given that the several states would need to combine forces and defend against "attacks made upon them, or any of them, on account of *religion,* sovereignty, trade, or any other pretense whatever" (emphasis added), which is to say, they understood the establishment of religion to be a permanent and normal thing worthy of fighting wars over.

But the story goes back a lot further than the official documents of the United States of America. The inexorable links between religion and politics and government extends as far back as 1620 when William Bradford took a bended knee on "firm and stable earth" and thanked God for delivering his small band of immigrants to what they believed to be a New Zion.

Of course, before landing ashore, Bradford needed to establish order among the passengers on the *Mayflower,* some of whom had grown impatient and unruly. In doing so, Bradford appealed to God Almighty and established what was to become the first written government document in our nation's history, the Mayflower Compact. This short document is dripping with church-state unification:

IN THE name of God, Amen.

We whose names are underwritten, the loyal subjects of our dread sovereign Lord, King James, by the grace of God, of Great Britain, France and Ireland king, defender of the faith, etc., having undertaken, for the glory of God, and advancement of the Christian faith, and honor of our king and country, a voyage to plant the first colony in the Northern parts of Virginia, do by these presents solemnly and mutually in the presence of God, and one of another, covenant and combine ourselves together into a civil body politic, for our better ordering and preservation and furtherance of the ends aforesaid; and by virtue hereof to enact, constitute, and frame such just and equal laws, ordinances, acts, constitutions, and offices, from time to time, as shall be thought most meet and convenient for the general good of the colony, unto which we promise all due submission and obedience.

Not a Christian nation? From the very first, civil order in America was established "for the glory of God, and advancement of the Christian faith."

OF POLITICS AND PIETY

From that time on, religion and politics were not only mixed together with great fervency but they became, and have remained, almost inseparable throughout our history. Presidents from Washington through George W. Bush—including many Democrats such as Franklin Roosevelt, Harry Truman, and Jimmy Carter— would furrow their brows if today's theophobic scolds admonished them not to mix the Gospel and the stump speech.

Can you imagine a Democratic Party even existing from the mid-nineteenth to the mid-twentieth century without the influence of big-city Catholic politicians? Or an ascendant GOP in the modern era without the influence of the Religious Right? Of course not.

Where would the abolitionist movement or the women's suffrage movement have gone but for the powerful moral highroad granted them through their Christian foundations? Would Martin Luther King's civil rights crusade have been as fruitful as it was without his intimidating, honorific title of reverend and the moral authority that rightfully came with it? We rarely hear about the important role Christianity played in these historical political movements. The Left would have us believe that the march toward freedom and human rights has been a secular humanist exercise.

It has not been. Charming humanists such as Joseph Stalin believed wholeheartedly in their own ability to shape events and control the trajectory of progress. In truth, however, it is the United States, with its unique Christian heritage, led by believing men and women, that has advanced the cause of human freedom. It is inconceivable that little black boys and little white boys would drink from the same water spout, let alone attend school with one another, let alone marry little white girls and little black girls if the profound understanding that we are all created in God's image were an alien one to America and Americans.

As Clyde Wilcox acknowledges in his fair but largely disapproving study of the Religious Right, "America remains a nation with a strongly established civil religion. Religious imagery, language, and concepts pervade public discourse, appear on currency, and are present in the pledge to the flag. Many Christians see America as somehow chosen to fulfill God's will. The Puritans frequently likened their new covenant with God to that of God with Abraham and sought to create 'God's New Israel.' This infusion of religious belief and national purpose persists today."[23]

In the preparation of this book, I came to realize that the first item on the Left's demonization of the Religious Right "To Do List," is manifestly to deny Christian conservatives any claim to our share in cultural-political heritage. If the Left were ever given the chance finally and thoroughly to cross this item off their Demonization "To Do List," they could then credibly paint today's Christian conservatives as politically heretical to our nation's founding principles.

That would not necessarily neuter the Religious Right politically, but it would go a long way toward painting the Religious Right as "weird," "out of touch," or even "dangerous"; charges the Left has lobbed at the Religious Right for decades but which apparently have not had an impact on the majority of the American public.

Ask yourself, If this is not a Christian country, why must atheists like Michael Newdow resort to court challenges as opposed to legislative action in furtherance of his life's goal to remove "under God" from the Pledge of Allegiance? Why did Pres. Bill Clinton take great pains to be seen coming out of church, Bible in hand, during the Monica Lewinski scandal? Why did Pres. Franklin Roosevelt choose to announce on 6 June 1944 that Operation Overlord was underway with a tear-jerking prayer for the million American soldiers fighting to "prevail over the unholy forces of our enemy"?

And why did Pres. Abraham Lincoln so frequently quote from the Bible and use religious imagery such as in his letter to Lydia Bixby of Boston who lost five sons in the Civil War: "I pray that our Heavenly Father may assuage the anguish of your bereavement, and leave you only the cherished memory of the loved and lost, and the solemn pride that must be yours, to have laid so costly a sacrifice upon the alter of Freedom"? Why does one of our most beloved national songs, Samuel F. Smith's "America," include the verse "Our fathers' God to thee / Author of Liberty / To Thee we sing. / Long may our land be bright / With freedom's holy light / Protect us by Thy might / Great God, our King"?

Why? There is no convincing answer the theophobes can give.

If, at this point, you remain unconvinced that America is a Christian nation, all I can say is that you are in the minority. According to the Pew Research Center, by a margin of 51 to 44 percent, most Americans believe churches should express views on political matters. Moreover, a whopping 67 percent of all Americans believe the United States is indeed a Christian nation.[24]

At the beginning of this chapter, I asked a question: Is America a Christian nation? I also asked you to weigh the evidence before answering. Now that the evidence has been submitted, we can all render a judgment:

Of course it is. Don't be ridiculous. What a stupid question.

3

GOP—GOD'S OWN PARTY?

We have seen that from our nation's founding, two figures stood most assertively against religion playing a significant role in public life: Thomas Jefferson and James Madison. Nearly unique among the Founders, these two shared an inordinate fear of organized religion, and it is clear that their revolutionary spirit spilled over into dislike for the Church of England.

But Jefferson and Madison were also the two most prominent Republicans in the early-American era, which is to say they were founders of what we today call the Democratic Party. (The Democratic Party was originally called the Republican Party, then the Democratic Republicans, then the Democracy, then the Democratic Party.)

Today's radical Left has grossly distorted the worldviews of Thomas Jefferson and James Madison, but these two figures were to the "left" of their fellow Founders on this important issue. We can see their radical progeny in today's Democratic Party, jam-packed with wild conspiracy theories about "theocracy," a religious-based "war on science," and a "war on objectivity."[1]

And so where Jefferson and Madison stood apart from the other Founders merely for wanting to prohibit the several states from establishing official religions, present-day leftwing activists, such as the Message Group of Northern Virginia (whom we met in chapter 1), are egged on by radicalized showstoppers such as Michael Newdow, the ACLU, and Americans United for Separation of Church and State.

Make no mistake, the modern American Left is openly hostile to religion and religious folks who take active roles in politics and public life. That doesn't mean all Democrats are hostile to religion. There are certainly millions of Democrats who are also devout, believing Christians. But too many in the Democratic Party leadership either share this leftist hostility to Americans of faith or are too beholden to leftwing activists to stand up for people of faith when they are under fire.

And while Republicans are hardly uniform in their support for faith in the public square, there seems to be something rather fated about the GOP's relationship with Americans of faith.

"THE FIFTH CATHOLIC"

Just before Christmas in 2005, federal judge David Hamilton ruled that the Indiana House of Representatives could not include the name of "Jesus Christ" in its invocation, something it had been doing for two hundred years.[2] The lawsuit was brought by the American Civil Liberties Union.

Around the same time, a Texas-based atheist group filed a lawsuit against the Utah Highway Patrol and the Utah Department of Motor Vehicles for erecting white crosses along the highway in honor of slain UHP officers.

Anecdotes like these are all too common in our culture. But where do they come from? Not the Right; that much we know for sure. They come from two groups: people animated by the paranoia we observed in chapter 1 or people who have a political interest in encouraging that paranoia.

All too often, those with the political interest in stoking the flames of paranoia are Democratic Party politicians and office holders. For example, Supreme Court nomination and confirmation battles have become inquisitorial affairs about whether respective nominees are too pious.

Pres. George W. Bush nominated three people to the high court during 2005: John Roberts, Harriet Miers, and Samuel Alito. The religious convictions of each of these three became the fixation of a great many liberals. To many, it looked like an attempt by the radical Left to apply a religious test against these nominees for high public office.

A great deal was made of the fact that Samuel Alito would be the fifth Catholic on the Supreme Court. Under the headline, "Alito would tip court to Catholics," Rachel Zoll of the Associated Press lamented that "more than 200 years of Protestant domination on the Supreme Court would end if Samuel Alito is confirmed as its next justice."[3] National Public Radio contributor Dahlia Lithwick reported that "[p]eople are very, very much talking about the fact that Alito would be the fifth Catholic on the Supreme Court if confirmed."[4]

What people? No one that I spoke to. Perhaps the hallways at NPR were filled with newsies abuzz over "the fifth Catholic," but normal Americans hardly seemed to notice. What stood out in the nomination and subsequent confirmation of Alito (as well as that of Chief Justice John Roberts, also a Catholic) was how remarkably ordinary he was.

In the case of John Roberts, Senate Democrats brought out the religious test during the Senate Judiciary Committee confirmation hearings. As noted in chapter 1, Senator Diane Feinstein invoked Pres. John F. Kennedy, the nation's first Catholic president in an apparent effort to corner Roberts into denouncing his faith.

"At the time," said Feinstein, "he [Kennedy] pledged to address the issues of conscience out of a focus on the national interests, not out of adherence to the dictates of one's religion. And he even said, 'I believe in an America where the separation of church and state is absolute.' My question is: do you?"

Feinstein could only have been implying one thing here: Roberts, and all other nominees to the Supreme Court, must check their religious faith at the courthouse steps. As justices of the Supreme Court don't make laws and merely make decisions about the constitutionality of laws (or, that's the idea, at least), Feinstein's question was utterly irrelevant unless it is her contention that a person's religious faith can play no part in his public life and decision making.

But isn't this and the "fifth Catholic" whisper campaign against Samuel Alito obvious attempts by the political Left to turn the Constitution's religious test prohibition on its head? The original purpose of the prohibition was to prevent anyone from being disqualified for high public office because of his religion. Alito's persecutors and Senator Feinstein instead implied that a judicial nominee's religious faith should keep him out of office. Whereas the original intent was to protect dissenters from being denied their right to stand for public office, Feinstein et al. believe it was designed to prohibit *believers* from doing so.

It doesn't end there. Deeply antireligious rhetoric has been a hallmark of Democratic Party speeches and public utterances for years. In the aftermath of the Terri Schiavo tragedy, Democrat National Chairman Howard Dean asked publicly, "The issue is: are we going to live in a theocracy where the highest powers tell us what to do? Or are we going to be allowed to consult our own high powers when we make very difficult decisions?"[5]

Berkeley activist and commentator Bob Burnett summed up the

Left's collective delusion about religious conservatives when he wrote, "Fundamentalist have taken over the Republican Party and, in the process, consummated the Devil's bargain. They get to implement a conservative Christian theocracy. And Republican politicians get to keep the money."[6]

What has been the public's attitude to the political Left's unveiled hostility to Americans of faith? They don't much care for it. Only 28 percent of respondents to a late August 2005 Pew Forum on Religion & Public Life survey believe Democrats are "concerned with protecting religious values," and only 29 percent believe Democrats are a "religious-friendly party."[7] Their opinions and attitudes on this issue are clearly reflective of the public dialogue that has been going on for the past three decades over the country's shared values and moral trajectory.

Americans simply do not trust Democrats on matters of religious tolerance and the preservation of our moral values.

And while the level of animosity has grown exponentially since the early days of the Democratic Party, the truth is, Democrats never really "got" religion in the first place.

THE VIRGINIA MAFIA

As much as this Democratic belligerence toward Americans of faith seems like a new phenomenon, an alternate explanation may be that this has always been the case. The Democratic Party is our nation's oldest political party. Formed during the presidency of George Washington over ongoing policy disputes between Thomas Jefferson and Alexander Hamilton, the Democratic Party—then called the Republican Party—became Jefferson's political vehicle and was characterized by regressive, populist, agrarian, and, as we have noted, vaguely anticlerical sentiments.

Whatever else one might say about Jefferson, he was indisputably a political genius. In short order, the Sage of Monticello transformed this political movement from a backwater gaggle of malcontents localized in Virginia's Piedmont region into America's only national political party.

From his triumph in the turbulent 1800 presidential contest to his anointing of his successor, James Madison, and the subsequent political ascension of James Monroe, Jefferson's Republican Party controlled what some historians have called "the Virginia Mafia," an early-age political machine that did away with its hapless rivals, the Federalists. So dominant had the Republican Party become that during the presidency of James Monroe, the United States became a one-party nation and contemporaries heralded "the Era of Good Feeling," a period of time with little or no political dissent. Monroe was reelected in 1820 with all but one electoral vote.

This period of relative harmony is attributable in great part to the Republican Party's aptitude for gobbling up and championing issues of its erstwhile opponents. But it would be a mistake to assert, as many historians do, that "the Era of Good Feeling" was a period of complete political and cultural homogeneity. Slavery started to become an issue in Monroe's second term, highlighting sectional discord and divergent views of America's moral compass.

Loosely coterminous with Monroe's second presidential term came another historical cultural event, one that would have far longer lasting implications than the Era of Good Feeling. The period many historians call the "Second Great Awakening" began around 1820 and inexorably changed America's moral and political visage for decades.

The Second Great Awakening was a period of intense religious revival in which many Americans—particularly in New England, New York, and Appalachia—came to Christ. The causes of the

Second Great Awakening were many. With the westward expansion of the United States, many religious leaders felt it necessary to spread Christianity "from sea to shining sea," and this required active evangelism on their parts.

Because of the American West's broad land mass, the building of churches and strict adherence to denominational doctrines became less relevant to the practice of worship. This had an important impact back East, as well. Rigid ceremony seemed to subside in importance in the Northeast and old church buildings were replaced with revival tents; formal prayer books with the Old and New Testaments.

Revival meetings necessarily took on a nondenominational, even entrepreneurial, tone. This had the impact of reducing doctrinal disputes among denominations and generated what we might call a "mere Christianity" that had held broad appeal to Americans of many walks of life (though by no means did all denominational distinctions evaporate). It also placed greater emphasis on shared moral values than on doctrinal disagreements.

It's not hard to see how these changes helped to create a unifying atmosphere among religious groups. And when we consider this development in light of the fact that Jefferson's Party held, at best, a skeptical eye toward religion, we can begin to see the formulation of a political-religious convergence, which in many ways foreshadows our present political dynamic.

Under America's one-party rule, many religious leaders came to see a certain godlessness among the nation's decision makers. From its early roots as a Puritan outpost to the colonial establishments of religion to the clear invocation of the Divine Creator in most of the nation's founding documents, a new breed of more secular leaders had emerged from Virginia who were at first—in the case of Jefferson and Madison, Deists—and later—in the case of Monroe—not religious at all.

For the health and future of this great country, many religious leaders felt compelled to alter America's moral trajectory. And so some of them began to poke their noses around in politics, just as their religious forefathers had.

One such leader was the Reverend Ezra Stiles Ely, a Presbyterian minister from Philadelphia who endeavored to create a "Christian party in politics."

"I do not wish any religious test to be prescribed by constitution, and proposed to a man on his acceptance of any public trust," said Reverend Ely in a sermon on 4 July 1827. He continued:

> Let the religion of the Bible rest on that everlasting rock, and on those spiritual laws, on which Jehovah has founded his kingdom: let Christianity by the spirit of Christ in her members support herself: let Church and State be for ever distinct: but, still, let the doctrines and precepts of Christ govern all men, in all their relations and employments. If a ruler is not a Christian he ought to be one, in this land of evangelical light, without delay; and he ought, being a follower of Jesus, to honour him even as he honours the Father. In this land of religious freedom, what should hinder a civil magistrate from believing the Gospel, and professing faith in Christ, any more than any other man?[8]

Stiles encouraged a great many Americans of faith to stand for high public office and reestablish Christian morality in American public policy.

The lesson here is that during a period when one-party rule in the United States began to ebb, one serious contender to play the role of protagonist against the secular Jeffersonian Democrats was an outright Christian party. This says something profound about how far Jefferson's party had drifted from the public attitudes of Americans of faith.

It bears noting that no serious political thinker today wants a Christian party in politics. Jim Pfaff, who handles mobilization efforts for Focus on the Family, told me flat out, "We don't want a Christian party. We want politicians in Washington and in the states to stand up for traditional families."

Once again, we have an example in which the modern-day Religious Right would have represented a moderate voice if they had spoken in an earlier era.

LEGISLATE THIS!

Stiles failed to establish his Christian party, but several political movements began to emerge from this convergence of religiosity and politics. The most important of these political movements was the cause of abolition.

There is no argument that can be made to diffuse one fact of American history: the growth and ultimate success of the abolition movement was the result of Christians imposing their moral values on their fellow Americans.

This is not a difficult thing for Christian conservatives to say. In fact, they feel rather comfortable when they tell others that imposing the biblical value that all men were created in the image of God and are therefore worthy of equal and just treatment led to other Americans discovering the illogic and un-Christian nature of slavery.

But this ought to be a difficult thing for today's liberals to *hear*. Nary an election cycle goes by without a present-day Leftist grumbling about Christian conservatives attempting to "legislate morality" or "impose their moral values on the rest of America."

Members of the ultraliberal World Council of Churches, for

example, admonished American churches on 4 November 2004 for helping to reelect Pres. George W. Bush. Reuters reported: "God has no place in politics and should not have been used by churches in the United States to influence the presidential election, a council representing 342 Christian groups around the world said."[9]

Imagine how remarkably destructive such a sentiment would be to our nation if it had prevailed during the decades-long debate about slavery in the United States. Or on civil rights for Southern blacks.

Would today's secularists and theophobes shout down the Reverend Martin Luther King with pious hoots of, "Quit trying to legislate morality"? King believed his political cause was endorsed by the Man Upstairs Himself. "I still believe that standing up for the truth of God is the greatest thing in the world. This is the end of life," King once stated. "The end of life is not to be happy. The end of life is not to achieve pleasure and avoid pain. The end of life is to do the will of God, come what may."[10]

The blending of religion and politics became necessary because the Democratic Party, which came to dominate America's political scene, lost touch with the nation's Christian roots and grew distant from a huge segment of the population that had grown increasingly religious and active in the imposition of their morality on its secular government.

At the same time, large segments of what had now become known as the Democratic Party had begun to defend slavery. In some cases, Democratic senators used their political clout to expand slavery into new territories. This had the two-pronged impact of expanding their political base and creating a more pronounced backlash against human bondage.

Meanwhile, a new political party emerged, which called itself the American Whig Party. Not unified in its support for abolition, however, the Whigs were more a party in pursuit of "national greatness" through fiscal policy and internal improvements. Abolition became too powerful an issue for Whigs to remain silent on, and they either needed to take charge of this message or dissolve. They dissolved. And by the early 1850s, the American Whig Party joined the Federalist Party in the dustbin of American political history.

Abolition had become the sole unifying theme among those Americans who were disinclined to support the Democratic Party. Other parties existed and threatened to control regional balances of power: the Know-Nothing Party, the Free Soil Party, the Temperance Party, and some leftover pockets of the Whig Party. But no party could mount a credible national challenge to the Democratic Party.

For its part, the Democratic Party had become intensely Southern. While still strong in some dispersed areas throughout the North and the West, the Democrats saw their national strength diminish badly because of their obstreperous defense of slavery. This once dominant party, which had exclusive control on the seat of power from 1800 through the Van Buren administration ending in 1841 and again for twelve of the subsequent twenty years, had atrophied into an angry, chauvinistic, un-Christian party.

ENTER: THE HOLY SPIRIT

Worse still for Southern Democrats was the fact they faced not only morally high-ground pronouncements from their Northern antagonists but an increasing amount of Negro slaves had come to accept Jesus Christ as their Savior, as well. While Southern white Democrats were doing everything in their power to keep their Negro slaves from getting "uppity," Northern evangelists, fueled with the fervor of the Second Great Awakening, had converted thousands of black slaves to

Christianity and filled this aggrieved underclass with the power of the Holy Spirit. Many slaveholders came to learn that there is no Negro more uppity than a Negro filled with the Holy Spirit.

It was an ironic discovery because the prevailing view among Southern slaveholders had been that African religions represented a threat to the Peculiar Institution. They didn't understand these religions, which involved odd rituals and resulted in groups of African slaves skulking away into dark corners of the plantation to worship and perhaps even plot against their white slave masters. Better to Christianize them and teach them the Gospel, make them understand that slavery is just a part of God's divine plan. Southern slaveholders welcomed evangelists, thinking that Christian Negroes would be easier to control than pagan Negroes.

Surely, you might say, proud Southern slaveholding Democrats believed they were Christians and used Christian precepts to justify their advocacy of African slavery. Yes. But this turned out to be a very stupid thing for them to do. For it underscored the unsustainable hypocrisy of their position.

Uppity Negroes such as Fredrick Douglass could now state with impunity, "A slave-holders profession of Christianity is a palpable imposture. He is a felon of the highest grade. He is a man-stealer. It is of no importance what you put in the other scale."[11] Better, noted Douglass in a letter to William Lloyd Garrison, for the slaveholder to keep his trap shut: "The naked relation of master and slave is one of those monsters of darkness, to whom the light of truth is death! The wise ones among the slaveholders know this, and they studiously avoid doing anything, which, in their judgment, tends to elicit truth. They seem fully to understand, that their safety is in their silence."[12]

With the North growing increasingly intolerant of the South's racists ways, Negroes in the fields singing Christian spirituals and the

high-ground long since swept from under their feet, all that was left
was a powerful political force to put it all together and challenge the
decades-long political strength of the American Democratic Party.

Enter Abraham Lincoln and the Republican Party.

DID YOU SAY "ABE LINCOLN"?

The nation's sixteenth president was also its most eloquent. Almost
150 years after his dominance of the American political scene, his
speeches still give history buffs goosebumps. And nowhere did
President Lincoln's language inspire more than when he spoke about
the moral struggle of the War between the States.

To Lincoln, the Civil War was redemptive penance made necessary for centuries of un-Christian transgressions against our fellow
man. What made Lincoln such a powerful critic of our national
tragedy was his liberal use of biblical language to explain to the
American people why this terrible war was so necessary. In virtually
every speech he delivered as president, Lincoln peppered his remarks
about the war and its ultimate end—the abolition of slavery—with
biblical allusions that put the lie to the modern-day Left's assertion
that Pres. George W. Bush is the "most outwardly religious president
in history."

Here was Lincoln explaining the horrors of war and why it was
required by God for the nation's past sins.

> The Almighty has his own purposes. "Woe unto the world
> because of offences! for it must needs be that offences come;
> but woe to that man by whom the offense cometh!"
> [Matthew 18:7 KJV]. If we shall suppose that American
> slavery is on of those offences which, in the providence of
> God, must needs come, but which, having continued

through His appointed time, He now wills to remove, and that he gives to both North and South, this terrible war, as the woe due to those by whom offence came, shall we discern therein any departure from those divine attributes which the believers in a Loving God always ascribe to him? Fondly do we hope—fervently do we pray—that this mighty scourge of way may speedily pass away. Yet, if God will that it continue, until all the wealth oiled by the bondman's (slaves) two hundred and fifty years of unrequited toil shall be sunk, and until every drop of blood drawn with the lash, shall be paid by another drawn with the sword, as was said three thousand years ago, so still it must be said, the judgments of the Lord, are true and righteous altogether [Psalm 19:9].[13]

Lincoln spoke of battlefield bloodshed like it was a sacrifice for heinous sins against the Father. And today's liberals claim Pres. George W. Bush uses too many religious allusions in defense of the war in Iraq! Can't you just imagine the American Civil Liberties Union or Americans United for Separation of Church and State faxing off press releases castigating President Lincoln for claiming to have been doing God's work by launching the preemptive war against the South and thereby committing the unpardonable civil sin of blending church and state?

That's what they essentially accused President Bush of in June of 2003 when a story (apocryphal, in all likelihood) emerged from the president's meeting with Palestinian officials.

Nabil Shaath, then-Palestinian foreign minister, told the BBC that Bush said, "God would tell me, 'George, go and fight those terrorists in Afghanistan.' And I did, and then God would tell me, 'George, go and end tyranny in Iraq,' . . . and I did."[14]

Liberals all over the world went berserk. Never mind that Shaath later backed off from this statement. "In one sense, however, it doesn't matter what he actually said," wrote leftist columnist Paul Vallely in the *Canberra Times* of Australia. "What is alarming enough is that it is the kind of thing he would say. Every line of it is entirely consonant with George W. Bush's religious world view."[15]

Esther Kaplan, a contributor to the leftwing opinion journal the *Nation,* pointed out that "these were not the only instances of Bush inserting his Christian beliefs in American diplomacy."[16] And then she rattled off a few more examples intended to outrage liberal secularists but which were really no big deal and, anyway, had only been "reported" by this or that crankish left-leaning newspaper.

The above story has been circulated as fact in countless liberal opinion articles, blogs, books, and MoveOn.org meetings. Each time a secular liberal reads or hears it—always without the disclaimer that Shaath distanced himself from his own account—she is aghast. "So what exactly did Bush say in those private meetings, his first serious interventions with two leaders engaged in a bloody conflict, each egged on by extremists?" Kaplan asked darkly.[17]

If we accept the first, unasterisked version of the story, his answer was essentially the same thing that Lincoln had said about the Civil War.

Later, of course, Lincoln would sign the Emancipation Proclamation, setting in motion the ultimate freedom of African slaves. In it, Lincoln actually claims God's endorsement of his public policy:

> And upon this act, sincerely believed to be an act of justice, warranted by the Constitution, upon military necessity, I invoke the considerate judgment of mankind, and the gracious favor of Almighty God.

Read that again: "the gracious favor of Almighty God." Has George W. Bush, a man whose religiosity is the source of great anxiety for liberals in America and abroad, ever claimed Divine endorsement for his domestic policies? Of course not. But Lincoln did. Often.

If today's theophobic liberals were true to their paranoia, they would hate Lincoln as much as they do President Bush. Who knows, maybe someday activists will gather outside the Lincoln Memorial in Washington DC with placards and sandwich boards that read "God is not a Northerner" and "keep your rosary off my slavery."

. . . LONG TIME AGO

Don't misunderstand. The Democratic Party has not been entirely hostile to Americans of faith throughout its history. Democrats accepted new Catholic and Jewish Americans during the great waves of American immigration, whereas Whigs, Native Americans, Know-Nothings, and even Republicans were not so open-armed. No one political party can claim to have an unblemished record in its treatment of religious Americans.

On the flip side, many Religious Right leaders recoil at the assertion that they are partisan one way or the other. I sat down with Jim Pfaff of Focus on the Family in preparation for this book. Pfaff heads up mobilization efforts for Focus.

"The parties just don't get it," he told me. "To them it's just a numbers game. They see thirty million evangelicals as thirty million prospective voters. And so, at the highest level, they pander to us." Pfaff said that many of Focus's closest "friends" in the political process are Democrats in state governments, not Republicans in Washington.

But still, trends are trends, and they cannot be denied. The Democratic Party's secularist tendencies—characterized historically by its espousal of extreme separationism, its defense of slavery, its modern ties to decidedly anti-Christian activist groups, and acquiescence toward anti-Christian policies—has made it an afterthought for serious Americans of faith.

And as for the GOP? Well, Democratic Party Chairman Howard Dean was sort of correct when he said the GOP is "basically a white, Christian Party."

But do Republicans themselves even recognize this fact? When Dean roared his attack, Republicans did not respond by asking "so what?" Instead, they barked back that it simply wasn't true. Well, of course it isn't true. The GOP is a loose coalition of many factions and voting blocs. But clearly the Republican Party has been the default home of Christian conservatives for decades. Why had the GOP suddenly denied them?

Well, it wasn't so sudden. Perhaps because of intellectual intimidation, perhaps for aesthetic reasons, or perhaps out of their enduring compulsion to be all things to all voters, the modern Republican Party has always been in various degrees leery of conservative Christians.

For example, in the rush to define their political success after the 2004 election, many Republicans and conservatives claimed President Bush's reelection and his congressional coattails amounted to a ringing endorsement of his foreign policy. And yet of the two foreign policy options in a 2004-exit-poll, "Most Important Issue" question—"the War on Terror" and "Iraq"—President Bush's foreign policy seemed nearly as unpopular with the American public as it had support.

On other issues—"the Economy/Jobs," "Education," and "Health Care"—voters overwhelmingly supported Senator John Kerry (D-MA) over President Bush. Even on "Taxes"—a perennial Republican powerhouse issue—voters only supported President Bush over Senator Kerry by a margin of 57 percent to 43 percent. It was only when we came to the family of issues called "Moral

Values" that we see President Bush walloping Senator Kerry (80 to 18 percent).

Nevertheless, anxious to credit Bush's reelection to his foreign policy proposals they, in part, helped construct, many "neoconservatives" claimed the exit polls were all screwed up. Conservative columnist Charles Krauthammer was principle among these. Declaring the impact of moral values voters a "myth," Krauthammer cleverly asserted the "Bigoted Christian Redneck" was merely a fictional character created in the "Blue State media" to soften the blow to their egos created by the GOP victory. But in order to follow Krauthammer's storyline, one must first accept the Left's characterization of conservative Christians as "Bigoted Rednecks"—a view Krauthammer seems to accept. In this infamous postelection piece, Krauthammer does not defend conservative Christians against this hateful smear. He merely says conservative Christians had a marginal impact on the outcome of the election!

Krauthammer was not alone. David Brooks from the *New York Times* stated a similar case. As did David Boaz of the Libertarian think tank the Cato Institute. Indeed, even President Bush himself appeared to misidentify the reasons for his political fortunes. Almost immediately after the 2004 election, President Bush launched a nationwide campaign to reform Social Security, hardly an issue of great consequence to the events of 2 November 2004. Some conservative Christians were outraged and viewed the president's misplaced priority as evidence that the GOP had merely used conservative Christians to win another election.

And perhaps it was. After a campaign so dominated by cultural conflict, the gay-marriage controversy chief among these, Senate Majority Leader Bill Frist scheduled a vote on the federal Marriage Amendment a full nineteen months after that fateful election. Curiously, however, the vote also happened to fall five months before the next election and, scheduled for late June, would be one of the last acts of the current Congress before its members headed home to campaign for reelection.

Does this sound like a party committed to its base? Or like a party taking its most loyal voters for granted?

Dean was speaking for the modern, extremist faction of America's oldest party. Its founders—Thomas Jefferson and James Madison—at least recognized America's unique Christian founding and, irrespective of whether or not they agreed with it, respected it as a fact that they'd have to work with.

It is, therefore, secular leftists, theophobes, and church-state fetishists—not the Religious Right—who are the political heretics of our day. But of course, as we have seen, the history behind that statement is long and tangled.

The Democratic Party, which had come to dominate American politics during the first half of the nineteenth century, became too secular, too Southern, and too un-Christian to maintain its political hegemony. The Republican Party, formed out of the Christianized political causes of the late-Second Great Awakening—especially the abolition movement—became the national alternative to the Democratic Party. And the two impulses have worked their way through the body politic now for 150 years.

To put it as it might appear in Genesis, opposition to Jeffersonian Democratic secularism begat the Second Great Awakening, the Second Great Awakening begat the abolition movement, the abolition movement begat the Republican Party, and the Republican Party begat Abraham Lincoln, America's most crusading president.

This history is important as we now move to a discussion of politics in a more recent time: the 1994 election. It is important because we must understand that the rise of the modern Religious

Right was not surprising, not unprecedented, not unexpected, wholly predictable, good for the country, predictive of the 2004 campaign, responsible for a great number of social improvements over the past decade, and, above all, further evidence in support of the idea that the GOP is, perhaps, God's Own Party.

4

1994

The hot gas expended by political analysts about the 1994 campaign could clear out a football stadium.

As far as the Democrats are concerned, the most consequential political realignment since the New Deal was merely a tactical victory for the Republicans. Just enough legislative obstruction and redistricting by the GOP, we hear from the likes of Nancy Pelosi and Howard Dean, was enough to smash the Democratic Party's forty-year hammerlock on Washington. Imitation is the sincerest form of flattery, and so we see Pelosi's Democrats playing the obstruction game in Capitol Hill in hopes of capturing 1994's lightening in a bottle in 2006.

A second analysis of dubious validity comes from the mainstream media. These folks would have us believe that the mythical "angry white males" rose up from their slumber to realize the nation had been taken over by blacks. For whatever cockamamie reason, some media types still believe that racial quotas were the defining issue of the 1994 Republican electoral takeover of Congress.

This analysis is too bizarre to take seriously any longer and, as we will see, masks the very genuine outrage many Americans felt toward the Clinton administration and its policies, outrages that had nothing to do with race.

A third questionable analysis comes from libertarian-leaning

Republicans. These folks, right-thinking on a great many things, nevertheless have a fabled view of recent history. To them, 1994 was a year of the great libertarian revolt, the year in which mainstream Americans finally came to see the world as they did. As far as these market-driven Republicans are concerned, government spending was the key issue in 1994 and, finally, Americans had said, "Enough!"

This analysis is one I wish I could believe. But developments after 1994 demonstrate that this idea was a pipedream. It requires an enormous amount of faith to believe that Americans told Congress to "spend away" for thirty-nine years of Democrat control but on the fortieth they said, "Too much."

In this chapter we are going to look at these three analyses and identify the ways in which they crack under the weight of the facts. Then, we're going to look at the real issues that allowed the GOP to claim control of Washington for the first time in forty years and maintain control ever since: moral values.

APING NEWT

In January 2005, Pres. George W. Bush launched a nationwide campaign to win support for the principle of Social Security privatization. The politically astute White House had recently been emboldened by the GOP's strong showing in the previous November's elections in which Republicans increased their majorities in the US House of Representatives and the US Senate and Bush himself earned more votes than any previous presidential candidate in history.

The Bush folks decided to dedicate that "political capital" (as the president called it) toward giving Americans an element of choice and ownership in their own retirement planning. The president himself launched a "Sixty Cities in Sixty Days" tour to promote the idea.

Some members of Congress began filing legislation that would reform Social Security. Washington's right-of-center think tanks launched into high gear, producing issue papers and advertising campaigns to promote this idea, which many think tanks had been advocating for years. Progress for America, the powerful Republican-leaning 527, launched an ad campaign, as did the Coalition for the Modernization and Protection of America's Social Security. The Club for Growth established a blog dedicated solely to Social Security choice. New groups in favor of reforming Social Security began to pop up on college campuses. Many conservative columnists tried to convince Americans that the president was on to something.

Congressional Democrats and other liberals would have none of it. From the very beginning, almost immediately after President Bush identified Social Security reform as his 2005 legislative priority, House Minority Leaders Nancy Pelosi and Senate Minority Leader Harry Reid announced that Democrats would not negotiate with Republicans. "There is no Social Security crisis" became the mantra of the Left, despite all economic data to the contrary.

As polls began to demonstrate that most Americans really did recognize the very real fiscal problems with Social Security, however, Democrats and their liberal supporters had to change their tune.

The powerful senior lobby group AARP launched an ad campaign claiming the Bush plan for "privatization" would exacerbate many of Social Security's fiscal problems that Bush claimed his reform would repair. And Democrats now claimed that they would negotiate with the president and Republicans in Congress, but only if privatization of Social Security was definitively "taken off the table."

Fat chance of that. From the earliest days of the Social Security fight Democrats were quite open about their goal of obstructing President Bush's Social Security initiative in much the same way Newt Gingrich and his Republican minority in Congress had obstructed President Bill Clinton's plan for socialized healthcare in 1993. To Democrats, this was their opportunity to stymie the president they had grown to hate with an incomparable hatred.

From day one of the president's initiative, moreover, the mainstream media drew lusty comparisons to the defeat of President Clinton's healthcare scheme. "President Bush will officially open today the Republican version of a domestic policy brawl that will rival in scope, intensity and political difficulty the 1993–94 effort by then-President Bill Clinton to remake the nation's health care system," wrote Carolyn Lockheed in the *San Francisco Chronicle*. ". . . [T]he enterprise faces all the land mines of Clinton's failed effort: The idea of individual accounts, like universal health care, may sound popular, but the devil is in the details. The financial and technical challenges are enormous."[1]

Every time some middle-of-the-road Democrat gestured to the Republican congressional leadership that he might be willing to negotiate on a compromised plan, Nancy Pelosi, Harry Reid, or their attack dog surrogates would slap them down. When Senator Joe Lieberman (D-CT) indicated to the media that he was privately discussing a compromise alternative with Senator Lindsey Graham (R-SC), liberals attacked him with a vengeance.

"He has given aid and comfort to the Republicans on multiple occasions. If there were a ten strikes and your (*sic*) out rule he would have been carted off months ago," chimed one typical liberal blogger.[2] Most of the anxiety about Senator Lieberman's position on Social Security was not relative to the senator's actual position on Social Security privatization, which he claimed to oppose. Rather, liberals were furious that he was even open to the concept of discussing Social Security reform with a Republican.

What would make so many aggressive liberals turn on the senator from Connecticut, a man they, only four years earlier, insisted was the uncrowned vice president of the United States? It had nothing to do with Social Security and everything to do with "party unity." Dems wanted to replicate the Republican success of 1994.

In order to understand this mania for party unity, we need to understand what the Democrats and their liberal pep squad believe happened in 1994. According to their view, Newt Gingrich and a new breed of mean-spirited partisan Republicans in Congress whipped their GOP colleagues into opposing anything then-President Bill Clinton wanted to do. Clinton even made a fool of himself in a 1993 press conference by childishly pounding the podium and whining that every time he tried to do something wonderful, the Republicans in Congress, still in the minority, just said, "No, no, no, no, no."

The obvious example everyone points to is the aforementioned ClintonCare proposal, which First Lady Hillary Clinton cobbled together and which Republicans indeed and rightly savaged. But according to Democrat revisionists, it wasn't savaged because it was an awful idea. Clinton lost this issue merely because he was outmaneuvered by the GOP. "The take-away lesson was the insistence on the initial plan and the failure to engage in a real dialogue," Clinton White House chief of staff Leon Panetta told USA Today.[3]

This analysis is absurd.

The nation clearly rejected the idea of socialized medicine in 1993. Polls showed that popular support for the plan plummeted not because Republicans were clever but because they didn't want the nation's healthcare system in the hands of a federal government that had the compassion of the Pentagon and the efficiency of the post office.

Moreover, this analysis ignores the fact that the so-called obstructionist Republican minority that ended up sweeping into power during the 1994 election actually put forth a positive, forward-looking agenda called the Contract with America. In retrospect, perhaps it would have been easier not to put so many conservative ideas down on paper as a promise to voters. Maybe legislative obstruction was all that was required of Gingrich and his team. But we will never know, because that's not what happened.

There are other indications that the Left believes the Republicans have just been more tactically imaginative than Democrats over the past couple of years. Al Franken and his gang of liberal blowhards on Air America Radio honestly believe that Republicans win elections because they have conservative talk radio hosts like Rush Limbaugh and Sean Hannity endorsing their ideas for several hours each weekday.

Franken and company fail to understand that Limbaugh and Hannity are broadcasting entrepreneurs who found a hunger out there in America that needed feeding: conservative news and comment on the car radio. If people didn't agree with what they were saying and didn't enjoy listening to them, they would have dried up and gone away like so many of the liberal talk-radio hosts who have tried to emulate their success.

We shouldn't rob Newt Gingrich of recognition for his innovative tactical genius. He did use new techniques to distribute messages more effectively: C-SPAN, small circulation newsletters, talk radio. But state-of-the-art tactics were not sufficient to produce the ground-shifting changes that came in 1994 and every serious political observer knows that.

GRRR! ANGRY WHITE MALES!

The press propagates a second legend about the 1994 election: that millions of "angry white males" turned out on Election Day and rejected Pres. Bill Clinton's liberalizing agenda, especially as it related to black people.

Clinton, you will recall, boasted upon taking office that he would have a cabinet "that looked like America." Most journalists and Americans took that to mean that Clinton would populate his inner circle with people from all walks of life, from every race and creed, and then some. Clinton nominated Zoe Baird, a woman, to serve as attorney general of the United States. He also nominated a black woman named Lani Guinier to serve as assistant attorney general for Civil Rights. Ron Brown, a black man, would head Commerce. Henry Cisneros, a Latino, would become the head of Housing and Urban Development. Hazel O'Leary, a woman, would run Energy. Donna Shalala, another woman, would head Health and Human Services. Joycelyn Elders, a black woman, would serve as Clinton's surgeon general. Stature-challenged Americans even earned a voice in the cabinet when President Clinton named Robert Reich to be the next secretary of labor. (If you find my incessant labeling of each of these cabinet members gratuitous, imagine how most Americans felt back in 1993.)

The media loved it. It fit perfectly inside the narrative they had created about American politics, which, they believed and asserted whenever possible, was principally an exercise in race and class division. If the GOP made gains in this environment, it could only have been through stoking the flames of resentment against those up-and-coming minorities who were lucky they weren't checking coats at the Old Boys Club.

Hollywood even got in on the act with the 1993 film *Falling Down*, starring Michael Douglas as a frustrated workaholic who goes bonkers after a series of small but escalating obstacles prevent him from seeing his daughter after work. Douglas's character goes on a racially motivated violence spree. The film's tagline tells the story: "The Adventures of an Ordinary Man at War with the Everyday World." Message: white guys are getting angry and boy, are they dangerous!

After the 1994 election, and I mean *immediately* after the 1994 election, *USA Today* ran the declarative headline, "Angry White Men: Their Votes Turned the Tide for the GOP." It would take a while for the professionals to challenge that assumption. John DiIulio of the University of Pennsylvania explained in 2000, "supposedly what the angry white males were most angry about was affirmative action. Never mind that between '86 and '94 women as well as men, and blacks as well as whites, and Democrats, independents, and Republicans all became less supportive of affirmative action. And never mind that by 1994 the so-called gender gap between males and females had actually shrunk. The claim was 'the white guys are angry.'

There is something annoyingly dismissive to the tone of this analysis of the 1994 election. Oh sure, the Republicans might have won, but only because those angry white men felt threatened by Bill Clinton's openness to diversity.

But in addition to being annoying, this analysis is also wrong.

The truth about America's reaction to their new president's cabinet had nothing to do with the cabinet members' gender or pigment of skin, but rather about what they stood for. Many Americans thought they had voted for a moderate Southern Democrat who promised to cut taxes for the middle class and get the economy rolling again. Instead they seemed to get the very worst in stereotypical Ivory Tower academic leftism. The annoying apple-polishers from high school were now running the country.

Joycelyn Elders, for example, Clinton's choice for surgeon general, was anathema to the American public not because she was a black woman but rather because she came across as having an unwholesome enthusiasm for condoms in public schools. She supported the legalization of some illicit drugs. She advocated for "safer bullets" to curb gun violence. Elders would later go on to advocate the teaching of masturbation in public schools.

Health and Human Services Secretary Donna Shalala didn't help much either. In May of 1994, she boasted that the Clinton administration—her department in particular—had paved the way for do-it-yourself abortion drug Mifepristone to enter the US market. In April 1993, homosexual activist Larry Kramer had "outed" Shalala at a gay rights march in Washington DC by saying, "Donna Shalala, you know you're a lesbian, and we know you're a lesbian. So why don't you just come out of the closet and admit it?" And before that, almost immediately upon taking office, Shalala flushed the so-called abortion "gag rule" down the toilet and encouraged federally funded "family planning clinics" to counsel (read: encourage) young women about abortion as a birth control mechanism.

Is it any wonder that a public anxious to recover from a recent recession began to scratch their heads and wonder, *What have we gotten ourselves into?*

It didn't end there. In 1993, Clinton nominated Ruth Bader Ginsberg to the Supreme Court of the United States. Ginsberg was by any measure a movement Leftist in America's culture wars. Having served in several linchpin positions at the American Civil Liberties Union, Ginsberg's fingerprints were all over the Left's attempts to litigate morality.

It went on like this. Jane Fonda represented the United States at the Cairo Population conference, where she took a decidedly pro-abortion stance. Clinton himself revoked the ban on homosexuals in the military and replaced it with the "don't ask, don't tell" policy. Generals in the United States Army were forced to sit through training videos with titles like *On Being Gay.*

Contrary to Clinton's promise to have a cabinet that "looks like

America," Clinton built a team that, in the words of national radio personality Don Imus, "looks like the bar scene in *Star Wars*."

Liberal political analyst Ruy Teixiera had to admit that "[c]ontrary to the hopes invested in the 'gender gap,' non-college-educated white women also deserted in droves. For both white women with a high school diploma and those with some college, Democratic support dropped 10 points. Thus, to ascribe the falloff in Democratic support to 'angry white guys,' as many commentators did, is to miss the point. Large numbers of non-college-educated white men and women alike abandoned the party."[4] White guys were no angrier at the Clinton administration than their female counterparts.

Clinton's cabinet surely did offend many Americans, but not because they were black or because they were women or because they were black female lesbians. Americans recoiled from Clinton's inner circle because these people were so drastically removed from the mainstream of America.

THE LIBERTARIAN FANTASY

The third prominent flawed analysis of the 1994 election comes from the Religious Right's sometimes friends and allies on the market-driven Right. These folks hold that 1994 was a libertarian uprising in which the American people finally had it with Washington DC's big government ways and threw the liberal bums out. According to this story line, the Contract with America, which was essentially an antigovernment manifesto, painted a clear contrast between the pro-big-government Left and the antigovernment, pro-individual Right. And the Right won. Pres. Bill Clinton himself seemed to endorse this analysis and tip his hat to market Republicans when he stated emphatically during his postelection State of the Union Address, "the era of big government is over."

As Hemingway once wrote, isn't it pretty to think so? I would love to believe this, but events subsequent to the GOP takeover should have swiftly disabused any enthusiastic libertarians of this chimera. Postelection polls showed that very few American voters, and even a minority of *Republican* voters, had even heard of the Contract with America, coverage of which didn't really take off in the mainstream press until *after* the election.

Moreover, when Clinton's name next appeared on the ballot in 1996, this deft political survivalist did not dance rightward on fiscal issues, but rather on values. Clinton talked up dress codes in public schools, antiviolence chips in television sets, and welfare reform, for its character-building effects. The message from Clinton was clear: I understand what you the public said in 1994 and I've changed, I've really, really changed. And he won. On values.

Moreover, perhaps having breathed too much of its own libertarian exhaust, the GOP leadership in Congress, especially in the House of Representatives, proceeded to advocate for significant spending cuts in some truly deplorable programs. Newt Gingrich and his revolutionaries did not just target the low-hanging fruit of "waste, fraud and abuse" either.

Republicans slated full federal departments for elimination, the federal department of Education most famously. And they got their heads bashed in by a revived Clinton who had no intention of presiding over a massive reduction of the federal government. Serious discussions of budget cuts have not graced the halls of Congress since.

PRELUDE TO 2004

To understand what happened in the 1994 election, political observers need to dispense of the long-held conventional wisdom that the Religious Right hurts the Republican Party as much as it helps it on Election Day. Yes, this has sometimes been the case. But it certainly was not the dynamic in effect in 1994.

What each of the above analyses ignore is the tremendous anxiety in America at the time that our cultural values were eroding at a rapid pace, that Pres. Bill Clinton and his team in Washington were somehow complicit in this cultural degradation, and that if left unfettered our country would devolve into a corrupted Las Vegas-style bender.

Reflect back on the state of American culture during Bill Clinton's first term. The hottest play in the country was *Angels in America*, a drama dripping with homosexual indignation and scorn for mainstream American cultural values. One of the hottest films of the year was *Philadelphia*, another tale of homosexuals in America in which the majority of villainous characters are stereotypical gay-hating conservatives. Other prominent films of the time seemed to mock American values: *Pulp Fiction, Kalifornia*, and *True Romance* were gratuitously violent; *Cape Fear* featured a murderous, Bible-quoting Christian in the villain role; *Indecent Proposal* dared to ask Americans how much money would it take to allow your wife to sleep with another man; *Natural Born Killers* celebrated the surreal depravity of its psycho killer main characters; *Threesome* continued the sexual liberation theme. . . .

The message from the Left Coast was clear. America is falling apart and we love it. But lest any slow-witted Americans refuse to blur fiction with reality, many of the same stars behind these unpleasant cultural achievements also became increasingly active in politics. On behalf of the Democrats, of course.

Moreover, America's decadence wasn't just the stuff of Hollywood magic. Stories of metal detectors being installed at schoolhouse doors and armed policemen having to roam the halls of public schools shocked Americans.

Other stories would have been humorous, had they not foretold of the aggressive secularist attacks on Americans of faith that are commonplace today. A schoolgirl in Nevada was barred from singing "The First Noel" at a school Christmas pageant. Other public schools began to ban Christmas celebrations altogether. Courthouses were barred from displaying the Ten Commandments.

High-profile stories of grisly murders, especially the murders of two South Carolina toddlers, added credence to the cry of conservatives that our nation was becoming awash in a culture of death (and it wasn't just about abortion). Meanwhile, the hapless Clinton administration offered up midnight basketball as some sort of criminal therapy and filled its campaign coffers with Hollywood dollars.

Americans were growing increasingly concerned about this decadent celebration. Meanwhile, another trend had begun to crest that would channel this annoyance and anxiety toward good use at the ballot box: Evangelical Christians and other Americans of faith had begun to express a keener interest in politics than perhaps ever before. Through the advanced political training and superior organizational skills of organizations such as Pat Robertson's Christian Coalition, Christians had begun to emerge as the strongest force in American politics.

THE LEFTIES GET ONE RIGHT

The 1994 election was the first in history in which a given voter's religious faith was a greater determiner than his class or income of how he would behave on Election Day. *Almanac of American Politics* coauthor Michael Barone wrote in his analysis of the 1994 election, "If you want to know whom American voters are for, ask what they believe, that is, in the religious sense of belief. For nothing—not economic status, not region, not even race—divides American voters as starkly as their religious beliefs."[5]

It has remained this way ever since. The more "religious" you are—measured by the frequency with which you attend church and the orthodoxy of your belief—the more likely you are to vote Republican. To this day, the greatest distinction between Republicans and Democrats has more to do with their religious views and practices than with any other tool political professionals use to identify voting blocs. This trend only became obvious in 1994, but it was in development for many years before that. Jim Pfaff from Focus on the Family told me, "It manifested itself in 1994. But it really started to blossom under Ronald Reagan."

To be sure, the Clinton administration's obliviousness to our nation's cultural decline under his watch (and perhaps with a few nudges from members of his cabinet) played a big part in erasing any lingering partisan ambiguities in the hearts and minds of religiously motivated voters. But it didn't happen in a vacuum. Conservative Christians had been building a political operation for decades, and at just about the time the GOP was prepared to take control of Washington DC in 1994, this political operation had become a well-oiled machine.

The growth of the Religious Right's political strength and its subsequent "take over" of state and local Republican Party committees led to the overwhelming revival of the Grand Old Party, which, in 1993 and 1994, had precisely zero power in Washington DC. Moreover, to deny the Religious Right its due with regard to the GOP revolution in 1994 is to ignore election data and to discount some of the most observant *liberal* political reporting during that time.

Hysterical news stories began to surface in 1993, warning Americans of an assertive new breed of Republican activist known sometimes as evangelicals, other times as fundamentalist, and some identified as members of the Christian Coalition (whether they were or not). Most of these articles were breathlessly paranoid and obnoxiously dismissive at the same time. Liberal opinion journalists were hearing stories about Christian activists "taking over" local Republican Party committees after the devastating GOP loss in 1992. One such journalist was liberal fire-breather Joe Conason, who in March of 1993 wrote about "the resurrection of the Christian right, a political movement pronounced dead at the end of the Eighties" for *Playboy*.[6]

Conason chronicled the movements of the Christian Right starting with the Reverend Pat Robertson's failed bid for the Republican presidential nomination in 1988, whence upon he founded the Christian Coalition and began to organize conservative Christians to take part in American politics. Had Conason been writing about any other group of Americans—say young people or blacks—this trend would have been regarded as an uplifting display of civic responsibility. But because these folks were believing Christians, Conason saw them as "a movement far more ominous then any represented by [George H.W.] Bush or Ronald Reagan."[7]

In Conason's telling of the story, local and state Republican bosses who were seeing their chapters taken over by Christians were innocent victims, the good guys even.

"These not-so-isolated incidents foreshadow a change taking place in American politics—a shift that has nothing to do with bounced checks, smoking bimbos, talk shows, dirty tricks or any other floating ephemera of campaign 1992," Conason explained. "Across the nation, in primary after primary, stunned Republican leaders echoed the lament of one longtime party activist in Texas, a personal friend of Barbara Bush, who suddenly found herself ousted by the fundamentalists. 'They organized and we didn't,' she said. 'I didn't think it was going to be this bad.'"[8]

At the time of Conason's writing, the Christian Coalition had about 550 chapters and hundreds of thousands of members across the country.[9] Those numbers would continue to grow throughout the early years of the Clinton presidency and, contrary to Conason's predictions of Republican dissolution, would turn the party committees they had "taken over" into powerful groups of activists, campaign volunteers, and voters.

Conason was dismissive of their ability to reform America once in power. "There may not be much chance that a majority of Americans would willingly vote to overturn the Constitution and to surrender their freedoms to a band of religious zealots," he wrote.[10] It's a fine thing, then, that overturning the Constitution was not the goal of these "religious zealots" at all.

Writing for the leading leftwing opinion journal, the *Nation*, Greg Goldin covered the goings on in small Republican-leaning suburbs like Vista, California, where religious conservatives had begun to "take over" local boards and commissions. "The same day Bill Clinton won the White House, the Christian right captured seats on school boards, hospital boards, county party committees, from Alaska to Minnesota, Washington to Texas," wrote Goldin.[11] "While national attention focused on George Bush's resounding defeat, few noticed that the fanatics who'd brought him to his knees at the Republican Convention in Houston were jubilant."

The Christian Coalition and other organizations, Goldin wrote, had targeted lower elected offices, and it was from these positions of power that Religious Rightists would "convert America to Christendom."[12]

"It is there that the local concerns dovetail with Pat Robertson's national strategy, and the counter revolution to the Clinton administration is taking shape. To the drumbeat of Rush Limbaugh, Christian militants are shaping the fears of white flight suburbanites into an electoral juggernaut."[13]

Seventeen months later Bill Clinton would suffer the worst off-year humiliation in the history of American politics.

Minus the vituperations, Conason and Goldin were reporting on a genuine phenomenon. Christian conservatives had been dispropor- tionately active in American politics for over a decade leading up to the 1994 campaign. Sometimes organized well, other times not, Christians seemed especially motivated by Bill Clinton's public flout- ing of America's traditional values. While Clinton won the presidency in 1992, the Democrats lost seats in the House of Representatives, a trend that foreshadowed the 1994 revolution and one for which the Religious Right must be given credit.

Conason and Goldin were virtually alone in seeing this growing electoral strength among Christians. Most pundits at the time believed (as many pundits still believe) the Religious Right was a net negative for Republicans. Doomsday predictions that the GOP would suffer because of Christian conservative influence have not panned out as feared, or in the case of folks like Conason and Goldin, as hoped.

Some Republicans publicly disassociated themselves with the Religious Right. Upon announcing his retirement from the United States Senate in 1993, John Danforth, an Episcopal priest, warned against the possibility of the Religious Right taking over the GOP. In conceivably the worst prophecy of all time, Danforth argued that the GOP should avoid the Religious Right "if you want to be a majority party." The GOP became a majority party less than two years later with significant help from the Religious Right.

Campaigns & Elections magazine claimed in 1994 that the Religious Right was the dominant faction in eighteen state Republican Party organizations and had substantial influence in thirteen more. Christian conservatives had only "minor influence" in nineteen states. The story took on additional significance when after the election we learned that those states that had been "taken over" by the Religious Right prior to the 1994 election contributed a greater number and greater share of new members of the legendary Republican freshman class of 1994. That is to say the Religious Right's takeover of the GOP led to a GOP takeover of Congress.[14]

WHO NEEDS A MACHINE?

When the 1994 campaign finally rolled around, all this increased activism within the Religious Right climaxed with an explosion of campaign activity that had no parallel in previous off-year elections. Though the number sounds slight by today's standards, political scientist John Green estimates that Religious Right groups spent as much as a combined $25 million on their grassroots efforts.[15]

These resources helped to motivate over seventy-five thousand activists nationwide. The Christian Coalition alone distributed fifty-seven million of its widely regarded voter guides, which laid out the candidates' positions on controversial issues in clear language. The Coalition also hosted "Citizenship Sundays" in sixty thousand churches during the two weeks leading up to the election in order to register Christians to vote.

The state of Georgia started to emerge as a two-party political system for the first time in its history thanks to aggressive efforts by the Religious Right, which began to bear fruit in 1994. In their essay titled "Georgia: The Christian Right and Grassroots Power," Charles S. Bullock III and John Christopher Grant quote a "senior political journalist" who estimates, "At least a third of the state's lawmakers owe their allegiance to the Christian Coalition. So do three of the five members of the Public Service Commission and at least four constitutional officers."[16]

"To these members could be added at least three members of Congress and a US Senator," add Bullock and Grant.[17]

During the General Election in Georgia, the Christian

Coalition distributed upward of two million voter guides and deployed hundreds—if not thousands—of volunteer activists. So powerful a political force had evangelical Christians become that Bullock and Grant reported that many Democrats chose not to run in 1994 for fear of alienating themselves from their churches.

Same for Texas. In 1994, 62 percent of white evangelicals helped heave a young candidate by the name of George W. Bush into the governor's chair. In the four years leading up to the 1994 election, the Christian Coalition grew their membership from nine thousand to seventy thousand in the Lone Star State. Nevertheless, intraparty squabbles during the summer of '94 dramatized great division within GOP ranks. Democrats giggled as Christian conservatives took over county and local parties operations and even "seized control of the state party apparatus" in June. It was widely believed that the Religious Right's "capture" of the GOP reigns would damage Bush and other Republicans in November.

The "experts" were wrong. Bush upset the popular Democrat Gov. Anne Richards. What is more, Republican Kay Bailey Hutchison sailed to reelection to the US Senate. Republicans gained seats in the state House and state Senate; they retained one constitutional office and won another for the first time in history.

In Oklahoma, the Religious Right was largely responsible for an historical paradigm shift in the state's political culture. On the morning of 8 November 1994, Oklahoma Democrats controlled the executive and legislative branches of state government and enjoyed a 5-3 majority in the congressional delegation. When the votes were counted, the Republicans had won the governor's office and the lieutenant governor's office, they gained seats in both chambers of the state legislature, and they won all but one seat in the congressional legislation.

As if to remove any doubt as to who was principally responsible for this revolutionary turn of political events, congressional victors Steve Largent, Tom Coburn, J.C. Watts, and Frank Lucas were committed Christian conservative candidates, and conservative Mormon Ernest Istook unapologetically accepted the enthusiastic support of conservative Christians. Moreover, Jim Inhofe, whose sister was a well-known Religious Right political organizer, crushed his Democrat opponent by fifteen points.

At first glance, Virginia appeared to have been a mixed bag for the Christian right. Their favored candidate for US Senate was Col. Oliver North who lost to embattled Democrat incumbent Chuck Robb. But the results were actually rather encouraging. According to exit polls and postelection opinion research, North lost more because of his troubled past involving the Iran-Contra scandal during the Reagan presidency, which dogged him throughout the campaign. Moreover, former Office of Management and Budget director Jim Miller, who lost to North in the Republican primary, ran to the *right* of North on several values issues, especially abortion. Nevertheless, most pundits concede, Miller would have posed a more difficult challenge to Robb than North did.

In addition, because Virginia conducts their state elections in the "off-year," it is instructive to see how the 1993 state elections turned out in the context of our examination of the Religious Right during that era. In 1993, Republicans enjoyed success across Old Dominion. George Allen and Jim Gilmore won the governorship and lieutenant governorship respectively with strong public backing from Religious Right groups. Republicans also gained seats in the state legislature.

Republicans began a long dynasty of domination in South Carolina in 1994 behind the dedicated activism of Christian conservatives. Wrote James L. Guth, "Early in the 1994 campaign, South Carolina Democratic humorists quipped that only two skills were required to win a Republican gubernatorial nomination: speaking in tongues and handling snakes. . . . [O]n November 8 the joke was on them."[18] Like Georgia, Texas, and Virginia, South Carolina emerged into a two-party political system in 1994 largely due to the efforts of the Religious Right.

States like Michigan, Minnesota, Iowa, California, and Washington saw the number of Republicans in their congressional delegation grow substantially in 1994 as well.

Curiously, the state Republican Party operations in each of these states were reported by *Campaigns & Elections* magazine to have been "taken over" by the Religious Right by 1994. Journalists Conason and Goldin were dead right in their reporting of the same. Predictions that this Religious Right "takeover" would result in huge Democratic victories were dead wrong.

Those who benefited from the electoral hard work of the Religious Right in 1994 recognized their efforts. According to Clyde Wilcox, "When the new Republican majority took office in the House and Senate in January 1995, Christian Right lobbyists suddenly had access to the majority party. A significant portion of the new GOP majority were active evangelical Christians."[19]

STEALTH CAMPAIGN?

How could this have happened? How could a party that just got walloped out of office in 1992 and had subsequently been taken over by religious wackos mount such an extraordinary political realignment?

To begin with, these premises are incorrect. Republicans did not get bounced from office in 1992; President George H.W. Bush did. Republicans actually gained seats in the Congress that year. And the idea that the religious conservatives who "took over" the

GOP in the early 1990s were nutty is certainly subjective: among the people who comb the halls of mainstream media outfits in New York City and who frequently find themselves on casting couches in Hollywood, yes, religious conservatives are crazy. But to a great many Americans, and in some congressional districts, even a majority of citizens, the Religious Right was the mainstream culture in 1994.

Nevertheless, the types of people who would even pose such questions generally lack the critical thinking skills to get beyond the shock of the 1994 election. So they created a myth: Christian conservatives ran for office in 1994 in great numbers and many of them succeeded, but only because they ran "stealth" campaigns and hid the fact that they were Christians or even conservative at all.

If the Religious Right planned a sneak attack on the American people, it was—at least in that regard—wildly unsuccessful. In a July 1994 column, Dr. James Zogby wrote, "In an effort to define an issue that will shape their campaign strategy for the 1994 congressional elections, the Democrats have launched a well-orchestrated campaign criticizing the Republican Party for being taken over by 'radical right-wing religious elements.'"[20]

Throughout the summer Democrat leaders, including members of the Clinton administration, delivered high-profile speeches repeating the criticism that the GOP was under the influence of Christian extremists. Zogby was unequivocal: "Democrats will attempt to make the strength of the Christian right within the Republican Party an issue in this fall's elections."[21]

At a speech at the National Press Club in June, Representative Vic Fazio, then head of the Democratic Congressional Campaign Committee, lambasted Christian conservatives and predicted they would cost the GOP votes in November. The Democrats would be "picking up seats that are being fought out over issues of intolerance, issues related to the agenda of the radical Right as the agenda of the Republican Party."[22] Joycelyn Elders, DNC Chairman David Wilhelm, and President Clinton himself all repeated the charge within a couple of weeks. On a St. Louis talk-radio program, Clinton compared the Reverend Jerry Falwell to the money-changers in the temple who drew Jesus's fury. Sydney Blumethal, who would later join the Clinton White House, joined in on the fun writing in the *New Yorker,* "the Religious Right is winning a holy war in the state Republican parties . . . how far will they go?"

The Democrat's message in 1994 was clear, and they distributed it with Clintonesque campaign discipline: vote Republican in 1994 and you are voting for the "radical Religious Right."

Americans voted Republican anyway.

FAITH PLUS HARD WORK

But it would be a mistake to conclude that the success of a Christianized GOP in 1994 was merely the result of hardworking "zealots" in the Christian Coalition and other conservative religious groups.

While it is tempting merely to credit the organizational skills of Ralph Reed, the Christian Coalition's visionary Executive Director, as well as other Religious Right leaders, all the money and all the activist man-hours in the world cannot fundamentally alter the makeup of our representative form of government in a democratic society in which the people decide who their leaders will be. Voters must be willing participants for a revolution like 1994 to occur.

And they were.

This is the hardest part about the 1994 election for liberals to swallow. Ascendant Republicans didn't lie about who they were and what they had in mind in terms of public policy. The very fact that Republican politicians were honest about their public policy positions and that most Americans *agreed* with them created the anxiety among American liberals, which today has turned to rage.

In a preelection poll conducted in September by Peter D. Hart Research, 51 percent of all respondents agreed that the nation's most serious social problems "stem mainly from a decline in moral values," as opposed to 34 percent who agreed that they "stem mainly from economic and financial pressures on the family." Seventy-four percent said they would be more willing to support a candidate who puts "top priority on returning to traditional moral values." And over 60 percent of respondents said that the "declining role of religion in America" was a serious problem.

Here's the really interesting part. The poll was commissioned by People for the American Way, the self-assigned archrival of the Religious Right in America.

Democrats had spent the entire summer attacking Republicans for being puppets on Christians' string, and by the end of the summer most Americans told pollsters that's exactly what they were looking for.

Several nonpolitical events and trends also foretold of an increasing desire for more religion, specifically more Christianity, in American life. The Promise Keepers, a Christ-centered organization dedicated to introducing men to Jesus Christ and helping them to be better husbands and fathers, attracted fifty thousand Christian men to Boulder, Colorado, for their annual gathering in 1993. In 1994 that number ballooned to almost three-hundred thousand men, and Promise Keepers filled six stadiums across the country.

The Christian book industry exploded, as well. *Christianity Today* reported on a 92 percent increase in Christian book sales between 1991 and 1994, a year in which 70.5 million Christian books were sold.

By 1993 there were over 1,200 Christian radio stations. One out of every ten radio stations categorized itself as "religious." This boom in Christian radio stations supported a blossoming Contemporary Christian Music industry that by the early 1990s had begun to develop superstars all its own like Amy Grant and Michael W. Smith.

And in the two decades ending in 1990 conservative evangelical churches had established a trend, which has not abated since. Between 1971 and 1990, evangelical churches added more than 6 million new members while liberal mainline Protestant churches lost 2.6 million members.

Religion in America was on the rise in the early 1990s, period. The Religious Right's "take over" of the GOP and the GOP's subsequent "take over" of Washington DC were but two manifestations of this trend.

In her book *With God on Their Side*, Esther Kaplan laments, "The White House, Senate, and Congress are all now in Republican hands, and most states have Republicans in the governor's office. In 2002, Republicans won enough local races to outnumber Democratic state legislatures for the first time in fifty tears. Control over these state bodies will likely tilt to the US Congress in an increasingly Republican direction as well, since state legislatures, in most states, draw the lines for Congressional districts. And with the Republican Party decisively under the sway of evangelical conservatives, who now run everything from the state parties to the national party platform committee, Republican Party rule means ongoing political influence by the Christian Right."[23]

But enough with history. We can now move on to the section that can reasonably be called "current events." We'll fast-forward ten years to the rancorous 2004 presidential campaign between Pres. George W. Bush and Democrat Senator John Kerry. The election has kicked of a new round of intense debate about the Religious Right, the role of religion in public life, and just how far the Democrats have distanced themselves from Americans of faith.

5

JANET VS. MEL

The tone and tenor of the 2004 presidential campaign was set on Sunday, 1 February. On that day, aging pop star Janet Jackson and already-past-his-prime boy-toy Justin Timberlake performed a raunchy Super Bowl halftime show that culminated in Timberlake ripping of the right cup of Jackson's leather bustier to expose her breast on national television.

Now, the Super Bowl is the most watched television event every year, and ninety-nine million Americans happened to watch this particular Super Bowl. In many households, it was the only football game a wife watched all year. In addition, the Super Bowl is an odd and unexplainable bonding moment between fathers and sons. So when Janet Jackson's bare breast came bouncing out, there were lots of embarrassed and enraged parents. Industry types immediately tried to spin the incident as a "wardrobe malfunction." But Americans aren't stupid. Timberlake sang, "I gotta have you naked before the end of this song" just before the infamous "costume reveal."

Moreover, the halftime show was only one incident in a uniquely ribald Super Bowl event. The Super Bowl commercials that year—an annual attraction in and of themselves—were notoriously raunchy. One ad for the Web domain registry GoDaddy.com featured a "well-endowed" actress before a congressional hearing asking for permission to appear in a GoDaddy.com commercial.

When the actress stood up, the strap of her tank top came undone. She then performed a dance number for the committee reminiscent of a striptease routine to show off her "talents" to the committee. The members were depicted as easily offended old fogies who needed to get with the times. Art imitating life imitating life imitating art, I suppose. The tasteless ad ran during the first quarter when millions of children were still awake and hoping to catch a glimpse of their gridiron heroes in the biggest game of the year.

The entire Super Bowl affair was a powerful moment in culture war symbolism. Here was that annual moment of classic Americana—the Big Game—drenched in licentiousness and soft-core pornography. Christian groups were up in arms. And middle-of-the-road Americans shared their disgust.

Howard Dean, by then a flailing contender for the Democratic presidential nomination, wasn't too bothered by it, however. He called a Federal Communications Commission investigation into the Super Bowl's primetime porn "silly."[1] Rep. Sheila Jackson Lee (D-TX) said she was "proud" of the "family oriented entertainment" her hometown of Houston provided the country as the host city of the Super Bowl.[2] And as for Senator John Kerry, who by this time had the Democratic nomination for president pretty well wrapped up, he couldn't be bothered with such concerns. Instead, Kerry wrung his hands in worry at a Los Angeles press conference over whether or not Mel Gibson's *The Passion of the Christ* contained anti-Semitic messages.[3]

TWO AMERIKAS

Mel Gibson's putative anti-Semitism dominated leftwing water cooler confabs in 2004. Leon Weiseltier, the literary editor of the *New Republic,* argued, "In its representation of its Jewish characters,

The Passion of the Christ is without any doubt an anti-Semitic movie, and anybody who says otherwise knows nothing, or chooses to know nothing, about the visual history of anti-Semitism, in art and in film."[4] *Time* called it "the goriest story ever told."[5] Abe Foxman of the Anti-Defamation League said, "The film can fuel, trigger, stimulate, induce, rationalize, legitimize anti-Semitism."[6] David Edelstein of the leftwing online magazine *Slate* dubbed *The Passion of the Christ,* "*The Jesus Chainsaw Massacre.*"[7]

The Super Bowl? Grow up, America. Can't you see your *religion* is the hateful scandal?

Electoral politics are about symbols. Most Americans are altogether too busy to focus on the minutia of politics. Few people outside the think tanks of Washington DC recall the myriad twists and turns of Pres. Ronald Reagan's foreign policy during the final decade of the Soviet Union's existence. Instead, they remember that he stood in West Berlin and said, "Mr. Gorbachev, tear down this wall."

I do not mean to suggest that the American people are shallow or that our politics are vapid. On the contrary, I believe Americans lead complex lives, and our national affairs are so immeasurably complex that we rely on these kinds of potent symbols to burn through the clutter. Symbols are good. They are important. And I can think of no more potent culturally symbolic moments that sum up America in 2004 than these two symbols: reactions to Janet Jackson's "reveal" and the buzz around Mel Gibson's powerful movie.

With the Super Bowl incident, we had everything that is wrong with our liberated society, so obsessed with radical personal autonomy. It is of no surprise, of course, that the aging pop star chose to expose herself in a vain attempt to revive her career. But two things cause distress for Americans who think these kinds of things are better left to pay-per-view television.

First, someone—or more probably, *someones*—at MTV, who

produced the show, the NFL, who hosted the show, or CBS, who aired the show, thought this was a great idea. While executives from each of the three culprits took great pains to distance themselves from this foolish decision, no one emerged to say, yeah, they ran this idea by me and I thought it was really stupid and that we shouldn't do it. It appears that no one in these massive communications outfits had the critical thinking skills to realize some Americans might actually be offended by public nudity on a primetime family television program.

Second, lest we forget, a great many Americans remarked the next morning "how cool" Janet's surprise was. I recall many coworkers and peers chattering about "how awesome" the "reveal" was.

But remember, the Janet Jackson affair was just a symbol. It worked as a pervasive cultural symbol because so many Americans saw it at the same time (rather like the old days when American tastes were not so atomized and we all watched the same three news broadcasts) and because it was indicative of the general decline in our public morality.

Consider the March 2004 study by the Parents Television Council, which profiled, among other outrages, "In 171 hours of MTV programming . . . containing 3,056 depictions of sex or various forms of nudity and 2,881 verbal sexual references. That means that children watching MTV are viewing an average of nine sexual scenes per hour with approximately 18 sexual depictions and 17 instances of sexual dialogue or innuendo. To put this in perspective, consider that in its last study of sex on primetime network television, the PTC found an average of only 5.8 instances of sexual content during the 10 o'clock hour—when only adults are watching."[8]

That was one week of programming on one channel.

Many Americans—especially many Christian conservatives—see these kinds of unwholesome images as smutty self-fulfilling prophecies.

If you expose your children to this kind of thing, they will want more of it. And they will get it. While Howard Dean et al. think smut TV is nothing to get worked up about, other Americans worry that it leads to an increased sexual adventurism among children.

In a recent survey of five thousand students in Hillsborough County, Florida, for example, nearly half of high-schoolers and one in five middle-schoolers say they have had sexual intercourse.[9] It is nearly impossible not to sense a correlation between these two phenomena. Reactions to smut TV (and its relatives in the music world, the publishing world, and the Internet) often manifest themselves in calls for government censorship, personal efforts at self-censorship, or, I believe, conservative behavior at the voting booth.

Certainly John Kerry is not responsible for the moral decline of America, you say. And in some respects you would be correct. But are not liberals in America uniquely indifferent to this decadence? Certainly Howard Dean's comments indicate he doesn't care. While we cannot assume Kerry enjoyed Janet Jackson's performance, didn't his silence say something profound to Americans who are concerned about our shared moral character?

The Democrats, remember, are notoriously reliant on the political and financial favors of the same Hollywood smut-peddlers who degrade our culture. At a star-studded gala that raised over $7.5 million for the Kerry-Edwards campaign in July, alleged comedienne Whoopi Goldberg unleashed a sexually charged attack against President Bush including puns about the president's last name.[10] She was not alone. Actress Jessica Lange referred to Bush as our "so-called president" and said she would do everything short of selling her children to defeat him in November.[11] That night Kerry himself said, "Every performer tonight . . . conveyed to you the heart and soul of our country."[12] John Edwards echoed Kerry's gratitude and claimed, "This campaign will be a celebration of real American values."[13] The

Kerry-Edwards campaign refused to release a videotape of the event to the public when challenged to do so by the Republican National Committee, knowing full well the public relations disaster it would create.

In another telling example, John Kerry's daughter Alexandra, who had an official role in her father's campaign, appeared at the Cannes Film Festival in France in a sheer gown that left her breasts completely exposed. Suddenly, Janet Jackson's primetime peep show and Democratic Party coarseness didn't seem so distinct.

In some ways it seems unfair to blame the Janet Jacksons of the world for the coarsening of American culture. She and Madonna and Britney Spears and the rest are but cogs in the entertainment money machine. But John Kerry? Well, he claimed leadership status in this country and even sought the highest public office in the land. And Kerry and company were deliberate in their decadence.

During an interview with *Rolling Stone* during the presidential campaign, candidate Kerry used "the F-word," ostensibly to convince readers he was hip. Later, Matt Drudge highlighted countless obscenities posted on the "Kerry for President" website. Kerry's classy wife, Teresa, told the press she didn't "give a shit"[14] whether they call her Teresa Heinz, Teresa Kerry, or Teresa Heinz Kerry.

The evidence piled high and deep against the Democrats in 2004 that they were part of what was wrong with America.

At around the same time that Janet Jackson exposed herself on national television, Mel Gibson began to market his forthcoming film, *The Passion of the Christ*. Moments after word escaped that Gibson was producing and directing a film about the last hours of Jesus's life, it became quite obvious to all that reaction to the film would be politically motivated.

New York Times sob sister Maureen Dowd was not a big fan of *The Passion of the Christ*. She claimed director Mel Gibson was "courting bigotry in the name of sanctity."[15] After watching the film, Dowd wrote, "you want to kick in some Jewish and Roman teeth. And since the Romans have melted into history . . ."[16] She then went on to compare Roman Catholicism to drug and alcohol addiction, calling the Stations of the Cross "the ultimate 12-step program."[17] To say that Dowd was out-of-touch with mainstream America in this regard would be an understatement, however. Dowd claimed her local theater at 84th Street and Broadway in New York City was only about a quarter filled on the night she caught *The Passion*.[18] That's odd because the film is the ninth top grossing film in history.

In a review by Charles Krauthammer, who is not normally inspired to comment on movies and such, the reader was led to believe Christianity itself is an anti-Semitic slur against Jews. "Christians have their story too: the crucifixion and resurrection of Christ. Why is this story different from other stories? Because it is not a family affair of coreligionists," wrote Krauthammer. "If it were, few people outside the circle of believers would be concerned about it. This particular story involves other people. With the notable exception of a few Romans, these people are Jews. And in the story, they come off rather badly. Because of that peculiarity, the crucifixion is not just a story; it is a story with its own story—a history of centuries of relentless, and at times savage, persecution of Jews in Christian lands."[19]

Krauthammer went on to implicate the Gospels in the Holocaust: "The blood libel that this story affixed upon the Jewish people had led to countless Christian massacres of Jews and prepared Europe for the ultimate massacre—6 million Jews systematically murdered in six years—in the heart, alas, of a Christian continent."[20]

Leftwing drama queen Andrew Sullivan thought the film was pornographic. "I repeat that there is something deeply disturbed about this film," Sullivan wrote on his blog. "Its extreme and un-Biblical fascination with human torture reflects, to my mind, not devotion to the message of the Cross but a kind of psycho-sexual obsession with extreme violence that Gibson has indulged in many of his other movies and is now trying to insinuate into Christianity itself."[21]

Reaction to *The Passion of the Christ* was indeed decidedly political. How then were Christian admirers of the film expected to behave on Election Day, which loomed only a few months in the distance? According to a prescient story that ran in the *Economist* a month before Election Day 2004, "The people who wept at Mel Gibson's 'The Passion of the Christ' will vote for Mr. Bush in November just as surely as those who cheered Michael Moore's 'Fahrenheit 9/11' will not."[22]

Taken together, these two cultural moments, which occurred more or less contemporaneously, shone a light on the cultural differences between two groups of Americans. Let us call them Janet Jackson-Americans and Mel Gibson-Americans.

For years, armchair political analysts have tried to break America down into two groups: red vs. blue, north vs. south, urban vs. suburban, "Metro" vs. "Retro." In truth, however, the main distinction between the two largest groups in America is not how much they make or the color of their skin or where they live or their gender, but rather the way they view their relationship with God. Religious people and irreligious people are different. In many ways they inhabit different countries.

When these two Americans clash, we call it a culture war. On my blog, I dubbed the combatants of this culture war Janet Jackson-Americans and Mel Gibson-Americans because these two stars and their recent newsworthy antics were perfectly emblematic of the warring factions in the culture war.

UNDER WHOM?

The battle fronts of this culture war took Americans to Elk Grove, California, where avowed atheist publicity hound Michael Newdow sued the school district because it invited his daughter to participate voluntarily in a Pledge of Allegiance every morning. The Pledge includes the words "under God." This, as far as Newdow was concerned, was a clear violation of his daughter's constitutional rights.

The Ninth US Circuit Court of Appeals—the most overturned court in the federal circuit and often referred to derisively by conservatives as the "Ninth Circus"—agreed with Newdow, saying, "the coercive effect of the policy here is particularly pronounced in the school setting given the age and impressionability of schoolchildren."[23] The decision was put on hold pending a Supreme Court challenge, but as far as the federal judiciary was concerned at that point, uttering "under God" in a classroom was unconstitutional.

This all happened in 2002. By 2004 the case was before the Supreme Court. And conservative Christians were not at all confident that the gang of black-robed elitists would do the right thing. In the end, the court punted. In June, the court ruled unanimously that the case be dismissed. However, a majority of five justices ruled that because Newdow was estranged from his wife and daughter he did not have standing to contest the Elk Grove School District's policy. The Ninth Circus's decision was tossed in the trash can, like so many of its other decisions. But the Court left open the possibility that some other disgruntled atheist with a closer relationship with his children could pursue a similar case.

Charles Lane of the *Washington Post* reported that the "outcome means that the pledge remains as it is—and that a potentially incendiary election-year debate over religion, patriotism and the federal courts has been defused."[24] This was an important hope for American liberals. A Gallup poll earlier that spring indicated that 91 percent of Americans wanted "under God" to remain in the Pledge. Only 8 percent thought it should be expunged.[25] For liberals, the sooner this issue went away the better.

But it didn't go away. While many conservative Christians were relieved that the decision of the Ninth Circus was tossed out, they were furious that the Court kept open the question of whether or not "under God" offends the US Constitution. They knew full well that theophobes would take another bite at the apple. Almost immediately after the decision was announced, Barry Lynn of Americans United for Separation of Church and State warned, "The justices ducked this constitutional issue today, but it is certain to come back in the future."[26]

James Dobson typified Christian frustration with the Supreme Court's nondecision. "I am certainly pleased that the US Supreme Court has overturned the decision of the Ninth US Circuit Court of Appeals," he said. "However, the Supreme Court does not emerge from this case the defender of America's moral and Christian heritage—in fact, it showed a lack of principle that is truly appalling. Instead of settling this question once and for all, the Court has left the nation to wonder if God's name will be found unconstitutional if another challenge is brought in a procedurally correct fashion. By refusing to rule on the substance of the case, the Supreme Court has left the door open for additional challenges to our nation's godly foundation—one which is reflected on our currency, in our government buildings—including the Supreme Court's own chamber—and in the oaths we take."[27]

Newdow himself seemed to take pleasure in stoking the flames of Christian frustration. "There's no problem bringing the case right back," he told Paula Zahn of CNN.[28]

ALSO RANS

Finding no satisfaction within the unelected, unaccountable branch of the federal government, conservative Christians were motivated by these events to participate with even more energetic vigor in the electoral process. There was also a cluster of smaller issues that brought people to the polls that we should not let escape our notice.

Remember that the Ten Commandments also found themselves in the Star Chamber in 2004. One year before the 2004 election, a federal judge in Montgomery, Alabama, ruled that a 2.6 ton granite monument to the Ten Commandments had to be removed from a state judicial building because it violated the church-state separation principle and therefore offended the US Constitution.

Alabama Chief Justice Roy Moore's refusal to remove the monument created a highly publicized conflict between the federal and state courts. The federal court won when agents of the federal government forcibly removed the monument on 12 November 2003. Barry Lynn of Americans United for Separation of Church and State was there again taunting religious conservatives, calling the removal of the Ten Commandments "a tremendous victory for the rule of law and respect for religious diversity. . . . Perhaps Roy Moore will soon leave the bench and move into the pulpit, which he seems better suited for."[29] And yet, as with the Janet Jackson and "under God" controversies and the war over *The Passion of the Christ*, leftwing theophobes found themselves on the wrong side of public opinion. A CNN-*USA Today*-Gallup poll found that 77 percent of Americans opposed the federal court's mandate to remove the monument.

Conservative Christians found themselves in the right and in the clear majority, yet they were hobbled and overruled by an unelected and unaccountable branch of the federal government.

And during the summer of 2004, a coalition of feminist and

pro-abortion groups held a gathering, which they dubbed "the March for Women's Lives" on the National Mall in Washington DC. In the same week, that left-of-center pollster John Zogby began to recognize growing public support for the unborn,[30] thousands of aggressive, angry feminists waved placards and wore sandwich boards saying things like, "Barbara should have had an abortion," "Get your rosaries out of my ovaries," and "Hands off my Bush."

The mainstream media did its best to portray the march as a thoughtful, upbeat gathering of concerned female citizens. But uncensored pictures of the event were easily obtained and published online by bloggers, which revealed "the March for Women's Lives" to be a macabre freak show complete with scowl-faced women waving coat hangers and one female member of Congress urging the president of the United States to "go to hell."

One cluster of marchers wore white lab coats and waved boastful signs that read, "We are tomorrow's abortion providers."

THAT'S OUR BUSH

All the while, leftwing pundits and liberal politicians hurled snide insults at Pres. George W. Bush for his public displays of faith. To be sure, Bush is one of the more religiously expressive presidents in history. Most Americans appreciate this level of religious conviction in their president. According to the Pew Research Center, 72 percent of all Americans agree that a "president should have strong religious beliefs." And only two months before the 2004 election, only 24 percent of all Americans thought President Bush mentioned his faith "too much."

Evangelicals, of course, love it when President Bush slips passages from Scripture or stanzas from popular Christian hymns into his speeches. Catholics tend to think it's okay; some think it's pretty cool, in fact. But many Catholics still express a level of concern about the infusion of religion in public life, or, rather, more concern than Protestants tend to express. Most Jews are historically hostile to any blending of church and state. Given the particularly oppressive history of that religious group, one can certainly understand why. Conservative and orthodox Jews tend to be far less worried about it than secular Jews.

But now we come to the category that's often marked "other," which includes most members of the mainstream media, liberal politicians, and opinion molders in general. At best, they think President Bush's religious expression is some kind of weird code language spoken between him and his evangelical base, worthy of the occasional teasing and derisive snark. At worst, they see Bush's religiosity as a dangerous threat to America.

At times, the political chattering class has been downright cruel to the president.

Leftists have had a lot of fun with the idea that then-Governor George W. Bush claimed to have heard "the call" to run and serve as president. "Even if the president does not literally believe," writes Esther Kaplan, "that God told him to strike at al-Qaeda and Saddam Hussein, his unwavering certainty about every decision he has made regarding the war on terror is likely bolstered by the prevalence of such beliefs within his administration and among his most fervent supporters."[31]

"He became convinced that God was calling him to engage the forces of evil in battle, and this one time baseball-team owner from Texas did not shrink from the task," Tom Carver of the BBC has said.[32]

"So Iraq's a mess and half the country hates you. Just keep praying," cackled Rick Perlstein in the *Village Voice*.[33]

"Are the White House and the Bush campaign actively encouraging the idea that Bush has been put there by God? Bush has been careful to never say anything close to that in public. And yet the combination of passages in carefully vetted speeches and quotes from close friends or supporters indicate that this is the understanding," wrote Steven Waldman in *Slate* shortly after the Republican National Convention.[34]

Liberal pundit Bill Press has even questioned President Bush's religious conviction, suspecting it is little more than slick packaging. "Skepticism about the calculated nature of Bush's faith is further fueled by the fact that he belongs to no congregation [Note: this isn't true. Bush belongs to a Methodist church in Texas] and does not regularly attend church services [Note: President Bush reads the Bible and prays every morning at 6:00 AM]—compared with John Kerry, for example, who wears a crucifix, carried a rosary and Bible with him on the campaign trail, and goes to Mass every Sunday. On the other hand, why should Bush bother going to church? He's apparently got a direct hotline to God."[35]

Absent from any of these taunts is any critical understanding of what many evangelicals believe about providence. Evangelicals believe God is the author of all things. So while American voters literally choose their presidents at the voting booth, God has already written down the outcome beforehand. Given this understanding, it would be irrational and unnatural for Bush and his evangelical supporters to believe he was not chosen by God, for whatever purpose.

Many Christians believe that God indeed chose George W. Bush to be president of the United States during this time, just as He chose you to be a plumber or a doctor or a teacher. But liberal pundits, anxious to make Bush look stupid or backward, simply smear him for expressing a worldview that is completely consistent with his Christian faith.

Another common attack directed at President Bush's religious conviction during the 2004 campaign was the charge that Bush claims God told him to invade Iraq. "President George Bush has claimed he was told by God to invade Iraq and attack Osama bin Laden's stronghold of Afghanistan as part of a divine mission to bring peace to the Middle East, security for Israel, and a state for the Palestinians," Rupert Cornwall unambiguously averred in the *Independent*.[36] This story is based on the probably exaggerated retelling of President Bush's meeting with two Palestinian leaders who claim Bush justified his mission by claiming God, indeed, told him what to do. Sounds crazy, huh? This guy must be nuts. Let's vote him out of office.

But forget for a moment that one of the participants in this conversation later recanted. What if I told you I talk to God every day? That might sound a little weird to the average secularist, but Christians know I'm simply saying that I pray to God every day. All Christians do it. Shoot, before my wife and I sold our house in Maryland and moved north to New Hampshire, we prayed on it together. We asked God for His guidance and wisdom. I would find it rather discomforting if President Bush *hadn't* prayed to God for guidance before sending our fighting men and women off to war. After we put this story in its most probable context, it doesn't sound so weird, does it?

These dishonest and deceptively demeaning attacks on President Bush's Christian faith were not lost on evangelicals and conservative Catholics when it came time to choose the next president of the United States.

You could hear the disdain for President Bush's faith in big media's collective bowel clenching when the president used the word *crusade* to describe the war on terror shortly after 9/11. See, it *is* a holy war, we knew it! Forget that Dwight Eisenhower used the word *crusade* to describe our call to arms during World War II and even wrote a book titled *Crusade in Europe*. Forget also that Osama bin

Laden quotes the Koran to justify killing Americans and Jews. Bush's religiosity was something to get *really* worked-up about.

Against the backdrop of this Christian-baiting, I ask, how were evangelical Christians and conservative Catholics expected to behave on Election Day?

DEFINING MARRIAGE DOWN

But the biggest battle in the culture war of 2004 started on 18 November 2003 when the Massachusetts Supreme Court struck down a state law banning same-sex marriage as unconstitutional.

This decision offended conservatives of all stripes for several reasons. Here was another example, like the "under God" controversy and the Ten Commandments battle, in which the unelected and unaccountable branch of the government decreed what was right and what was wrong to an American public with no democratic recourse.

Worse, the people feared that once legalization stuck in one state, the Supreme Court justices would find a "right" to gay marriage under the full faith and credit clause of the US Constitution. And the other forty-nine states would have to get with the program.

The principle reason most conservatives—indeed most Americans—recoiled at this decision by the Massachusetts Supreme Court was because they simply opposed gay marriage, period.

I am not here talking exclusively about religious conservatives or only people who identify themselves as conservatives. The majority of *all* Americans opposed gay marriage when the decision came down in Massachusetts, and continue to do so. In a December 2003 poll conducted on behalf of CBS News and the *New York Times*, 61 percent of Americans said they opposed gay marriage.[37] In a similar poll taken by a partisan operation on behalf of National Public Radio, 56 percent said they opposed gay marriage.[38]

For their parts, pro-gay-marriage liberals knew not how to react. Perhaps knowing the issue would be sheer poison for them in the 2004 election, they employed a two-pronged strategy: First, they declared the Massachusetts Supreme Court to be no big deal. Second, they attacked Republicans for trying to make political hay while the sun was shining.

Americans weren't buying it. Gay marriage remained unpopular throughout the 2004 election. Eleven states placed questions on their ballots inviting their citizens to write a ban on gay marriage into their state constitutions (all eleven would pass overwhelmingly). President Bush publicly backed a constitutional amendment at the federal level, which did not pass. Liberal politicians across the country were forced to answer the question: what are you going to do about this?

The guy who was really in the hot seat on this issue was Senator John Kerry, who represents Massachusetts, and was named by *National Journal* in 2004 as the Most Liberal Member of the United States Senate. Americans were deeply suspicious of Senator Kerry's assertion that he had the same position on gay marriage as V.P. Richard Cheney, whom Kerry-boosters were erstwhile attacking for being an irresponsible rightwing warmonger.

The most liberal senator in America, who also happened to be from the offending state in question, claimed to have the same position on one of the most important issues of the election as the man he was trying to toss out of office, and for some reason the Democrats expected Americans to just say, "Oh, okay then. That settles that."

Obviously, voters were unconvinced.

FIGHTING THE WRONG WAR

This was the backdrop against which the 2004 campaign took place. The politicians focused heavily on the Iraq war, as did the press. But here at home culture war bombs were going off left, right, and center.

So when the media began to talk about the exit polls showing a plurality of voters citing "moral values" as the principle motivation behind their Election Day behavior, some of us expressed little surprise. There has always been a strong contingent of values-driven voters in presidential elections. Why should 2004 be any different, especially with so much obvious wear and tear to our society's moral fabric?

Nevertheless, the press was shocked. Moral values!? This election was supposed to be about Iraq and healthcare. It was supposed to be about how George Bush lied us into war and failed to capture Osama bin Laden. This election was supposed to be about how President Bush dodged the draft and went AWOL as a member of the National Guard. This election was supposed to be about how George W. Bush willingly allowed sick Americans to die because he opposed embryonic stem-cell research.

How could this have happened?

Suddenly, the Religious Right had everyone's attention.

6

THIRTY MILLION JESUS FREAKS CAN'T BE WRONG

The best way to think about the postelection analysis from 2004 is of two armies. One army advances on a piece of terrain and swiftly takes it. The second army girds its forces, complete with superior firepower and overwhelming troop strength. This second army not only retakes the lost ground, but then proceeds to decimate opposition forces, hopeful none will live to retell the tale of their inspiring, if short-lived, victory.

This first army represents the immediate conventional wisdom after a 2004 exit poll showed that 22 percent of all voters were motivated to vote by "moral values" issues, as opposed to 20 percent who said the "economy and jobs" motivated them, 19 percent who said "terrorism," and 15 percent who said Iraq.[1]

"What does Bush owe the Religious Right?" asked Karen Tumulty and Matthew Cooper in *Time* magazine. "They helped reelect the President, and Christian conservatives want payback."[2]

"I think the rise of what was called moral values in the polls on this election defined a group of people whose families face, who want to live, and do live in what we would call an old-fashioned life . . . more 'Father Knows Best' and less 'The Times They Are A Changin',' " historian and writer Richard Reeves, who studies politics and presidents, told CBS News. "And 'Father Knows Best' held on."[3]

"Voters focused on four issues: moral values, the economy, terrorism and the war in Iraq. The issue most voters thought was most important was moral values," observed Dan Rather. "For those voters, the choice was lopsided: 79 percent went for Mr. Bush, and only 18 percent for Kerry."[4]

Some of the duller lights of this analysis emanated, of course, from liberal pundits. These folks accepted the idea that moral values won the election for Bush. Yet they resented the fact because they themselves very publicly reject America's moral values. "Can a people that believe more fervently in the Virgin Birth than in evolution still be called an Enlightened nation?" cried Garry Wills.[5] The ironically named novelist Jane Smiley used the I-word to explain what happened: "The election results reflect the decision of the right wing to cultivate and exploit ignorance in the citizenry."[6] Columnist Michael Kinsley said Christian voters were more "arrogant" than people on his side of the aisle who are "crippled by reason and open-mindedness."

Finally reaching the acceptance stage of grief, Katha Pollitt wrote in *Slate*, "If a voter wants Christian Jihad, he may not be willing to desert the cause for health insurance—especially with Republicans telling him 50 times a day that the plan is really a socialist plot to raise his taxes and poison him with Canadian drugs."[7]

"Let's be clear: Bush ran on a moral agenda—God, guns, gays, and true grit in fighting the evils of Saddam Hussein and terrorism," echoed Robert Reich.

THE "MYTH" MYTH

So that was it, eh? Case closed? Evangelical Christians turned out in record numbers, motivated by "moral values" and an inordinate fear of progress to reelect Pres. George W. Bush?

Not quite. The counter-analysis came swift and hard. It came from the Left and the Right and the Center. Whatever the 2004 election was about, these election spinners demanded, it was *not* about "moral values."

"The morality gap didn't decide the election," declared Professor Paul Freedman of the University of Virginia. "Voters who cited moral issues as most important did give their votes overwhelmingly to Bush (80 percent to 18 percent), and states where voters saw moral issues as important were more likely to be red ones. But these differences were no greater in 2004 than in 2000. If you're trying to explain why the president's vote share in 2004 is bigger than his vote share in 2000, values don't help."[8]

Alan Abramowitz of Emory University concluded, "It may take years to determine whether the 2004 election signaled the beginning of a new era of Republican domination of American politics or was simply a normal election in an era of intense competition for the support of a closely divided electorate. However, data already available suggest that Republican claims that 2004 was a landmark election are overstated and raise doubts about the notion that Republicans won the election on the strength of a massive turnout of social conservatives."[9]

New York Times op-edster David Brooks declared the "moral values" story line "certainly wrong." He explained, "Much of the misinterpretation of this election derives from a poorly worded question in the exit polls. When asked about the issue that most influenced their vote, voters were given the option of saying 'moral values.' But that phrase can mean anything—or nothing. Who doesn't vote on moral values? If you ask an inept question, you get a misleading result."[10]

Jim Wallis also objected to the wording of the exit poll, writing in his book *God's Politics*, "The single moral values question was a whole different kind of choice that the rest of the 'issues,' ignoring the moral values inherent in those other concerns. Putting an ambiguous moral values choice in a list of specific issues skewed the results."[11]

The issue was put to bed in the minds of most pundits. The "moral values" army of analysts were wiped out completely when Charles Krauthammer declared it a "myth." Krauthammer was a hard-charging Bush enthusiast during the 2004 election. He is also recognized as one of the few genuine intellectuals within the American political commentariate. And so people paid attention to what he had to say:

> Whence comes this fable? With Pres. Bush increasing his share of the vote among Hispanics, Jews, women (especially married women), Catholics, seniors and even African-Americans, on what does this victory-of-the-homophobic-evangelical voter rest?
>
> Its origins lie in a single question in the Election Day exit poll. The urban myth grew around the fact that "moral values" ranked highest in the answer to Question J: "Which ONE issue mattered most in deciding how you voted for president?"
>
> It is a thin reed upon which to base a General Theory of the '04 Election. In fact, it is no reed at all. The way the question was set up, moral values were sure to be ranked disproportionately high. Why? Because it was a multiple-choice question, and moral values cover a group of issues, while all the other choices were individual issues. Chop up the alternatives finely enough, and moral values are sure to get a bare plurality over the others.[12]

It must be noted that many pundits had an ulterior motive in downplaying the role of moral values in 2004. Most liberal commentators fluffed off the impact the Massachusetts's Supreme Court's gay marriage dictate would have on the election. Allowing posterity to come to believe that 2004 was the year of the moral values counterrevolution would forever blemish their reputation as pundits.

Worse still, it would create a sense of finality on the issue of gay marriage, a very real sense that Americans don't want it, now and forever. And that wouldn't do because liberalism is all about breaking down social norms until the irregular becomes normalized.

David Brooks, whose conservative credentials are otherwise challenged only for his employment at the *New York Times*, supported legalized gay marriage. Even Krauthammer wrote a column in which he expressed opposition to the Federal Marriage Amendment in Congress.

But let us assume that these pundits were sincere and were not simply trying to protect their income-earning potential as political prognosticators. Which analysis is correct?

Well, for reasons not really expressed by anyone in the public, the first army, the one decimated by the likes of David Brooks and Charles Krauthammer, were right, but not for the reasons they think. I alone have lived to tell the story.

Let us start by examining that "flawed" exit poll question. Was it, as Krauthammer explains, flawed because "moral values" covers a "group of issues"? Possibly. But isn't "Education"—one of the other options—a "group of issues"? And what about "the Economy"? Certainly Krauthammer wouldn't argue that the economy is a singular issue, right? And "Terrorism." Is that a single issue? Or a family of issues?

Krauthammer's analysis falls far short of debunking the "moral values myth."

What of Wallis's argument that the "moral values" option on the exit poll question was "ambiguous"? Perhaps it was . . . to Jim Wallis. But he is virtually alone in his confusion. Overwhelmingly, voters who cited "moral values" as their motivator voted for George W. Bush—80 percent to 18 percent. In other words, voters were very *unambiguous* as to the meaning of the question, at least as it related to their vote.

The fact that "moral values" registered on the exit polls and that those voters were so solidly behind one candidate over another tells us that there is something far more significant going on here than Krauthammer's "myth" and Wallis's "ambiguity."

The fact is George W. Bush won reelection because the Religious Right turned out in numbers previously unimaginable. Whereas 1994 was the Religious Right's first successful endeavor into *national* (as opposed to regional) election activity, 2004 was the year they took over American elections altogether. Two thousand four was the year in which the Religious Right established itself as the most consequential voting bloc in the nation, the GOP's indispensable voting bloc, the people standing between the modern Democratic Party and its hopes of ever again becoming the nation's dominant political faction. The 2004 election changed everything.

When we actually consider what happened in 2004—who voted and why—we can easily understand the visceral reaction of those who pursue an agenda antithetical to that of the Religious Right. Liberals have quite logically concluded that they need to nip this "moral values" thing in the bud. But the bud has bloomed. And it has spread its seed across the fruited plain.

As for Krauthammer, Brooks, Wallis, et al., I can only say that spinning an election is a lot different than winning one. They must never have worked on a political campaign in their lives and therefore can only postulate from the sidelines. The simple fact is, I have worked on scores of Republican campaigns for high public office, and I have never sat in a strategy session and said, "Gee, how can we get the neocons and the antigovernment libertarians engaged in our campaign?"

Republican political professionals always start a campaign by establishing a relationship with the conservative base. And those folks are found in churches, faith-based groups, and pro-life organizations. For Republicans to win, they must first talk to Christian conservatives. If that fact offends the sensibilities of the sophisticated commentariate, I suggest they look into another line of work.

TURN THIS MUTHA OUT

It would be literally impossible to overstate to impact the Religious Right had on Election Day 2004. According to exit polling data and postelection research, white evangelical Protestants, the linchpin demographic of the Religious Right, voted for President Bush over John Kerry by a margin of 78 percent to 22 percent. Catholics who regularly attend Mass voted for Bush over Kerry by 56 percent to 43 percent.

For the first time since Pres. Ronald Reagan's 1984 drubbing of Walter Mondale, the Republican candidate for president won a majority of all Catholic voters. Mainline Protestants who regularly attend church (among other behavioral indicators) favored Bush by 68 percent to 32 percent. President Bush benefited from an eye-popping 31 percent increase in his vote share among Latino Protestants and benefited from a 17-point swing in his favor among Latino Catholics from his previous performance.

The frequency with which a voter attends church was a greater predictor of his Election Day decision than whether or not he attended college, belonged to a union, served in the military, or was married with children.

These lopsided margins are hardly surprising, and yet they only tell a small piece of the larger story. Consider, George W. Bush won 100 percent of *my* household in 2004, but that was only two votes. Turnout and vote totals are far more important if we are truly to understand the 2004 election.

Very early on, political analysts and commentators realized the 2004 election would be unlike most previous presidential reelection campaigns. Whereas Pres. Ronald Reagan's victory in 1984 was an unmitigated wipeout of Mondale-style liberalism and Bill Clinton handily defeated Senator Bob Dole in 1996, no one believed President Bush's reelection would be a cake walk. Liberals still wore their frustration from the 2000 election on their sleeves. Moreover, that frustration had only grown stronger over time, as President Bush and congressional Republicans repeatedly defeated Democrats in Washington and at the ballot box. Democrats harnessed that frustration to develop one of the most impressive voter registration and mobilization machines in American campaign history.

MoveOn.org, for example, orchestrated an impressive Vote for Change Tour featuring top-shelf rock stars such as Bruce Springsteen, Dave Matthews, REM, the Dixie Chicks, and James Taylor. The tour was billed as "20 Artists. 28 Cities. 9 Battleground States." According to reporter Byron York, MoveOn.org operatives recruited concert-goers at postconcert house parties to draft five letters each to undecided voters in the all important swing states.[13]

MoveOn.org and other groups also teamed up with obese low-budget filmmaker Michael Moore to host special screenings of his anti-Bush film *Fahrenheit 9/11*. After these screenings MoveOn operatives recruited enraged and energized liberals from within the audiences to take part in Get Out the Vote activities.

George Soros infamously donated more than $27 million of his own money to finance various anti-Bush, pro-Democrat voter mobilization efforts. Soros was far from the only big Democratic backer to spend lavishly. Progressive Insurance chairman Peter Lewis donated almost $24 million. Hollywood heavyweight Steve Bing gave over $13 million. All told, Democrat-favoring voter mobilization groups raised and spent over $230 million to defeat George W. Bush.

During the 2004 election cycle, I consulted on a number of races with national implications. We occasionally processed much of the evidence York would later expose, and I would be lying if I said we were not concerned. Democrats were motivated in a way seasoned political professionals had never quite seen before. Word spread quickly that grad students and teachers and nonprofit employees were taking leaves of absence to move to Florida and Ohio to receive training for Election Day activities. People I know personally were contacted by complete strangers from Americans Coming Together or MoveOn.org, their names having been recommended by national associations of this sort and that. Many of these people packed up for the last two months of the General Election, gladly separating themselves from their families to live in motel rooms or the attics of fellow enthusiasts. This was "the most important election of our lifetime," an election of apocalyptic import for many liberals.

When Sally Baron of Wisconsin passed away that year, her family included a strange blurb in her obituary: "Memorials in her honor can be made to any organization working for the removal of President Bush."

"She thought he was a liar," Baron's daughter, Maureen Bettilyon, rationalized. "I think his personality, just standing there with that smirk on his face, and acting like he's this holy Christian, that's what really got her."

The obituary notice of Gertrude M. Jones contained similar language. "Memorial gifts may be made to any organization that seeks the removal of President George Bush from office," read the obit in the *Times-Picayune*. In short order, the campaign of General Wesley Clark, who had sought the Democratic nomination for president, reported receiving fifteen contributions in the name of Gertrude M. Jones.

The mania was not exclusive to rank-and-file leftwing hobbyists. It affected academics and celebrities, as well. Actor Vincent D'Onofrio, who stars in the NBC show *Law & Order: Criminal Intent*, plastered anti-Bush posters all over the set, and, according to the *Washington Post*, he attacked anyone who disagreed with him. D'Onofrio's behavior was so obnoxious that producers of the show put the kibosh on any political chatter at all on the set. (After the election, D'Onofrio apparently passed out backstage from anxiety over Bush's victory.)[14]

Air America Radio personality Randi Rhodes joked that other members of the Bush clan should take the president out in a row boat and shoot him in the head, like the character Fredo Corleone in *The Godfather Part II*.

At a MoveOn.org fundraising event, "comedienne" Margaret Cho rehashed the old leftist standby to huge applause from the crowd, "I mean, George Bush is not Hitler. He would be if he f———— applied himself."

The Dixie Chicks told a crowd in London that they were embarrassed that George W. Bush came from the state of Texas, from where they also hail.

Janeane Garofalo chimed in on the *Daily Show* with, "At this point, I think voting for Bush is a character flaw."

Let us not forget also the countless antiwar marches and nearly omnipresent comparisons of President Bush to Adolph Hitler. MoveOn.org even posted two television commercials on their website that directly referred to President George W. Bush as Hitler. The

"Bush is Hitler" charge became so ubiquitous in the run up to Election Day, many conservative bloggers, looking to save time while typing, coined the neologism "BusHitler."

Liberal behavior in 2004 was undeniably bizarre and over-the-top. Level-headed liberals will one day look back in embarrassment at the excesses of their rhetoric and wonder if they contributed as much to their defeat as their nominee's lack of clarity on fundamental issues of importance to regular Americans.

In their defense, the Bush-hating frenzy helped the Democrats register millions of new voters and exceeded their vote total from 2000 by more than eight million votes. It was one of the most successful electioneering performances in history.

It was, in fact, the *second* most successful electioneering performance in history.

Top honors would go to the Republicans of that year.

Perhaps because their voter registration and mobilization efforts in 2004 did not include A-list celebrities and rock concerts, much less attention has been paid to Republican efforts to increase turnout among their base. Looking at 2004 election results, we can only conclude on-the-ledge liberals were not the only people in America who thought 2004 was the "most important election of our lifetimes."

Republican turnout numbers were unparalleled. Whereas George W. Bush lost the popular vote in 2000 by five hundred thousand votes, he won the popular vote in 2004 by over three million. President Bush improved his vote total from 2000 by an extraordinary eleven-and-a-half million votes.

How did this happen? How did the GOP overcome the personal fortunes of eccentric billionaires, virtually the entire entertainment industry, and the reflexive hostility of the mainstream press?

SMALL IS BEAUTIFUL

The Religious Right hosted almost no mass demonstrations of electioneering like we saw among the MoveOn.org types and other liberal mobilization groups. Some conservative groups tried to harness patriotic sentiments by staging marches and vigils ostensibly for the troops in Iraq and Afghanistan, though clearly designed to show support for Bush administration policies. But these events were sparsely attended and achieved nothing close to the impact of the liberal public displays of outrage and energy.

So how could Katha Pollitt have been forced to confess, "Sometimes I wonder if political commentators do much more than rationalize their own worldview. While I was waiting with a huge crowd of volunteers for an Election Day bus to Pennsylvania, I ran into a famous pundit who told me Kerry would 'probably' win. I was so happy I kissed him! He told me he had traveled all over the country and had found no sign of the 4 million missing evangelical voters Karl Rove was trying to activate. Maybe they were hiding in the church basement?"

Why is it that no one could see this coming? How could the country's smartest and most experienced election observers not have predicted this extraordinary outcome, especially since presidential advisor Karl Rove telegraphed for them how he intended to construct a Bush reelection victory?

First, most of these observers have convinced themselves over time that the Religious Right is a marginal voter subgroup that rarely if ever influences national elections and is always on the verge of imploding on itself. Second, they knew not where to look. Their eyes were glued on the National Mall and downtown Manhattan and the streets of San Francisco where huge mobs of angry leftists insisted they were "taking back America."

Even after the election, when many in the media concluded the time had come to take Christians serious, these folks focused the majority of their attention on the megachurch phenomenon. Did you know there's a church in Colorado with twelve thousand members? Full house every Sunday! I heard there's one in California with fifteen thousand members. We need to go find out what this is all about!

The temptation to cover the growth in evangelical Christianity in terms of the megachurch phenomenon is great because the numbers are staggering. Two thousand five was the first year in which attendance at a single church topped 30,000 in one week (Lakewood in Houston). It was also the first year in which the number of megachurches in America (identified as having more than 2,000 attending worshipers) totaled more than 1,000. One church, Without Walls in Tampa, Florida, added 4,330 new members in 2005 alone.

This growth results in some impressive annual budget numbers. Lakewood's annual income in 2004 was $55 million. The Fellowship Church in Grapevine, Texas, has an annual budget of $30 million. It is only natural that this type of explosive growth attracts media attention. But while serious attention to these congregations is a welcome change in American media, it doesn't really help us understand how evangelical Christianity has become so synonymous with conservative politics. Only 13 percent of evangelicals attend a megachurch. So megachurches do not come close to explaining what's really going on out there.

Pundits and political commentators were thinking big. They ought to have been thinking small. Every night across America small gaggles of believers gather in a neighbor's living room or in some other mutually convenient place. They're there to worship, but this isn't church.

Christians call these gatherings small groups, and they play a significant role in the growth of evangelicalism in the United States. Small groups are attempts by modern believers to recapture the intimacy of early Christians who would literally gather in small groups (there weren't many of them in those early days, and they weren't very popular with outsiders) to worship.

Attendees at these small groups pray, read, and discuss the Bible. A given group may have started from Genesis 1:1 and decided to read and study and discuss all the way through to Revelation. Or a small group may center on a theme and scour Scripture for answers to life's questions.

There are small groups for men, women, and teenagers. Can't find a small group that concentrates on what you want to study? Talk to your pastor and form your own small group. Then invite other members of your church and set up regular meetings. Christians find Scriptural support for small groups in the Acts of the Apostles and in Jesus's teachings on fellowship.

The Winter/Spring 2006 Small Group catalogue for New Life Church in Colorado Springs, Colorado, is 185 pages long. Believers of every variety can gather to partake in worship while also engaging in hobbies, crafts, and pastimes.

"Golfers! Men who enjoy playing golf can meet & play with other golfers who share like faith in Christ," reads one blurb. "Using golf as a foundation, study God's Word on a regular basis and provide an avenue for outreach to non-Christians. . . . Monday @ 7:00 PM."[15]

"Secret Keepers . . ." reads another. "Girls in 8th grade & their mothers seeking the Lord's wisdom on topics facing teens. Wednesday @ 7:00 PM."[16]

There is a Spanish youth group, a marriage training group, an acting group, a volleyball group, groups to teach worshipers how best to pray for their children, or to pray for peace in Kashmir, a group for motorcyclists, and addiction support groups.

At a time when Americans mourn the loss of community, small groups create intimate, personalized gatherings of more or less like-minded Americans who actually seek out and enjoy one another's company.

Small-group meetings are not political in nature. Most of the small-group leaders I have encountered are surprisingly strict in terms of keeping their meeting on a snappy schedule and focused on the Word. Nevertheless, people being people, there is generally a great deal of chatting going on before and after a small-group meeting. During most months of the year, this chatter relates to what you might generally expect: the kids, work, *American Idol,* you name it. But during the months of August, September, and October, discussions before and after small-group meetings often turn to the subject everyone else is talking about at that time: politics.

Now, 80 percent of evangelical Christians are politically conservative and typically vote Republican. Research suggests that among small-group attendees the percentage is even higher. So you can imagine the slant of these conversations. Inevitably, someone at a small group will mention that they plan to attend a phone bank or drop literature for Candidate X that weekend and would anyone of you like to come with? And before you know it, one becomes ten. This happens in thousands of nameless nooks and crannies throughout the fruited plain.

As a Republican consultant, I cannot tell you how many times I have mentioned to a campaign volunteer during an election that we need a lawyer or a doctor or whatever to write a letter to his or her peers only to have them respond by saying, "Well, we have a lawyer in our small group and I know she's pretty conservative. Lemme ask her."

Not having grown up in the evangelical tradition, I was ignorant of small groups for most of my adult life. I finally attended a regular small-group meeting during most of 2004 in Annapolis, Maryland. I did not allow it to be known among my new friends that I was a Republican consultant. I told them I was in advertising, which was the truth. Nevertheless, every weekly meeting included informal and spontaneous discussions beforehand and afterward like the ones I describe above.

My theory is that small groups have not only helped the church to grow, but they have contributed incalculably to the growth in Republican campaign activism. What Democrats and liberals had to manufacture in 2004 at the monstrous cost and resource commitment of having to put together concert tours and the like happened spontaneously (and for free) every night all over the country. And it benefited George W. Bush and the Republicans mightily.

During our interview, Pastor Ted Haggard, an innovator in using small groups to build church communities, confirmed my theory. "New Life church has twelve thousand members and over one thousand small groups. That's the equivalent of a small town in America, complete with its own small communities and organizations," he said. "Small groups have an extremely powerful impact on the community at large because we meet every week and we actually believe something."

Moreover, what Bruce Springsteen, Al Franken, MoveOn.org, George Soros, and others spent millions and millions of dollars trying to affect in 2004 continues to this day on the other side every night of the year in hundreds of cities, suburbs, and exurbs.

This tendency among evangelicals to think small manifests itself in other ways. "Evangelicals believe in making a difference in the communities in which they live through volunteerism and community outreach. They prefer to engage in their local communities rather than undertaking projects to spread the gospel elsewhere in American and around the world," write Greenberg and Berktold.

In other words, contrary to the dominant thinking about evangelicals, they are less interested in global dominion than they are in having safe, clean, workable communities that reflect their own values. Again, we see Christians thinking small while the common culture's thinking *about them* is huge.

CATHOLICS COME HOME

Evangelicals are an important part of the story about Bush's victory. But they are still only part of the story. Bush also captured a majority of the Catholic vote in 2004. According to Kate O'Beirne, "John Kerry's liberal allies pin all responsibility for Bush's victory on evangelical Christians, and raise a hysterical alarm with their ridiculous predictions about the coming theocracy. But faithful Catholics were no less important in the Republican victory than Evangelicals; and Democrats should worry that an increase in Catholic defections from the Democratic flock may condemn the party."

The Democratic Party has slowly bled Catholic voters over the past decade. In 2000, Al Gore won a majority of Roman Catholic votes, though Bush managed to win a majority of Catholic voters who regularly attend church. By 2004, Bush could proudly strip that qualification away. He won an outright majority of Catholic voters—52 percent to 47 percent—over John Kerry, himself a Catholic.

But as many keen political observers have pointed out, the Catholic vote ain't exactly what it used to be. Catholics are no longer a monolithic bloc of votes that can be persuaded to vote one way or the other. So does it make sense even to talk about a "Catholic vote" anymore? And if so, who should be included in the Catholic votes?

First, yes, there is indeed a Catholic vote, and anyone who works in electoral politics knows it. Why else would George W. Bush have made such an effort to be seen by Pope John Paul II's side when he awarded him the Presidential Medal of Freedom in an election year? Why else would John Kerry have admonished the president by saying "faith without works is dead," an old-school Catholic retort to claims of quick and easy salvation?

But if Catholics in America are so atomized and no longer constitute a homogenous bloc, who should we consider "the Catholic vote"? It makes no sense to consider anyone other than those who exercise their faith. That means we need to think about people who regularly attend Mass, pray daily, read Scripture, and follow the teachings of the Church, no? It isn't enough to have an Irish or Italian last name and to have been confirmed in the Catholic Church. If we're going to talk about a Catholic vote, let's talk about people who behave like Catholics in every facet of their lives.

If we do that then we can see very clearly the emergence of an increasingly loyal Republican voting bloc, one which we must include in the Religious Right. Traditionalist Catholics, as John C. Green of the University of Akron labels them, supported President Bush overwhelmingly over John Kerry 72 percent to 28 percent. Even Centrist Catholics, who attend Mass less frequently and perhaps follow only many, but not all, teachings of the Church awarded Bush with 55 percent of the vote.

It is only when we get to Modernist Catholics, to use Green's phrase, those who attend Mass with little frequency and who only sparingly follow the teachings of the Church, that we see significant support for Kerry. But here's the catch. These Modernist Catholics supported John Kerry (69 percent to 31 percent for Bush) by almost the precise numbers as secular voters—who have no faith tradition at all—did (70 percent for Kerry, 30 percent for Bush).

Other polls have shown similar findings.[17] The bottom line is that some Catholics may have grown up in the Catholic tradition, but they have more in common with other, nonreligious political liberals than they do their fellow Catholics.

TIPPING THE SCALES

Just how important were religious conservatives to the GOP's success in 2004? So important, frankly, that without them, we would not be talking about the GOP's success in 2004.

In a postelection study titled, "The American Religious Landscape and the 2004 Presidential Vote: Increased Polarization," John C. Green, among others, segmented the 2004 American electorate by religious denomination—evangelical Protestant, Mainline Protestant, Catholic, and Jew—and by behavior and viewpoint—traditionalist, centrist, and modernist.

Green et al. assigned these labels to voter subgroups based on frequency of behaviors such as church attendance, prayer, etc. and on the relative orthodoxy and heterodoxy of voters' religious views. Their study reveals, "Four religious groups gave Bush more than two-thirds of their votes: Traditionalist Evangelicals (88 percent), Other Christians (80 percent), Traditionalist Catholics (72 percent), and Traditionalist Mainline Protestants (68 percent)." And that these four groups "combined for nearly one-half of his total ballots (47 percent)."

Almost 80 percent of the 28 million evangelicals who voted pulled the lever for Bush. That's 21 million evangelicals. If we add the 6.9 million Catholics who attend church on a weekly basis and who also voted for Bush, we end up with something close to 28 million conservative Christian voters—not quite half of Bush's total of 61 million votes, but close.

How does that compare to other significant subgroups within the electorate? African Americans who vote straight-ticket

Democrat number approximately 11.8 million. Straight-ticket Democrat union members number around 16.7 million. That is to say, conservative Christians are about as important to the GOP coalition as blacks and Big Labor are to the Democrats *combined.*

To look at it another way, almost no political organization has received as much media attention in recent years as MoveOn.org, the liberal activist group. References to MoveOn.org's aggressive electioneering were omnipresent in 2004. And yet, MoveOn.org boasts only 2.5 million members—less than one-tenth of the amount of Christian conservatives.

Let's look at it yet another way. If the United States had a parliamentary system of proportionate representation, a Religious Right party would have a perpetual plurality of seats in parliament and would be the natural party of government. No other single group would come close.

Steve Waldman and John C. Green wrote an article in the *Atlantic* not long ago in which they sought to itemize the religious constituencies of both the Republican and the Democrat Parties. Oddly ignoring conservative Catholics from their survey, Waldman and Green identified three groups on the right: the "religious right," "heartland culture warriors," and "moderate evangelicals."

These three "tribes" (as Waldman and Green call them) comprise roughly 35 percent of the total electorate, according to their analysis. Using 2004 turnout numbers, we're talking here about a whopping 42.3 million people (and, again, Waldman and Green left conservative Catholics out of the equation!).

What is remarkable about the Waldman and Green analysis, however, is that despite their segmenting of these groups, upon closer inspection we can see precious few distinctions among them. Their "religious right" consists of "traditional evangelical Protestants." Their heartland culture warriors "stand arm-in-arm with the religious right on most moral issues and are nearly as numerous." And their moderate evangelicals "are culturally conservative, but moderate on economic issues."[18]

If 42.3 million culturally conservative religious Americans voted on Election Day, why are the likes of David Brooks, Charles Krauthammer, and Jim Wallis surprised to see "moral values" pop up on an exit poll?

What drove anywhere from half to two-thirds of President Bush's voters to the ballot box that year? Pundits can claim social conservatives are pure fiction all they want. But facts are facts. "A majority of the top four Bush constituencies regarded social issues as very important to their vote, exceeding the figure for the entire sample," Green writes. "Each of these groups was also more likely to choose social issues as most important." Among Traditionalist Evangelical Protestants (47 percent to 29 percent) and Traditionalist Catholics (39 percent to 31 percent), social issues significantly outpolled foreign policy issues as most important. Additionally, 71 percent of evangelicals said their faith was more important than or as important as any other issue to their vote.

As Dr. James Dobson told me, "I believe that 2004 will be remembered as the year during which the great sleeping giant of the church woke up and made its presence known. Men and women of faith—what some have called 'values voters'—finally realized the stakes were too high to stay out of the battle."

Considering these staggering numbers from the 2004 election, Dr. Dobson's belief seems inarguable.

KERRY'S "RELIGIOUS" BASE

John Kerry, too, had a religious constituency. Waldman and Green sought to itemize Democratic religious voters in their article, as well.

"A deep-blue religious left is almost exactly the same size as the religious right but receives much less attention," they write.

Only there is a significant problem with Democratic efforts to cobble together a meaningful religious constituency: some of the Democrats' "religious voters," many of them in fact, aren't religious at all. Two of the Democrat "religious" constituencies are "spiritual but not religious voters" and "non-religious Americans, or seculars."[19] Combined, these two groups make up 16 percent of the electorate and well over two-thirds of the Democratic Party's "religious" base.

Now, it is a cardinal sin in America today to question someone else's faith, especially if they are liberal. But counting "spiritual but not religious voters" and "non-religious Americans" as "religious voters" is like counting Polish and Armenian Americans as black voters. It simply shatters credulity to include these coalitions in a religious base. I can understand the Left's desire to write about religion in public life with a kind of equivalence in mind. But this is just nonsense.

Polls show a more relevant trend than that of which religious groups supported which candidates. The more telling religious vote characteristic was a voter's religious behavior rather than his faith tradition. Based on five behaviors—worship attendance, financial support of a congregation, private prayers, Scripture reading, and participation of small groups—we learn that the more active one is in their faith, the more likely they were to vote for George Bush over John Kerry. That is to say, the "more religious" you were in 2004, the more likely you were to vote Republican.

The trend is so pronounced, I asked Green if it made sense even to call Kerry voters "religious" at all. In my experience, when religious participation is so low as to be almost nonexistent, it becomes more useful to categorize voters in other ways: income, gender, age, geographic region, and so forth.

Can someone who does not attend worship services with any regularity, does not pray, and does not read from Scripture really be called a "religious voter"?

"I think you are basically right," Green replied. "Which is precisely why we use multiple measures of religion to create the categories. While the absence of worship attendance may produce different political results, it doesn't mean that the less frequent and nonattenders aren't in some real sense religious—it is just that their religiosity is quite different. A century ago many Protestants would have questioned whether Jews were 'religious' because they were so different from Protestants. But of course Jews are religious, just in a different way that Protestants."

True enough, I suppose. But rather than expressing this study as a look at increased polarization among different religious categories, mightn't it make more sense to look at the results as evidence of a rift between Americans who exercise their faith more vigorously versus those who express it rarely at all or have no religion?

"Yes—and that is exactly what the study shows," Green concluded.

My mother-in-law, who is as ardent in her Catholic faith as she is in her disdain for George W. Bush, remarked to me once that she was so sick of hearing on talk radio that Democrats don't go to church. She is living proof that they do! Moreover, as Waldman told me in our interview, the Religious Left is certainly more cohesive, more self-consciously religious than it has been in the past. But anecdotes don't matter when looking seriously at election results. Trends matter. And there exists a hardening trend in American politics: the more you attend church, the more likely you are to vote Republican. Period.

John Kerry destroyed Bush among the 15 percent of Americans who never attend church (62 percent for Kerry to 36 percent for

Bush). Conversely, Bush (64 percent) beat Kerry (35 percent) by virtually the same margin among the 16 percent of the electorate who attend church more than once a week. This gap narrows and widens based on church attendance and virtually disappears among those who attend church monthly, who split their votes almost evenly: 50 percent for Bush, 49 percent for Kerry.

"HERE ARE THE FACTS"

David Brooks wrote after the election, "Here are the facts . . . there was no disproportionate surge in the evangelical vote this year. Evangelicals made up the same share of the electorate this year as they did in 2000."

Huh? In his postelection study, Dr. Green—using numbers provided by the Pew Research Center—writes, "Evangelical Protestants strongly backed Bush in both years, but their support increase by about 6 percentage points (from 74 to 78 percent). At the same time, their turnout grew by 9 percentage points (from about 54 to 63 percent)."

Moreover, according to exit polls from 2000, 14 percent of voters in that election identified themselves as "white Religious Right." Total turnout in the 2000 presidential elections was 105.3 million. That means roughly 14.75 million evangelicals voted. But in 2004, roughly 121 million total Americans voted. And the percentage of voters who self-identified as white evangelical Christians was 23 percent. That means almost 28 million evangelicals voted. The white evangelical Christian vote almost doubled in number and wildly outpaced increases for all other voter subgroups.

No surge?

I asked Dr. Green how Brooks could have concluded such a wildly off-the-mark analysis. Here's what I actually asked him:

Question:

> David Brooks wrote, after the 2004 election, that there had
> been no surge in evangelicals voting from the previous pres-
> idential election. He referenced Pew in this assertion,
> though he did not quote anyone and provided no numbers.
>
> Your postelection study was based on the Pew numbers,
> correct? Your poll shows a 9-percentage point increase from
> 2000 among evangelical Protestants. To me that represents a
> fairly significant surge. And, of course, the exit polls from
> 2004 show a remarkable surge in white born-agains from
> 2000. In 2000, white born-agains made up 14 percent of
> the electorate. In 2004, that number was, like, 26 percent (I
> don't have my notes with me right now, but it was some-
> thing like that.)
>
> Am I missing something here?

And here was Dr. Green's response:

> There are different Pew studies. The one Brooks looked at
> was an early one that simply compared the percent of the
> electorate in 2000 and 2004 that were evangelicals in the exit
> polls. *This was problematic because the exit polls did not use the
> same measures in 2000 and 2004.* In any event, their best
> measure suggested that the percentage of the electorate was
> about the same. But if so, then the 2004 percentage involved
> many more people because turnout was much larger. *Our
> data comes from more fine grained set of surveys that used the
> same measures in 2000 and 2004.* We did indeed show an
> increase in turnout (but then turnout went up across the
> board) and in support for Bush.

So here you have John Green, not Patrick Hynes, saying the "evangelical turnout was irrelevant" argument was based on "problematic" data. And, of course, Brooks was not alone.

Charles Krauthammer, too, made a mistaken claim in his analysis. "George Bush increased his vote in 2004 over 2000 by an average of 3.1 percent nationwide. In Ohio the increase was 1 percent—less than a third of the national average. In the 11 states in which the gay marriage referendums were held, Bush increased his vote by *less* than he did in the 39 states that did not have the referendum. The great anti-gay surge was pure fiction."

This point is irrelevant. George W. Bush was not running against the 2000 version of himself. He was running in 2004 against John Kerry. Republicans made a concerted effort in 2004 to place gay marriage bans on state ballots for the purpose of improving the president's chances of reelection. And Bush's vote share in gay marriage-banning states was 7 points higher than in other states (57.9 to 50.9). Moreover, Krauthammer assumes that the gay marriage debate did not play a role in voters' decisions in states that had no gay marriage ban in the ballot, that gay marriage was just a parochial wedge issue localized in eleven states. This is a dubious claim, at best.

Gay marriage was viewed by many Americans of faith as an issue of national concern. Most evangelicals supported an amendment to the US Constitution that defined marriage as between one man and one woman and believed that voting Republican would increase the likelihood of that happening. That was the very purpose of President Bush having endorsed the Federal Marriage Amendment—to nationalize the gay marriage issue.

In the end, the antimoral values forces won the postelection debate. Most of the cognoscenti in America now accept it as axiomatic that the Election Day exit polls were all screwed up and that conservative Christians are not as dominant a force in

American politics as they first feared. Which is why they will be so shocked when it all happens again.

AND STAY DEAD

One interesting development has come out of the 2005 off-year election. Whereas the idea that the Religious Right contributed handsomely to Bush's 2004 victory had been suppressed by our chattering class, it made a minor comeback in November of 2005 as an excuse to (you guessed it!) denounce Christian conservatives.

Political observers in the media and elsewhere tend to sum up elections in short, catchy blurbs. That's the only way they feel they can impart "what the voters said" on Election Day, even though "what the voters said" in one state or district is often contradictory to and inconsistent with "what the voters said" in another. Thus, 1992 became the "Year of the Woman," 1994 became the "Year of the Angry White Male," 2000 was the "Year of the Red-Blue Divide," and 2004 was, briefly, the "Year of the Moral Values Voters."

What will they say about the 2005 off-year elections? Well, certainly they will say that the Democrats mounted a bit of a comeback against the GOP, which had been enjoying a string of victories over the Democrats for the better part of the late-twentieth and early-twenty-first centuries. Democrats retained control of the governorships in Virginia (a red state) and New Jersey (a blue state). Meanwhile, California's Republican Gov. Arnold Schwarzenegger entered the *Jingle All the Way* phase of his political career. All four ballot initiatives supported by the Governator went down in defeat.

Though Election Day '05 was not the bloodbath Howard Dean and his cheering squads in the mainstream media have made it out to be, the Democrats did manage to stop their own bleeding. They had reason to celebrate.

So, what happened? Glenn Reynolds, the libertarian-leaning Instapundit, said, "I also think that I may have been right in suggesting that the GOP had lost its mojo with the Terri Schiavo affair. Things seem to have started to go south then, not only because of the issue itself, but because of the divisive venom that so many Schiavo partisans aimed at people who disagreed with them. I think it was very damaging to the GOP coalition, and they've continued to pay a price."[20]

With all due respect to Glenn, I don't see how he or anyone else can conclude the 2005 election results that the GOP has "lost its mojo with the Terri Schiavo affair," especially since there is zero evidence that it was even raised as an issue in any of the campaigns. Glenn also ignored the fact that nearly half of the House Democrats who were present voted in favor of "Terri's Law."

Rather, I'd argue that most voters in Virginia, California, and New Jersey, as well as in the larger cities across America, had long since forgotten about the Terri Schiavo affair and that it had virtually no impact at all on the election results. And to be quite frank, the social conservative wing of the conservative coalition came out of the elections in decidedly better shape than the libertarian-ish, fiscally conservative/socially agnostic side.

Taking a slightly modified tack, Bobby Ross Jr. suggested in a Religion News Service article that election 2005 was a bad one for religious conservatives. "Religious conservatives lost electoral fights to pass an abortion law in California, overturn gay-rights legislation in Maine. . . ." Ross quoted Boston College political scientist Alan Wolfe saying, ". . . maybe we'll look back and say the Bush first term was really the high point of the Christian right's influence in American politics."

Blaming the Religious Right for poor conservative Election Day performances, or accusing the Republican Party of being "too beholden to the Religious Right," is often the pro forma analysis offered up by almost all casual political observers. And declaring the Religious Right dead is the biannual sport of pundits everywhere. I suppose that strain of Wednesday morning quarterbacking will never die. But a closer examination of the results, including a referendum vote in Colorado, indicates that the GOP and conservatives in general succeed when they talk more about those dreaded social issues than when they promote a small government philosophy or advocate spending cuts.

To begin with, it is inaccurate to say that the Religious Right lost ground in 2005 because parental notification died in California and the repeal of a gay rights law earned only 44 percent of the vote in Maine. It would be more accurate to say that the growth in evangelical electoral strength has never permeated the political cultures of those two states. Evangelical Christians make up only 14 percent of the electorate in Maine and only 11 percent in California compared to the national average of 23 percent. To conclude that the Religious Right is "losing ground" from these two election results is a fallacy.

Second, all eight statewide ballot measures in California went down. This was the result of a massive advertising and Get-Out-The-Vote campaign conducted by the state employees and teachers unions. Curiously, Proposition 73, the measure requiring parental notification for a minor to have an abortion, was the top vote getter on the ballot, though it, too, went down in defeat: 47.4 percent of voters supported the ban. Six-hundred thousand more voters supported the ban than supported Proposition 76, a measure that "limits state spending to prior year's level plus three previous years' average revenue growth." Only 38 percent of voters thought that was a good idea.

Now let us turn to Texas. In 2005 the Lone Star State became the eighteenth in the nation to write a ban on gay marriage into its constitution. And Texans did so in a big way. Three-quarters of the voting population supported the ban. Only one county voted against it.

Compare this level of success on a compelling social issue with, say, Colorado's vote to remove the teeth of that state's once-ground-breaking Taxpayers Bill of Rights. By a vote of 52 percent to 48 percent, voters authorized the state to spend more money and, in effect, raise their taxes.

Meanwhile, the only high-profile candidate in the 2005 off-year to communicate an openly religious message was Democrat gubernatorial candidate (now Governor) Tim Kaine. To be sure, Kaine played fast-and-loose with the definition of "pro-life," among other things, but he advertised, ahem, liberally on Christian radio and spoke candidly about his faith in his commercials.

After the GOP's historic success in 2004—success attributable at least in part (though I would argue mostly) to almost thirty million religious conservatives—the Bush administration swiftly pivoted to a massive spending reduction proposal in the form of Social Security privatization. That pivot angered many evangelical Christian political activists who subsequently refused to engage in the president's national campaign-style effort in support of his Social Security reform, which is now all but officially dead.

Contrary to Glenn Reynolds's and Dr. Wolfe's analyses, Christian conservatives are alive and well and holding up their end of the big tent. It is the socially moderate, libertarian wing that looks a tad anemic.

7

MERE CHRISTIANS

Okay, so the Religious Right represents the largest bloc of votes in the governing party of the world's only superpower. By now I hope you are convinced this is a pretty powerful, electorally consequential group of people. As Kyle Fisk of the National Association of Evangelicals told me, after the election his organization considered using the motto, "What can thirty million evangelicals do for America . . . anything we want."

The NAE dropped the proposed motto over concern that it might come off as too belligerent. But in our interview, Fisk was no less sure of the power of his group. "We elected George Bush. Without us you'd have John Kerry as president of the United States. When we motivate thirty million evangelicals behind a cause or a public policy, there is nothing we can't do."

Who exactly are these people, then, who have come to dominate the global political scene?

To listen to many commentators you might conclude that the Religious Right consists of three people: Pat Robertson, Jerry Falwell, and James Dobson. And maybe their immediate followers, too. But at most we're talking about a few thousand people, right? All right, they will concede. It's a little bigger than that. All those tongues-talking, snake-handling fundamentalists, they're the Religious Right, too.

We're talking, what? Like a million people or so? In a country with almost three-hundred million, it's a pretty small minority.

There is a political agenda at work in this narrowing of the Religious Right. The smaller and fringier their enemies can make the Religious Right out to be to the public, the less likely politicians and key national decision makers will want to be seen with them, the less influence they will have in our democratic process. Pretty soon they'll just go away. "The electoral strength of the Moral Majority and the Christian Coalition was always exaggerated by themselves and the media, but now their ability to 'deliver' decisive blocs of votes is greatly diminished," writes Jim Wallis.

And he is correct in saying that those two groups have declined in influence. But Wallis looks silly, especially after the 2004 election, when he claims that Christians don't deliver votes. There was no more valuable place for a Republican politician to visit and shake hands in 2004 than their local Bible church, whether that church is of the mega or regular variety. This was true a hundred years ago, it is true today, and I would venture a guess that it will still be true in another hundred years.

Working with a very narrow definition of the Religious Right also allows liberals to demonize certain leaders and hold them up as symbolic heads of this zany movement. There is no greater proxy for the Christian stereotype than the Reverend Pat Robertson. Liberals have a good time highlighting Robertson's silly, incendiary remarks.

For example, in late August 2005, Robertson encouraged the assassination of Venezuelan President Hugo Chavez.[1] And in January of 2006, Robertson suggested God had smitten Israeli Prime Minister Ariel Sharon because "he was dividing God's land."[2]

Yes, Robertson says some very ill-thought things. He says them often, and they are broadcast all over the country almost immediately after he does. But as Wallis and others have pointed out, Robertson's organization the Christian Coalition was never as large as it was once made out to be, and it is not nearly as big today as it was, say, in the early 1990s. In its prime the Christian Coalition only consisted of three million members, tops. And that figure is vigorously contested by Robertson's detractors.

But the explosive growth in evangelical and conservative Catholic political activism between the 2000 and 2004 presidential elections cannot be attributed to the Robertson and the Christian Coalition. Robertson has not personally been involved in American politics at the activist level like he was in the late '80s and early '90s for some time now. Moreover, many Christian activists do not view Robertson with the same level of admiration that talking heads of the common culture assume they do.

In the case of the Reverend Jerry Falwell, we have a slightly less caustic voice who is even further past his prime. Falwell is the grand-daddy of modern conservative Christian political activism. In the late 1970s, his Moral Majority organization was the only game in town. Falwell's strength as a movement leader ebbed at some point during the Reagan presidency, and he was ultimately overcome by the huge publicity surrounding Robertson's campaign for president in 1987 and 1988. (Falwell had endorsed V.P. George W. Bush.) Despite several efforts to revive his movement, Falwell and his organization are small potatoes in today's highly developed world of Christian civic action.

Elsewhere, extreme rightwing activist Fred Phelps often receives mainstream coverage that treats him as just another pastor. So when Phelps shows up to the funerals of US soldiers who'd been slain in battle in Iraq with signs declaring these boys died dishonorable deaths in defense of a pro-gay country, he is almost always described simply as a "Christian activist." Rarely (in fact never) do we hear that Phelps also regularly protests outside Focus on the Family in Colorado Springs because, he insists, that organization is too "pro-gay," as well.

But constantly shining a light on the gaffes and wacky remarks of Robertson and Falwell creates a problem for liberals: most conservative Christians are as likely as not to be equally turned off by the impolitic remarks of these two aging political powerhouses. Pastor Ted Haggard of the National Association of Evangelicals explained to me that the energy within the evangelical movement has long since transferred from parachurch leaders such as Robertson and Falwell to local church pastors.

It is only a matter of time, Pastor Ted told me, before the media and the public at large recognize this shift in energy. Moreover, despite common stereotypes, conservative Christians are not stupid. They know what the media is up to when they mock Robertson, Falwell, or some other conservative cleric. "Just wait until one of our guys stumbles," Pastor H.B. London from Focus on the Family told me. "The media will be all over them." By casting a wide net and implying that conservative Christians are de facto Robertson-ists or Falwell-ites, the liberal media and their liberal political friends further alienate themselves from this important subgroup of the American electorate.

You don't have to take my word for it. Consider what pollsters Anna Greenberg and Jennifer Berkhold discovered about Christians' attitudes toward Robertson and Falwell. "Christian leaders more known to the general public, like Jerry Falwell and Pat Robertson, are viewed more skeptically by evangelicals," write Greenberg and Berktold. Instead, evangelical Christians are more positive in their thinking about other Christian leaders such as Franklin Graham and James Dobson.

Liberals have succeeded in diabolizing Robertson and Falwell, but at what cost? They have gravely damaged their credibility with a huge segment of Americans by attributing to this broad and diverse segment of the voting public the sentiments of leaders they themselves view skeptically.

By attempting to discredit the larger Religious Right by condemning proxies such as Robertson and Falwell, liberals only serve to discredit themselves among this increasingly consequential segment of the American electorate.

THE NEW RELIGIOUS RIGHT

But what happens when we broaden the definition of the Religious Right to include—as I argue we must—all politically conservative, religiously motivated voters? Suddenly, we see stereotypes begin to crumble. And we see an extraordinary amount of diversity.

For example, in a shockingly fair segment of *Dateline NBC* titled "In God They Trust," Tom Brokaw interviewed a deeply faithful evangelical couple in October 2005. Considering this was a mainstream media production featuring one of America's elitist news personalities, we can assume the couple was a pair of poorly educated, white, lower-class Southerners who placed all their faith in bizarre superstitions and all their money in oleaginous televangelists, right?

Surprisingly, no.

Brokaw introduced us to Leon and Venezia Lowman, an attractive African American couple so soft-spoken it was at times difficult to hear the husband, Leon. The Lowmans worship at New Life Church in Colorado Springs, home base for evangelical leader Pastor Ted Haggard. Leon gave up 50 percent of his salary to quit his corporate job to work at Focus on the Family, also located in Colorado Springs. The Lowmans also started a small business: a spa, which they struggle to keep afloat. "The financial side of it was very hard, but the other benefits that came out of it have been a huge blessing for us," said Venezia.

Added Leon, "What it's turned out to be is an increase in every aspect of our lives in terms of personal relationships, family relationships. Being able to participate with the events at the kids' schools. All those things have been a big increase for us."

Incidentally, if the Lowmans hardly sound stressed about their financial challenges, they are not alone. According to a study by the National Bureau of Economic Research in Cambridge, Massachusetts, religious involvement provides a kind of insurance from "wealth shocks," such as a demotion or a lost job.[3] Attending church and maintaining a faithful relationship with God keeps Christians such as the Lowmans on the sunny side of life.

The Lowmans can serve as a great example to shatter existing stereotypes, but we should not make the mistake of replacing those stereotypes with new ones. The truth is, the Lowmans are like other conservative Christians, but not in the ways you might think. As Anna Greenberg and Jennifer Berktold point out in their study "Evangelicals in America," "They are a diverse group, sharing many characteristics of Americans in general."[4]

In our interview, Dr. Dobson told me, "Evangelicals are certainly more ethnically diverse today, and . . . more informed and involved in the political process as well. During the 2004 election, Focus worked with a significant number of African American pastors who, like us, had grown increasingly concerned about the issue of judicial activism, especially as it related to the redefinition of traditional marriage. The liberal stereotype that all conservatives are 'old, rich, white men' is completely off-base."

Yuri Mantilla, also of Focus on the Family, told me that evangelical Christianity is booming in the Latin American community. And

Pastor Ted Haggard told me that the level of ethnic, socioeconomic, and cultural diversity in the forty-five-thousand-plus member churches of the National Association of Evangelicals only increases with each passing year.

In other words, in many ways, the Religious Right is rather, well, regular.

THEY WALK AMONG US

When we look at the 2004 electoral map we formulate some pretty obvious conclusions that conservative Christians are concentrated in the South, the Southwest, and the Plains. Indeed, a postelection cartoon map depicted blue America as part of "The United States of Canada" and red America as "Jesusland."

There is some justification for this caricature. More evangelicals, for example, indeed live in the Deep South than, say, in New England. A Southerner is more likely to call himself "a born-again Christian" than a Northeasterner[5] (54 percent to 24 percent), for example. Southerners are also more likely than Northeasterners to attend church and read the Bible.

Curiously, however, Southerners are not especially more likely to do these things than Midwesterners and Westerners. According to the Barna Group, 48 percent of Southerners attend church on a regular basis, compared to 46 percent of Midwesterners and 41 percent of Westerners. It is only when we look at Northeasterners that the number falls to 35 percent.

Same goes for Bible reading. Whereas, Midwesterners (41 percent) and Westerners (44 percent) attempt to keep pace with Southerners (52%) in this category, Northeasterners fall way behind (33 percent).[6]

The deeper we look at regional differences among Christians, the more we have to conclude that the Northeast, rather than the South, is the anomaly here. It is less the case that the South is hyper-religious than it is that the Northeast is less religiously active than the rest of the country, with Southerners being slightly more active than everyone else.

Moreover, the dispersion of the evangelical population closely mirrors that of other Americans. "White evangelicals are not overly concentrated in the South, despite popular assumptions," write Greenberg and Berktold. "Rather, white evangelical Christians are evenly spread out throughout the country."[7]

According to their research, whereas 28 percent of the nation's population lives in the Deep South, 31 percent of evangelicals live there. Whereas 16 percent of the nation's population inhabits the East North Central, 19 percent of evangelicals live there. And whereas 16 percent of the nation's population lives in Pacific states, 14 percent of evangelicals call the West Coast home.[8]

The largest evangelical megachurch is Saddleback Church in the town of Lake Forest in deep blue California. Over fifteen thousand people attend worship services there. Anecdotes such as this make stereotyping difficult to sustain.

One stereotype does hold up under the research, however. According to Greenberg and Berktold, evangelicals are more likely to live in suburban or rural areas than urban area.

Where do those Christian conservatives live? Chances are, they live right next door.

MARS AND VENUS AT CHURCH

Another common stereotype is that conservative Christians are dis-proportionately male. We pointed out in chapter 4, for example, how easy it was for armchair analysts to confuse conservative

Christian behavior at the ballot box with a revolution of "angry white males."

Is this true?

No.

I always found the archetypal white male Religious Right zealot a bit fantastic. Having worked on scores of campaigns for high public office, my interaction with the Religious Right has always disproportionately been a female thing. In my experience, the most energetic, religiously motivated campaign activists have been women; not exclusively, of course, but predominantly.

As I argue vociferously in this book, however, anecdotes don't make for cogent arguments, so I dug further to find some data that would either substantiate my impressions, or shatter them. I found that I was not imagining things. Conservative Christianity is a female-dominated sport.

Pastor H.B. London of Focus on the Family told me that he worries about what he calls the "feminization of the church," because "only 27 percent of men attend church."

And he's right. Female Christians outnumber men by a substantial margin of 57 percent to 43 percent.[9] Automatically, therefore, the Religious Right has a larger pool of female Christians than male Christians from which to draw its informal membership.

But that doesn't mean that the Religious Right is disproportionately female. It might just mean that Christian men are so much more conservative than Christian women, politically and theologically, that we are talking about two separate churches: a male-dominated conservative church and a female-dominated moderate to liberal church.

Except the exact opposite is true.

Within the evangelical community, women are more conservative then the men in both beliefs and behaviors. Write Greenberg and Berktold:

There are strong differences in formal and informal religious activity by gender among white evangelicals. Women evangelicals are more likely to hold a literal interpretation of the Bible (71 percent versus 62 percent of men). Women evangelicals are somewhat more likely than their male counterparts to attend church services at least once a week (74 percent versus 69 percent). Women are also more likely to regularly incorporate religious informal activities into their lives, such as pray before meals daily (64 percent versus 58 percent) and read the Bible at least once a week (81 percent versus 68 percent).[10]

Moreover, women are more likely than men (55 percent to 41 percent) to believe that the United States has special protection from God.[11] They are more likely to feel that a belief in God is necessary to be a moral person (53 percent among women versus 40 percent among men).[12] And women find less common ground between Christianity and other religions such as Islam.[13]

It is difficult to understand how and when the stereotype of the white male Religious Right zealot ever came about. As evangelical historian Douglas Sweeney has observed, "Women have always comprised a majority of the evangelical movement."[14]

It appears to be just one of those politically useful myths that, for whatever reason, remains as durable as it is wrong.

So not all conservative Christians are Southern white men. We can lump some Westerners and Midwesterners in there with them, and we can even concede that a majority of them are women. But we certainly all agree that we are talking about old people here, right?

I mean, only old geezers buy into this holy roller stuff, right?

Well, there again we have a common stereotype that is not easily substantiated. In a 2000 survey, The Barna Group[15] saw church population distribution that resembles the national average:

- 21 percent are "Busters" (between the ages of 18 and 33) versus 31 percent nationwide.
- 45 percent are "Boomers" (between the ages of 34 and 52) versus 42 percent nationwide.
- 24 percent are "Builders" (between the ages of 53 and 71) versus 19 percent nationwide.
- 8 percent are "Seniors" (age 72 or older) versus 6 percent nationwide.

While it is true that fewer "Busters" are Christians, Barna's scale shows that Christians grow in proportion to the national population as we move up the age ladder. Nevertheless, the plurality of Christians (45 percent) is within the age range of 34 and 52, and 65 percent are between 18 and 52. This hardly makes the church "old."

One thing we can tell for sure from the Greenberg and Berktold study is that like women, younger evangelicals are more orthodox in behavior. Younger evangelicals are more likely to attend informal prayer groups, are as likely to attend regular church services, and are more likely to hold a literal interpretation of the Bible than their parents or other older believers.[16]

When I visited Colorado Springs, the folks at New Life Church invited me to a Friday evening worship service for college-age people and twenty-somethings in the community they call "the Mill." Over 1,400 young people gathered at the megachurch on a blustery, below-zero night to chat, listen to live worship music, buy books, drink soda and eat bagels, and, yes, to flirt with one another.

I saw young people from every walk of life. One fellow wore a beard and his long hair in a pony tale. He wore a stud in his left eyebrow and tattoos on his arms. Figuring this guy was just there to pick up chicks, I asked him why he came.

"I like to be with other people my age who worship the Lord," he told me.

He was talking to an attractive young woman whose life goal was to be a stand-up comedian. I asked her why she was not out getting drunk at the bars like other folks within her age cohort.

"I used to go out and get drunk a lot," she told me. "But then I realized it's an empty existence."

Why this youth movement is not more widely known or recognized is a mystery. Many modern cultural observers credit the rise of aggressive conservative Christian recruitment techniques to the success of Campus Crusade for Christ (CCC). Formed in 1951 by Bill Bright, CCC became the nation's most aggressive parachurch organization designed to witness to students on college campuses and win young hearts, minds, and spirits over to Christ. An organizational genius by any measure, Bright managed to transform CCC from a UCLA-based ministry to a national movement that has managed to convert hundreds of thousands, if not millions, of American college students to Christianity.

While CCC was always a religious—and never a political—movement, obvious cultural and political differences between CCC activists and other campus activists became evident during the turbulent 1960s. It became impossible to ignore the dichotomy of buttoned-down Christian college kids on the one hand and wild-eyed beatniks and hippies on the other. Many of these CCC members saw it as part of their calling to involve themselves in political campaigns, specifically the Barry Goldwater presidential campaign of 1964 and the Ronald Reagan gubernatorial campaign in California in 1968.

And they weren't alone. Other youth-oriented organizations such as Navigators, InterVarsity Fellowship, and Youth for Christ emerged during the 1950s and 1960s to win souls for Christ. Inevitably, a great many of these students and youths involved themselves in political campaigns and social causes, often in reaction to the radical agitation of their counterculture peers.

The point is, since its early founding, the modern-day evangelical movement in general and the Religious Right in particular has relied on the energy and enthusiasm of young people.

MORTGAGING THOSE TREASURES IN HEAVEN

Okay, so conservatives Christians don't have to be Southerners, they don't have to be men and they don't have to be old. But we're talking about people on the lower end of the socioeconomic scale here, right?

Aren't we talking about people who don't have any money and don't have any prospects and are just hanging their last hope on the Cross? You know, like the inbred hicks Tom Frank was writing about in *What's the Matter with Kansas?*

Once again, we have bumped up against a common stereotype that doesn't match reality. As a group, evangelical Christians are not poor. Neither are they rich or middle-class. They are all three.

The dispersion of evangelicals by income level closely resembles that of the general population of the United States. Whereas 29 percent of all Americans earn $30,000 or less per year, 25 percent of evangelicals do. Slightly more evangelicals (36 percent) earn between $30,000 and $60,000 per year than do Americans as a whole (33 percent). And slightly less (22 percent) earn $60,000 per year and up than do Americans as a whole (23 percent).[17]

Interestingly, the percentage of adult born-agains from households making $60,000 per year or more has climbed dramatically from 13 percent in 1991.[18] We obviously cannot conclude from this that if you are born again and come to accept Jesus as your savior your income will go up. It might simply be the case that higher income earners have had born-again experiences in the 1990s and early 2000s.

But in a recent study conducted on behalf of the National Bureau of Economic Research, economist Jonathan Gruber uncovers a correlation between church attendance and "a better economic outcome."

Gruber argues that a household with double the rate of church attendance as another has on average 9.1 percent more income. "That extra participation in religious activity correlates with 16 percent less welfare participation than the usual rate, 4 percent lower odds of being divorced and 4.4 percent increased chances of being married."[19]

And for what it's worth, white evangelical Christians are more likely to give money to an organization that helps the poor or needy people than are non-Christians.[20]

BIND US TOGETHER

I have deliberately tried to shatter myths commonly associated with the Religious Right. It is simply incorrect to assert that the Religious Right is, as Michael Weisskopf asserted in the *Washington Post* some time ago, "largely poor, uneducated and easy to command." Neither is the Religious Right a collection of "angry white males," as the cognoscenti insisted after the 1994 Republican Revolution.

At the same time I have resisted the temptation to put forward a new stereotype of the Religious Right. Conservative Christians are simply too diverse a group of people to accurately label as belonging to any single demographic, regional, or socioeconomic group. It is useless and, frankly, irresponsible to try to stereotype evangelicals and other conservative Christians.

Here is the point I am leading up to: there is one thing that unites these people beside their faith in Jesus Christ; one thing that makes them alike more than their genders, their incomes, their levels of education, their ethnic heritages, or their regions of habitation. And that thing is the way they behave on Election Day.

Simply put, conservative politics brings these people together in a way that no other cultural indicator can. A Scotch-Irish, upper-middle-class, nondenominational female living in a Southern suburb may have absolutely nothing in common with a German, working-class, Lutheran man in Idaho except for the fact that on the first Tuesday after the first Monday every other year they draw similar, and in many cases the same, conclusions about the state of our nation and the remedies necessary for curing our collective ailments.

Think about that. The issues that so many talking heads in our common culture label "divisive" bring together people of every imaginable stripe and flavor. To further confound the common culture's conventional wisdom about "divisiveness," consider the fact that this uniting worldview is in the ascent in America. That is to say, conservative Christianity is growing while liberal denominations and churches are bleeding members and have been for some time.

Chalk it up to the common culture's unhealthy fixation with irony, but political expression among conservative Christians—so often condemned as "intolerant" and "exclusionary"—is the glue that holds together some of the largest and most rapidly growing segments of our population.

SO FIVE MINUTES AGO

Why is the straw man set up by the common culture to symbolize the typical Christian conservative—the slow-witted, poor, Southern white male—so far off the mark? To be sure, there is tremendous value in making this imaginary troglodyte the poster boy for the Religious Right. But I believe there is something else going on here.

The common culture and the mainstream media have fixated on passing fads over the last forty years as though they were genuine cultural trends. Meanwhile, they have missed the story of the greatest social movement of our era. Over the past forty-plus years, tens of millions of Americans—generation after generation—have turned their lives over to Christ. Unlike, say, disco or other dance crazes, this social movement has been sustained for decades. Many sociologists believe we are even amidst another Great Awakening.

And yet, this revival, to the extent it is covered at all, it generally characterized as parochial, weird, and underground. Meanwhile, boomlets that were little more than passing fancies made headlines.

Consider the 1960s. That era is commonly considered to be a period of massive counterculture activity. Hippies were everywhere. A whole generation had "tuned in, turned on, and dropped out." Really? As we observed above, the Christian movement on college campuses was every bit as organized and perhaps even more populous than the hippie movement.

Billy Graham urged thousands of young people to "tune in, turn on to God" at massive youth rallies throughout that troubled decade. And he succeeded. To this day, Billy Graham is one of the most recognized and respected public figures in America. Counterculture icon Abbie Hoffman, on the other hand, was arrested on drug charges in the 1970s and lived on the lam through much of that decade. He committed suicide in 1989.

The 1970s evoke images of John Travolta in a white three-piece suit, one hand on his hip, the other pointing in the air. When the entertainment industry attempts to immortalize that era, it turns to "Son of Sam" serial killer David Berkowitz or Studio 54's Steve

Rubell. That was the decade in which everyone was doing drugs. That was the decade America lost a war to a Third World country. That was the decade the president of the United States shamed his office and humiliated his country.

Well, yeah . . . but.

It was also the decade in which evangelical Christianity started to become a powerful force in public life. An unapologetic evangelical born-again Christian, a Democrat even, was elected to the highest office in the land. This was the decade in which Martin Luther King Sr. stated, while nominating Jimmy Carter at the 1976 Democratic National Convention:

> Surely the Lord is in this place. Surely the Lord sent Jimmy Carter to come on out and bring America back where she belongs. I'm with him. You are too. But as I close in prayer, let me tell you, we must close ranks now. If there's any misunderstanding anywhere, if you haven't got a forgiving heart, get on your knees. It's time for prayer.

This was the decade that the Reverend Jerry Falwell began to inspire conservative Christians to take political action, Francis Schaeffer called them to take on a larger role in pubic life, Pat Robertson's Christian Broadcasting Network began to attract hundreds of thousands of viewers, and Phyllis Schlafly mobilized thousands of Christian women to thwart the Equal Rights Amendment. This was a period of extraordinary maturation for Christian conservatives, and yet the era is characterized by camp and goofy clothing fashions.

To the extent that anyone in the common culture thinks about or talks about religion in America during the 1980s, they generally reflect back to the televangelist scandals involving Jimmy Swaggart and Jim and Tammy Faye Bakker. Few observers of that era had any inkling of the explosive strength of Christian conservatives until Pat Robertson went from obscure entrepreneurial reverend to presidential frontrunner at the end of the decade. Robertson's campaign fizzled out, but not until after he had raised more money (almost all of it from small individual donations, mind you) than any other presidential candidate up until that time.

The growth of conservative Christianity became even more obvious during the 1990s to anyone with eyes to see. When culture vultures were talking about grunge rock, Promise Keepers were holding mass rallies with hundreds of thousands of Christian men. While political talking heads carried on about the brilliance of Bill Clinton's "triangulation," the Republican Party took over the United States Senate and House of Representatives for the first time in forty years, largely on the shoulders of politically active conservative Christians.

All the signs were there in the 1960s and continued on for four-and-a-half decades since, but the sharpest observers of popular trends have either ignored or have been too dull to recognize this massive social movement of the last half-century.

And here comes the ultimate irony. While the chroniclers of the common culture have made big deals out of flashes in the pan, they have simultaneously reported on conservative Christianity as though it was the passing fancy, an oddball reaction to cultural change—"progress" they often call it—that will certainly fizzle out and die off soon.

"Signs Hint Christian Coalition Influence Has Peaked," read a *Chicago Tribune* headline on 13 September 1996.

"The problem, of course, for Republicans is that despite maintaining their strength and hold in the GOP, the popularity of the religious right has been diminishing amongst the majority of voters," opined James Zogby in March of 2000.[21]

"Religious Right on the Ropes," rang out an optimistic headline on AlterNet on 31 October 2001.[22]

"Their interest and their influence fading, Christian conservatives are struggling to regain the power that not long ago helped Republicans elect a president and win control of Congress," wrote Steve Thomma of the Knight Ridder Washington bureau in October of 2002. "[T]he movement has declined rapidly in recent years," echoed *National Journal's* Hotline that same month.

"Maybe we'll look back and say the Bush first term was really the high point of the Christian right's influence in American politics," said Professor Alan Wolfe of Boston College after the 2005 off-year elections.[23]

Curiously, the Religious Right never seems to go away. It has been pronounced dead more times than Jason Voorhees. But its enemies should not hold out hope that it will disappear from America's political scene any time soon.

At last count, the Religious Right is 30 million religiously motivated conservative voters. According to exit and postelection polling data, we can conclude that they are roughly 23 million evangelical and conservative mainline Christians and 6.9 million conservative Catholics. They represent the growing wings of their respective denominations and faith traditions. They are black, white, and brown. They live in parts North, South, East, and West. They are wealthy, middle class, and poor. They are highly educated and poorly educated. They are, in short, Americans.

8

I SCREAM, YOU SCREAM, BUT WE ARE THE MAINSTREAM

So I have convinced you that common stereotypes about conservative Christians are not supported by the facts. Conservative Christians are not necessarily surly, poor, old, uneducated, Southern men. There are some of those. But just as many members of the Religious Right are middle class as among the general population. Many are young. Most are women. They live in all regions of the country. While a dominant majority is white, an increasing number are Latino, Asian, and African American.

And we have determined that the thing that holds these disparate people together is a shared concern for the future of America and her culture and values, manifested through conservative political activism—those so-called divisive wedge issues. Certainly, the uninformed would argue, *this* is where the Religious Right gets weird. Here is where the Religious Right is different from the rest of America, right? Sure conservative politics has helped to bring disparate folks together, but only in turn to differentiate themselves from normal people. Their espousal of these "divisive" and "extreme" issues is what places them at the fringe of society. Doesn't it?

No, it doesn't.

The Religious Right is very much in the middle of mainstream American opinion. While the culture wars in America often find talking heads from opposing viewpoints screaming at one another on cable talk shows, conservative Christians are increasingly speaking for Middle America, defending shared American values against extremism from the political Left.

If that sounds counterintuitive that's because the people who control the flow of information in the United States are far, far outside the mainstream. A study by the American Society of Newspaper Editors found that 62 percent of editors and reporters are liberals. And 86 percent of elite journalists attend religious services seldom or never. Almost half have no religious affiliation at all.[1]

Meanwhile, 38 percent of all Americans say they attend church every week.[2] Fully 62 percent say they attend church at least once a month.[3] Ninety-two percent of Americans believe in God, 85 percent believe in heaven, and 73 percent believe in miracles.[4]

America is a deeply religious society, but our journalists are deeply secular. Is it any wonder that their perspectives are so different? Why when the *New York Times* announced in early 2005 that it was going to offer more and deeper coverage of religion, this was greeted with giggles and smirks? What did the *New York Times* know about religion? Would their reporters even know where to look? As expected, the *Times* generated a series of stories about liberal spiritual movements that contained frequent potshots at conservative Christians.

This dissonance reached comical out-of-touchness when *Times* columnist Nicholas Kristof penned a snobbish piece lamenting the fact that more Americans believe in the Virgin Birth than believe in Darwinian evolution. "The faith in the Virgin Birth reflects the way American Christianity is becoming *less intellectual* and more mystical over time," wrote Kristof (emphasis added). "I'm troubled by the way the great intellectual traditions of Catholic and Protestant churches alike are withering, leaving the scholarly and religious worlds increasingly antagonistic."

Yes, I'm sure that's it. The increased friction between Americans of faith and secular academics is the result of American Christians and Catholics becoming dumber. Well, the *Times did* say it would run more religion stories.

Regardless of whether Mr. Kristof's worries are justified or not, though, he makes a point that is fundamental to this book. Conservative religious viewpoints are not out of the mainstream. While Kristof used his data to demean Christian Americans for being unintelligent, they actually reflect the view of all Americans as a whole. The 83 percent that believe in the Virgin Birth of Jesus versus only 28 who believe in Darwinian evolution referenced in Kristof's column are among *all Americans*, not just rightwing Christian nuts.

As Kristof makes clear, much to his dismay, if you want to gauge what mainstream Americans are thinking, find out first what conservative Christians are thinking—then turn it down just a notch.

Former US Senator Gary Hart characterizes his essay, "God and Caesar in America," as "a critical analysis of the dangers of one minority wing of one religion subverting one part, and eventually the political system, to its beliefs."[5] He is, of course, talking about the Religious Right. The idea that a small minority of overzealous, rightwing Christians imposes its extreme agenda on an unwitting and unwilling American mainstream is omnipresent in our pundit-dominated public dialogue.

Frank Rich made essentially the same point on the pages of the *New York Times*. "All this is happening while polls consistently show that at most a fifth of the country subscribes to the religious views of those in the Republican base whom even George Will, speaking last Sunday on

ABC's *This Week*, acknowledged may be considered 'extremists.' In that famous Election Day exit poll, 'moral values' voters amounted to only 22 percent."[6]

Leave aside for a moment the question of whether any pollster could find 22 percent of Americans who agree with Frank Rich on cultural and moral values matters. The real question germane to this book is this: are Senator Hart and columnist Rich right in their argument that the Religious Right is a small, extreme minority?

Of course not.

As Rich might say, "polls consistently show" that the majority of all Americans share the political views of the Religious Right. Mainstream Americans do not feel as stridently as the Religious Right on many issues, perhaps; they may see some issues in some cases to be less black and white. But the fact remains on issue after issue, conservative Christians and mainstream Americans are on the same side of virtually every social and moral debate in our public dialogue.

As former Second Lady Marilyn Quayle once observed, "Not everyone joined the counterculture. . . . The majority of my generation lived by the credo our parents taught us: we believe in God, in hard work and personal discipline, in our nation's essential goodness."[7]

PUBLIC DISPLAYS OF AFFECTION (FOR GOD)

Let's look at some recent controversies in the culture wars to see on which side most Americans fall.

In recent years, we have seen secular liberals and atheists attack words and phrases that they claim breach the church-state wall. Displayed on or spoken within public property, words like "under God," "In God We Trust," and the various "Thou shalts" and "Thou shalt nots" of the Ten Commandments violate the First Amendment, they insist.

Atheist activist Michael Newdow has led the charge to have the words "under God" declared unconstitutional when spoken by students voluntarily in public schools. Newdow managed to convince the Ninth US Circuit Court of Appeals to agree that the Pledge of Allegiance is unconstitutional, though he failed to convince the US Supreme Court that he had standing to bring the case up at all. He hasn't quit though. Newdow, a lawyer, has convinced other parents with standing to bring up the case again.

Same for the words "In God We Trust" engraved on our national currency. In his 162-page lawsuit filed against the United States Congress, Newdow argues, "The placement of 'In God We Trust' on the coins and currency was clearly done for religious purposes and to have religious effects" and therefore must be scratched off our coins by an act of law or judicial intervention.[8] As with the "under God" controversy, Newdow is shopping for a judicial venue that will rubberstamp his latest instigation.

As for the Ten Commandments, challenges to their public display have cropped up in Texas, Kentucky, and, most famously, in Alabama. The Supreme Court recently ruled that some displays of the Ten Commandments are okay while others are not. Their convoluted decision is sure to keep the controversy alive until a uniform understanding of their constitutionality is established.

We can pretty easily guess what the Religious Right thinks of these efforts. Their first instinct is to giggle. Certainly Newdow is some kind of busybody wacko with too much time on his hands. But when federal circuit courts start endorsing Newdow's bizarre understanding of the First Amendment to the Constitution, their emotions sway from humor to fear and anger.

Where do most Americans stand on these issues?

According to the Barna Group's study titled "How 'Christianized' Do Americans Want Their Country to Be?" "Less than one out of every five adults (18 percent) supports 'removing signs that list the Ten Commandments from government buildings.'"

Seventy-nine percent of all Americans opposed "removing the Ten Commandments from public displays." Sixty percent were "strongly opposed." Even non-Christian faith groups responded negatively to the idea of removing the Ten Commandments.[9] The effort to remove "under God" from our nation's Pledge of Allegiance has an even steeper hill to climb. Eighty-four percent of all Americans reject the idea, and only 15 percent of Americans support it. Newdow hasn't even convinced his compatriots to support his pet cause. Only 40 percent of atheists and agnostics want "under God" removed.

Another 84 percent reject the idea that "In God We Trust" should be removed from American currency, with only 13 percent endorsing the proposal. Again, Newdow is in the minority even among his "faith group." Only 37 percent of atheists and agnostics want "In God We Trust" erased from legal US tender.

You could argue that in these three circumstances I have cherry-picked some no-brainer issues. But these are genuine controversies in which federal courts have—or will soon—expressed opinions that deviate from the overwhelming desires of the American public.

It bears repeating, the Ninth US Circuit Court of Appeals believes the words "under God," when voluntarily spoken in government schools, should be unconstitutional.

Who's out of the mainstream?

Now let's look at some other controversies that are perhaps not so clear cut.

UNINTELLIGENT DECISIONS

The issue of human evolution creates severe anxiety for Americans of every stripe: Catholics and evangelicals reject Darwinian evolution in big numbers. (Although Catholics generally embrace the idea of evolution, they reject Darwin's idea of random natural selection.) Secular humanists of course think biblical creationism is an absurd superstition.

Belligerent atheist evolutionist Richard Dawkins summed up quite nicely the dominant thinking among this crowd when he stated, "It is absolutely safe to say that, if you meet somebody who claims not to believe in evolution, that person is ignorant, stupid or insane (or wicked, but I'd rather not consider that)." A great many American secularists and liberals would gleefully add "wicked" to Dr. Dawkin's litany.

Now, this being America, you can think whatever you want to think. You can believe we evolved from apes. You can believe we were molded by God from clay. You can believe Earth is a petri dish and earthly plant and animal life are all part of some experiment by space aliens. That's the beauty of America—you can believe what you want.

Or can you? A great conflict arises around the question of how we got here when that question becomes a matter of public policy. You see, many secular humanists believe teaching creationism in public schools is unconstitutional. In 1982 the US Supreme Court made it the official law of the land that it is unconstitutional for a school board to demand equal time for evolution and creation science.[10] Indeed, the federal judiciary has made it plain in a number of cases that one version of how we got here can be taught in public schools: Darwinian evolution.

The issue became white-hot again in the mid-2000s. School boards across the country endorsed the ideal that Intelligent Design should be taught alongside Darwinian evolution in their state or district's science classes. Intelligent Design is the theory that holds that evolutionary development is so complex—"irreducibly complex,"

ID-ers call it—that we simply could not have arrived at where we are through a series of totally random mutations. Some intelligent force had to have guided the process along the way.

One school district, the Dover Area School District in Eastern Pennsylvania, mandated Intelligent Design be taught as an alternative theory to Darwin's. They were swiftly brought to court where Judge John E. Jones—a George W. Bush appointee—ruled that the teaching of Intelligent Design violated the Constitution because ID "cannot uncouple itself from its creationist, and thus religious, antecedents."[11] The case was so laden with culture war name calling, one witness at trial referred to Dr. James Dobson as a "theocratic extremist."[12]

Liberals and secularists cheered as the court system in America made absolutely clear once again its perspective on this battle of the culture war: anything other than Darwinian evolution is creationism and thou shalt not teach creationism in public schools.

The scientific community was elated. Their view of human biology had once again been validated by a federal court, at the expense of all others. And they maintained their monopoly on the flow of information in public schools. Why wouldn't they be thrilled?

And yet it is in this gaiety among secular liberals and scientists that we learn just how out-of-touch they are with the American mainstream. We know, for example, that 90 percent of the members of the National Academy of Sciences are materialists, that is to say 90 percent believe that only those things that can be observed and measured are real, a fundamental component of evolutionary theory. We also know that 56 percent of self-identified secularists believe "Humans and other living things evolved over time through natural selection."[13]

Do they represent the mainstream of America?
Hardly.

Seventy-eight percent of all Americans believe God created life on Earth, according to the Pew Forum on Religion & Public Life. And 60 percent of all Americans believe either "Humans and other living things existed only in their present form" or that their evolution over time was "guided by a supreme being." The only group in which more members believe in natural selection than believe humans and other living things have only existed in their present form is secularists. White evangelical Christians, white mainline Protestants, and white Catholics believe the opposite.[14]

But again, what someone believes isn't really the issue here. You can believe whatever you want. The question is what we can teach in America's public schools. And on this issue, the secularists are even further out of the mainstream. According to Pew, "64 percent support teaching creationism along with evolution in the public schools, while only 29 percent oppose this idea." Secularists and liberals have some proselytizing to do even in their own backyard.

Again, according to the Pew study, "Support for teaching creationism along with evolution is quite broad-based, with majority support even among seculars, liberal Democrats and those who accept natural selection theory."

So again, I must ask, who is it that is out of the mainstream?

DON'T GET ME TO THE CHURCH

I suppose I should bring up the issue of gay marriage at this point. There has been perhaps no more salient issue that broadcasts the secular left's out-of-touchness with mainstream America than the issue of gay marriage.

Liberals take solace in the spin that a combined 60 percent of Americans told 2004 exit pollsters that homosexuals should either be allowed to legally marry or form civil unions. But that "either" is pregnant with misplaced optimism. Only 25 percent of Americans who showed up to vote told exit pollsters they supported legalized same-sex marriage (which was a far lower number than most pre-election polls predicted).

The rest of the facts about this hot button issue need no asterisks. Americans don't want a public policy that recognizes same-sex marriage. Eighteen states have actually written a ban on same-sex marriage into their constitutions. On 2 November 2004, over twenty million Americans voted on ballot initiatives in eleven states to ban gay marriage. Combined, pro-traditional marriage won by a greater than 2-to-1 margin. In Oregon, the most liberal state to put the question to voters that year, 57 percent voted to write a gay marriage ban into the Constitution.

Federal policy dictates that marriage should be between one man and one woman, as well. Both Houses of Congress passed overwhelmingly, and Pres. Bill Clinton signed, the Defense of Marriage Act in 1996. This law, described by CNN at the time as "anti gay,"[15] codified traditional marriage. But liberals like Senator Carol Mosley Braun claimed the bill was "really about the politics of fear and division and about inciting people." Did you catch that? Traditional marriage is about "fear" and "division."

But who is causing the division? It's not the traditionalists who are merely adhering to, as Senator Phil Gramm referred to it, "5,000 years of recorded history." It's the 25 percent of gay marriage extremists who want to impose their permissive views of morality on the majority—make that the *vast* majority—of Americans.

What about the broad issue of faith-based initiatives, specifically the policy of allowing religious groups—even those associated with a Christian denomination—to apply for federal funding to carry out various social programs?

Many liberals hate the idea. "Nowhere has the Bush administration experimented more directly with theocracy than in the center-piece of Bush's compassionate conservatism: his faith-based initiative," charges leftwing polemicist Esther Kaplan.[16] "Essentially the faith-based initiative is a huge privatization scheme, a bait-and-switch," says Rob Boston of Americans United for the Separation of Church and State. Still other liberals have appropriated the term *faith-based* as an epithet for policies they hate. Thus the short-lived nomination of Harriet Miers to the Supreme Court was a "faith-based appoint-ment," and Bush tax cuts are called "faith-based economics."

This callous view is not shared by the majority of Americans, to be sure. Sixty-six percent of all Americans support policies "to allow churches to apply for government funding," according to Pew. A similar 66 percent say they believe houses of worship help solve "a great deal" or "some" social problems.[17] Curiously, to the extent that Americans want to deprive any religious organizations government funds for charitable work, it is Islamic groups whom they would deprive. Only 41 percent of Americans approve of giving Islamic groups taxpayer funds to combat social problems, versus 56 percent who oppose.[18]

LIFE OR DEATH

Issues of life and death come up a lot when Americans discuss the Religious Right. Religious conservatives are often said to be obsessed with these issues. But liberal priest Reverend John Paris doesn't see what all the fuss is about. In an interview with *Salon*, he stressed, "'We understand that life is not an absolute good and death is not an absolute defeat.' The whole story of Easter is about the triumph of eternal life over death. Catholics have never believed that biolog-ical life is an end in and of itself."[19]

Look, we're all going to die anyway, so what's the big deal, right?

Pull those plugs, abort those fetuses, clone and dissect those human embryos. They're in a better place now.

On the issue of abortion, leftist pundit Bill Press argues that Catholic and evangelical opposition to abortion is the result of centuries of religious oppression of women. "So religious opposition to abortion must be seen as part of a pattern—the churches' long history of talking down sex and putting down women," he writes.[20] And anyway, the pro-life position, like Intelligent Design, presumably, is so drenched in religious significance the government can't have anything to do with it.

That, Press explains, is "the most important principle of the entire abortion debate: *It's not the government's role to enforce by law what the churches can't deliver by faith or to replace churches as the primary moral agents of society.* Laws may not be based on religious orthodoxy. Congress should pass no law mandating that Americans obey what is essentially a matter of religious belief." It's an argument that seems to swim against almost every other argument in Press's book. He certainly does want the government to do the churches' job on helping the poor, for example. And he opposes capital punishment and the Iraq War on religious grounds.

Others have tried to use religious language in support of legalized abortion. In "An Open Letter to Religious Leaders on Abortion as a Moral Decision," the Religious Institute on Sexual Morality, Justice, and Healing writes, "We affirm women as moral agents who have the capacity, right and responsibility to make the decision as to whether or not abortion is justified in their specific circumstances."[21]

Still other ostensibly religious groups argue that the Bible mandates women have the right to an abortion. You see, because the Bible doesn't explicitly condemn abortion, the argument goes, but rather *does* mandate compassion for one another, we must allow women to kill their unwanted babies. Forget for just a moment that the Sixth Commandment proscribes against *lo tirtzack*, "any kind of killing whatsoever." This is what passes for serious thought on the issue of abortion.

Is it any wonder conservative Christians are winning?

Yes, conservative Christians are winning the national debate over abortion. Public perceptions may not convince you of that, but election results sure should.

When Bill Clinton defeated Pres. George H.W. Bush for the presidency in 1992, most pundits blamed the Religious Right for Bush's Jimmy Carter-like reelection performance. Bush had simply been too beholden to those religious nuts. It killed him with women, it scared mainstream Americans, and so forth. Political commentator James Pinkerton argued at the time that the Republican Party would never win the White House again unless it nominated pro-choice candidates.

Meanwhile, other political pundits began to think that the pro-life position was a Republican albatross. Republican political consultants advised their clients to run away from their pro-life stands and, in the event that they had not yet taken a public position on the issue, to declare themselves pro-choice.

In 1996, pro-abortion forces had Republicans on the run. A cabal of pro-abortion Republicans fought like hell to change the abortion plank in the Republican Party platform during the Republican National Convention that year. Senator Olympia Snowe's (R-ME) overheated concern for the looming political apocalypse if the Republicans didn't at least become agnostic on the issue of abortion was indicative of prominent thinking of the time:

> Well, it [the present abortion plank] does a lot of damage because we obviously have a significant gender gap. It sends a chilling message to women about how they perceive the Republican Party, that we're inflexible, intolerant, and that

this somehow represents a view of all Republicans when, in fact, it doesn't. The message that I'm getting here at home in the state of Maine is get my party back, it's moving in the wrong direction. And that's what we're trying to do.[22]

Obviously, things never worked out like the doomsayers thought *or hoped* they would. Yes, Bob Dole was crushed in 1996, but for reasons totally unrelated to the abortion plank. Moreover, the GOP's continued success as a pro-life party since then ought to be evidence enough that the pro-life position is not the electoral loser it has sometimes been thought to be.

And probably it never was. Liberals take comfort in the litany of polls that remind them that most Americans routinely describe themselves as pro-choice. But in point of fact that is the only abortion-related issue in which most Americans take the liberal position. Polls consistently put Middle America well into the Religious Right camp on parental notification, parental consent, partial-birth abortion, born-alive abortions, and the whole litany of ancillary issues.

And that "pro-choice" majority rejects the pro-abortion extremism of the Democratic Party and their liberal puppet masters. According to a Zogby poll from January 2001, 51 percent of respondents agreed that "abortion destroys a human life and is manslaughter" versus only 35 percent who said "abortion does not destroy a life and is not manslaughter."

Elsewhere we see that 77.7 percent of all Americans said physicians should notify parents if an underage girl is seeking an abortion.[23] Seventy-one percent oppose the use of federal funds to finance abortions.[24] Seventy percent of Americans think access to abortion should be limited to some circumstances versus only 16 percent who say abortion should be legal in all cases.[25]

Partisans Jim Carville and Paul Begala recently wrote in their book *Take It Back*, "Do Democrats need to make peace with as least some restrictions on abortion? If they want to show the overwhelming majority of Americans who support those restrictions that they understand and respect their values, yes. If not, they will continue waging a battle they've already lost, and risk losing the war they ought to win."[26]

Nevertheless, many pro-abortion pundits are putting a happy face on the slide. Liberal pollster Celinda Lake says, "Despite what anti-abortion activists and politicians would have you believe, the majority of Americans continue to support a woman's right to a legal abortion—as they have done consistently for the past 15 years. Polls show that those who strive to abolish a woman's right to the full range of family-planning services are fundamentally *out* of step with American opinion."[27]

So the question becomes, if Ms. Lake is correct and abortion is still the albatross weighing down the GOP, why did Hillary Clinton, who badly wants to be president of the United States, promise in April of 2005 to find "common ground" with pro-life Americans? Why did Senator John Kerry, who badly wanted to be president of the United States, urge his party after the election to change its messaging on abortion because too many Americans think Democrats are for it?

They did so because they are willing to admit what some pollsters and a great many liberal enthusiasts are unwilling to admit: "pro-choice" is a great brand, but it is an unsafe issue position in a conservative Christian America.

Another issue we have seen come up in the public dialogue recently is stem-cell research. Of course, there is nothing objectionable to the idea of stem-cell research, *per se*. Stem cells are just blank-slate cells that haven't fully formed and can therefore develop into the cells of almost any human tissue. Theoretically, blank stem cells could be used to generate new brain cells in patients with brain diseases. There is, for example, nothing wrong with using adult stem-cells or stem-cells extracted from umbilical cord blood. An ethical problem arises, however, when the federal government gives money to scientists who extract stem-cells from human embryos, thereby killing them. A deeper ethical problem arises when the federal government gives money to scientists to harvest embryos through human cloning in order to have more stem cells to extract and, thereby, kill more of them.

When you hear liberals talk about "stem-cell research," they are not talking about the okay kind of stem-cell research. They are talking about the use of federal tax dollars to clone and kill human embryos kind of stem-cell research, the kind so mired in ethical drawbacks it oughtn't even to be considered.

And that's pretty much President Bush's position on the issue. He allowed already allocated federal resources to be used to conduct research on already frozen human embryos (which would just be thrown away if the research wasn't allowed to continue, Americans were told). But the president prohibited taxpayer money to be used to kill human embryos for scientific experiments, and certainly not to clone any humans for scientific experiments.

Nevertheless, because a scientist (and quite a mad scientist, it turned out) in South Korea named Hwang Woo-suk claimed to have developed a fast and revolutionary cloning procedure which would advance Korean stem-cell research far beyond our own, many liberals began to panic. Fifty-eight US senators sent a letter to the president urging him to change his position. The promise of embryonic stem cell research was simply too great to be ignored, they claimed.

The extreme optimism about the "promise" of stem-cell research reached out-of-control proportions when 2004 Democrat vice presidential nominee John Edwards, sounding like a Pentecostal preacher, actually claimed at a campaign stop that if Americans would just vote for him and John Kerry "people like Chris Reeve will get up out of their wheelchair and walk again . . ."[28]

Are you getting the picture here? Liberals dressed up horribly unethical public policy in religious imagery in the hopes of fooling the American public into supporting clone-to-kill programs.

But Americans aren't fooled.

Democrats seemed to have it all going for them on the issue of stem-cell research in 2004. According to a Pew study, "By more than two-to-one (63%–28%), those who have heard a great deal about the issue believe it is more important to conduct stem-cell research that may result in medical cures than to not destroy the potential life of human embryos."[29] Well, yes. With so much talk during that dishonest election about people getting up out of their wheelchairs and former First Lady Nancy Reagan issuing calls for federal funding of embryonic stem-cell research to cure Alzheimer's, it seemed hard to be against it, didn't it? The people of the cash-strapped state of California even approved a ballot initiative to allocate $3 billion toward embryonic stem-cell research.

But three factors prevent Democrats from taking advantage of this seemingly overwhelming call for embryonic stem-cell research.

First, Americans oppose human cloning in a big way. Eighty-seven percent of Americans believe cloning humans should be illegal in the United States. Even 59 percent believe cloning *animals* should be illegal.[30] A huge majority also opposes cloning for "therapeutic" reasons. Advocates of embryonic stem-cell research cannot escape the fact that human cloning is the integral piece of the "Chris Reeve will walk again" argument. For example, South Korean pioneer Hwang Woo-suk's breakthrough was not in doing anything unique or clever with the stem cells themselves, but in putatively designing a faster and easier way of reproducing his human lab rats through cloning. (More on this in a moment.)

Second, any thinking person, regardless of what the Pew poll indicates, recognizes the moral dilemma at play here. Is it ethical to take life to save it? Should we be playing God in a laboratory? Isn't this something private industry should finance? Why do they need tax dollars?

Embryonic stem-cell research is a deeply complex issue, not only scientifically, but morally, as well. Talk to anyone with half a brain (and at least half a heart) and they will tell you, regardless of their position, that this is an issue to be *weighed*, not demagogued. And the people who appear to have weighed seriously the pros and the cons of embryonic stem-cell research are conservative Christians, emblemized by Pres. George W. Bush's "split the baby down the middle" position on the issue.

The moral absolutists on the issue of embryonic stem-cell research, those who appear to have given it no critical thought at all, are dogmatic liberals who promise miracle cures without considering the cost. So while many Americans have arrived at a similar conclusion as liberals on this issue, the way most liberals arrived at it, frankly, creeps them out.

And finally—and this is a big one—it's all a lie.

Well, okay, it's not *all* a lie. But pretty much. In late 2005, stem cell "pioneer" Hwang Woo-suk was exposed as a fraud who hadn't actually developed any advancements in embryonic cloning. He faked it. He faked it all. Now, the fifty-eight senators who signed a letter to the president, John Edwards, and all the rest certainly could not have known Hwang was lying. They are as much victims of the stem cell over-hype as the rest of us. But their groundless enthusiasm for what turns out to have been an extreme exaggeration underscores their lack of seriousness on the issue.

And lest you think the Dr. Hwang scandal is just a hiccup, read stem cell scientist Dr. Joseph Itskovitz's reaction to the revelation that Hwang was fraud: "The bottom line is that it's a major disaster to our whole field because the expectations were so high and now we are back to square one."[31]

Square one.

JUST SHOOT ME

If liberals have grown overconfident on abortion and their enthusiasm for embryonic stem-cell research is unwarranted, they have become downright cocky on so-called end-of-life issues, specifically their latest construction: the right to die (try finding *that* one in the Constitution).

So convinced are they of their own correctness on these issues, Democratic National Chairman Howard Dean actually told an audience of gay rights activists in West Hollywood, California, that "We're going to use Terri Schiavo later on" in 2006 and 2008.[32]

Terri Schiavo, of course, was the young Florida woman who got into a car accident fifteen years ago, leaving her brain dead and on life support. Er . . . no . . . wait. She wasn't brain *dead*, she was brain *damaged.* And she wasn't on *life support*, she was on *a feeding tube.* She wasn't dying.

But she did tell everyone under the sun that she wouldn't want to live like that, like a vegetable, right? Well, no. She only told her husband that, apparently. And both her parents and her brother and sister claim she told them something quite the opposite.

But Michael Schiavo, Terri's husband, was deeply committed to their relationship and would never misrepresent her wishes, right? Well, some people weren't so sure. Mr. Schiavo had a girlfriend and two children outside of his marriage to Terri. Some folks questioned his motives and his loyalty to Terri.

Now, considering all these misconceptions about the Schiavo case—that she was brain dead and on life support, that she said she never wanted to live like that, that her husband was a grieving spouse who struggled with his final decision—it's understandable that tidal waves of polling data showed that most Americans wanted Terri dead. Shoot, isn't that what she wanted?

So when Congress and the president of the United States convened to pass and sign legislation forcing the federal courts to review her case—to "err on the side of life," as President Bush urged—liberals can be forgiven for believing they gained a powerful leg up in the culture wars.

Frank Rich called the Republicans' behavior a "full-scale jihad,"[33] which is odd because Democrat members of Congress supported the measure, as well. When asked by *Salon* what he thought this case was really about, Reverend John Paris responded, "The power of the Christian right."[34] "This Republican party has become the party of theocracy," cried Rep. Chris Shays (R-CT).[35]

Forget for a moment that liberals generally oppose court-imposed death sentences when they are handed down on murderous criminals. And try to put it out of your mind that while they were cheering the death of Terri Schiavo, they were simultaneously urging for tax dollars for embryonic stem-cell research under the putatively compassionate (and not yet debunked) promise that stem cells from clone-to-kill programs could regenerate brain tissue.

When liberals pulled all the misinformation and contradictions out of the equation, they achieved their desired result. An ABC News poll was indicative of public reaction to Washington's intervention in the case. Sixty-three percent wanted Terri Schiavo to die. Sixty percent opposed the measure put forth by conservative members of Congress. And 70 percent said it was inappropriate for the federal government to get involved at all.[36]

The Religious Right was on the ropes. Pundits, bloggers, and liberal activists howled with glee that Republicans would now lose control of Congress. All because they intervened to save the life of this poor girl who was not brain dead, was not on life support, and had allegedly told her parents and siblings that should she ever be in this kind of situation, she would want to live.

Oh yeah, and a whole bunch of Democrats voted to intervene in her case, too. But no matter. Everyone knew this was a Republican problem.

As is their wont, liberals may have counted their chickens before they hatched in the case of Ms. Schiavo, however. I argued earlier that the way in which the mainstream media portrayed the Schiavo case was confused at best and willfully dishonest at worst. But when he presented Americans with a hypothetical scenario identical to Ms. Schiavo's actual case, pollster John Zogby discovered something disheartening.

Zogby asked respondents a straight forward question: "If a disabled person is not terminally ill, not in a coma, and not being kept alive on life support, and they have no written directive, should or should they not be denied food and water?"[37] An astonishing 80 percent responded that this hypothetical person should not be denied food and water. In the abstract at least, a huge majority of Americans wanted Terri Schiavo to live.

So why was it disheartening? Well, Ms. Schiavo had already been killed.

Some bloggers tried to bring attention to the poll. But the mainstream media didn't seem too interested.

NEW FEAR FRONTIERS

Perhaps recognizing that their shopworn attacks on cultural issues have alienated *them* rather than the Religious Right from the American public, liberal leaders have expressed a new unwillingness to start fights over the old cultural issues. Instead, they have shifted their focus to obscure matters of doctrine over which there is a great deal of controversy inside the church and for which their certainly is no consensus.

Liberal writers such as Michelle Goldberg from Salon.com wrote a book titled *Kingdom Coming: The Rise of Christian Nationalism* which posits all, or essentially all, Christians adhere to Dominion Theology—the idea that Christians are commanded to lord over unbelievers and have been prophesied to rule the United States of America. Others, such as Bill Moyers, make a big stink over premillennial dispensationalism—the eschatological worldview that involves believers sitting at the right hand of the Father during the Tribulation, in which unbelievers will suffer mightily.

And yet, as when they attribute to all Christians the political malapropisms of Jerry Falwell and Pat Robertson, liberals are misrepresenting the facts. It is simply untrue that all Christians or even all conservative Christians adhere to these two doctrines. It is untrue even that a majority of conservative Christians adhere to them.

I asked Peter Sprigg of the Family Research Council about Dominion Theology. "Do you feel driven by prophesy to rule the nation as a theocracy?" I asked him. He laughed. "We couldn't establish a theocracy even if we wanted to because we don't all agree on our theology," he told me. Dr. Bill Meier from Focus on the Family finds the charge equally absurd. "I have given entire speeches, conducted entire debates without ever once mentioning God, theology, or my faith," he told me. "All the things we have been talking about here at Focus can now be expressed just as easily using evidence from social science rather than the Word of God. For example, we can prove definitively that a high level of promiscuity in young girls leads to extraordinarily high rates of depression. That's not theology, that's social science."

When I sat down with Kyle Fisk of the National Association of Evangelicals and asked him about premillennial dispensationalism, he furrowed his brow and craned his neck back as though he was watching a bad and confusing *Saturday Night Live* sketch. "We never talk about End Times theology because there is so little consensus about it. I would say that is a minority point of view within the evangelical community, certainly among pastors."

Just as the Left's old attacks on cultural issues failed to marginalize conservative Christians, it appears their latest departure down a path of theological obscurities will not win them any converts.

TROUBLE AHEAD?

As I have taken great pains to illustrate, the Religious Right is, in sociologist Alan Wolfe's words, "part of the mainstream culture, not dissenters from it." On issue after issue, we have seen that the Religious Right speaks for mainstream Americans.

In fact, a growing number of evangelical Christians have become uncomfortable with the mainstreaming of their faith tradition. Evangelical leader Chuck Colson asked darkly in March of 2004, "Have evangelicals come full circle in just fifty years—from fundamentalist isolation to mainstream acceptance? Have we embraced a national creed that values personal growth over doctrinal orthodoxy?"[38]

He called it an "attractive proposition" for battle scarred culture warriors: "Just give us our lovely sanctuaries, our padded pews, and our upbeat music, and we'll no longer worry about society disintegrating around us. The culture will ignore us, and we'll ignore the culture, which will be nice when we socialize with nonbelievers who will no longer consider us backwoods fundamentalists trying to impose our morality on them."

Colson has a point. At this point mainstreaming would be so easy, but also wrong. Conservative Christians should never get complacent. The mainstream will follow them if they show the courage to lead society. But if they don't stay at least one step ahead of the common culture, the culture could absorb the Religious Right, dilute its values, and ignore its sermons by changing the channel.

9

ONWARD, SECULAR
SOLDIERS

Perhaps the most vexing feature in our nation's ongoing public dialogue is the notion that the Religious Right is trying to "impose its values on all Americans." The political Left and the mainstream media has worn this particular talking point raw. It is the most powerful weapon in their arsenal and the seedling for the full blown anti-Christian paranoia we observed in chapter 1. Here is one typical example:

> While most all Western and many other countries have more reasonable laws regarding sexual pleasure, in the US we are faced with moralists imposing their values on other people. If they can't reach us by knocking on our doors and preaching, then they will instead enact laws to prevent us from doing what they secretly wish they could. We oppose laws that violate our freedom as consenting adults to in private share intimacy and pleasure.

A homosexual rights group lamenting the criminality of sodomy in his home state? A Planned Parenthood spokesperson railing against an anticontraception campaign? A NOW representative lambasting abstinence-only sex education? Try none of the above. That salvo was launched by the Decriminalize Private Adult Sexwork Coalition,[1] an entity dedicated to mainstreaming prostitution.

Nevertheless, the "imposing their values" talking point has worked its way in from the fringes and is today an almost daily obstacle for conservative Christians to confront. Oh, you're pro-life? You're just trying to impose your values on me. Against gay marriage? Imposing your values. No sex education in the classroom? Imposing. Oppose indecency on broadcast television? Go impose your values somewhere else.

Consider former Pres. Jimmy Carter's depiction of the culture wars: "The irresolvable differences of opinion on abortion, homosexuality, and other sensitive issues have been exacerbated by the insistence of intensely committed hardliners on imposing their minority views on a more moderate majority."[2]

So pervasive is the irrational fear-mongering that the Religious Right is attempting to "impose its beliefs" on the rest of America—indeed, the rest of the world—that liberals even criticize otherwise uncontroversial policies that indisputably benefit humankind because they are supported by Christian conservatives.

The issue of international sex trafficking wouldn't even be on the federal government's radar screen but for the dogged lobbying of the Religious Right that America should lead the world against this unpardonable crime against humanity. Every year, hundreds of thousands of girls are sold into sexual bondage. Virtually all of them die of sexually transmitted diseases or drug overdoses before reaching adulthood. Nevertheless, some would prefer this grisly status quo to working alongside the Religious Right to eradicate it. Here is Melissa Farley, author of *Prostitution, Trafficking and Traumatic Stress*:

> [The critics] declare . . . that [we] are tainted by guilt by association. Evangelicals and feminists. If any cause is

endorsed by the Right—if we agree with them on any-thing—we are "in bed with them." Object to child pornog-raphy? Oops, so does the Christian Right, gotcha. Favor strong laws against prostitution and trafficking? Oops, so does George Bush, gotcha. This adolescent logic trumps carefully articulated policies based on years of evidence-gathering and analysis.[3]

At some point in the last forty or forty-five years a large number of liberal Americans came to believe that prior to the Religious Right's political ascent federal, state, and local governments did not legislate or regulate human interaction, that communities had no shared sense of the boundaries of acceptable behavior.

Liberal Ohio University history professor Kevin Mattson even argues that conservative culture war combatants are the descendents of 1960s radicals. "The looniest aspect of the far left during the 1960s morphed into the looniest aspects of the far right today," Mattson writes.[4] "An attack on intellect and objectivity grounded in a belief that everything was political (including the 'personal') fueled the student movements of the late 1960s. It's the excesses of that time that . . . the right's cultural warriors of today represent."

These liberals seem to think that before, say, 1960, America was some sort of sexually licentious, amoral, nonjudgmental, libertine dystopia in which all "values" were considered equal. But then rad-ical Christians rose up, snuffed out the cigarettes, poured the whiskey down the drain, clamped on the chastity belts, and spoiled the party.

And in large part the Left has succeeded in convincing many Americans that this is how it all went down. Didn't Patrick Buchanan stand there at the podium in Houston, Texas, at the 1992 Republican National Convention and declare a culture war on America?

In an insightful article published in the *Atlantic*, Brookings Institution scholar E.J. Dionne Jr. makes a point that there really is no genuine culture war in America. The real conflict, Dionne argues, is between those Americans who want a culture war and those who don't.[5] The majority of Americans, however, are quite content to remain in the middle.

Dionne has helped me to make the principle point of this chapter. As we saw in chapter 8, the Religious Right speaks for Middle America's values. They are on the vanguard of the mainstream, certainly. But on every social issue of public importance, the mainstream of America follows the Religious Right's lead. Whether or not this was Dionne's intention, his argument substantiates my point that this coalition of conservative Christians and Middle Americans represents what he calls "the non-warring middle."

Where conservative Christians and mainstreamers agree is in their shared adherence to tried-and-true traditional values. As president of the National Association of Evangelicals and Pastor of New Life Church in Colorado Spring, Colorado, Ted Haggard told me, "It's not as if evangelicals have come up with anything new, it's that the moral fabric of America continues to deteriorate. None of our grandparents would have even contemplated a doctor prescribing a pill to kill an old person or endorsed procedures to kill unborn babies."

In an era in our nation's history in which unchaperoned children are subjected to thousands of violent and sexual images, at a time when liberal activists and the judiciary are attempting to redesign the American family in unpopular ways, during an epoch in which one American president will forever be recognized for having wagged his finger at the American public and stating untruthfully, "I did not have sexual relations with that woman," it seems unfathomable that the Religious Right should be called out for "trying to impose its values" on the rest of America.

Pastor Ted provided me with another example. His organization, the National Association of Evangelicals, was involved in a dispute over the right of Air Force Academy chaplains to pray in the name of Jesus Christ and the right of Christian cadets there to evangelize. Some fifty students have complained over the past couple of years that they have been "inappropriately proselytized."

Now, proselytizing is not a new thing at the Air Force Academy. And neither is praying in Jesus's name. Indeed, the very idea of prohibiting or even restricting these activities is profoundly un-American. As Pastor Ted has stated, "Why in the world would we adopt a view that freedom of speech applies in every area except religion?"[6] But that's what some liberals, led by Long Island Democratic Congressman Steve Israel, are contemplating.

If we marry Gary Hart's concern about "restrictions on broadcasting" with Representative Israel's desire to curb the rights of people to exercise their religion freely, then we would live in an America in which gratuitous sex and violence were broadcast unfettered over federally regulated airwaves but that the name Jesus could not be spoken on a military campus. Who is imposing what on whom?

If we are to accept E.J. Dionne's premise—that some in America actually *want* a culture war—then who is launching the unprovoked attacks?

I believe secular leftists are determined to remake American culture and society in their own warped image, to tear down traditional pillars of America's moral strength, and to wage its culture war wherever they think the can win. The radical secular Left has launched a many-fronted culture war against the values conservative Christians share with mainstream Americans. Evangelicals and other conservative Christians are not looking to do anything new and different. They are merely trying to protect what our great country has already stood for, the values we have always cherished.

And while the secular Left believes some foolish things, they are not necessarily foolish people. They have seen the mainstream of America hug the Religious Right on social issues and have concluded that the squishy middle is persuadable. And since the 1960s they have tried to persuade, and often times tried to force, Americans to adhere to their belief systems.

In other words, they have tried to impose their values on the regular Americans—exactly what they have fraudulently accused the Religious Right of having done so many times before.

SHOCK AND AWE

The secular Left's most successful technique over the years might be labeled "shock and awe." These campaigns of deliberate desensitization to long-standing cultural taboos have helped secularists breakdown walls of societal resistance on issues from birth control to the homosexual lifestyle.

How does it work? Typically, activist groups will agitate on behalf of some cause, specifically an unpopular cause (popular causes don't require much agitating). This group might tinker with state legislators and Congress, but they are fully aware that their cause has no genuine popular support so they often go straight to the court system. There they shop for sympathetic federal judges and almost always find them on the Ninth US Circuit Court of Appeals.

Euphemisms start flying around. Suddenly, "gay marriage" becomes "equal rights" and "assisted suicide" become "death with dignity." Meanwhile, their pals in Hollywood will work storylines into television shows and sometimes even make movies dedicated to proselytizing for the cause. You can usually tell which shows these are by the networks depiction of them as "the most talked about episode of the season." Heartbreaking sob stories head down the leftwing talk show pipeline, with Oprah being the world's worst and most dangerous offender.

The secular Left's morbid fascination with euthanasia is a recent and classic example. The courts have been friendly to the idea of pulling the plug. In 2005 the family court system in Florida literally ordered the death of Terri Schiavo. The US Supreme Court upheld Oregon's assisted suicide law in early 2006. Hollywood joined the crusade with the Oscar-winning film *Million Dollar Baby*, in which a boxing trainer, played by Clint Eastwood, kills his pupil because she has a broken back and will never box again. Oh, yeah. Eastwood's character is the hero of the film. This gives the social commentators a chance to weigh in on the issue clandestinely by praising the film, not the cause.

"Clint Eastwood's drama about a grizzled boxing trainer and a spunky young fighter is the best movie released by a major Hollywood studio in years," raved A.O. Scott of the *New York Times*.[7] "An emotionally powerful drama about a woman boxer, a crusty old trainer and their journey of the heart," echoed Frederick and Mary Anne Brussat of—get this—*Spirituality & Practice*.[8] And of course, the Academy of Motion Picture Arts and Sciences famously passed over *The Passion of the Christ* to award *Million Dollar Baby* with the Best Picture Oscar.

The Left, the courts, and the entertainment business agree: if you aren't for euthanasia, there is something wrong with you.

Let's look at another example. Embryonic stem-cell research swept through the political and cultural scene in the early part of the new millennium. So powerful was the campaign in favor of embryonic stem-cell research, complete with disabled celebrity endorsements, that the secular Left managed to convince a huge number of Americans to support something they otherwise oppose strongly, as I highlighted in the previous chapter. Cloning programs started carrying the label "therapeutic." Wild and exciting promises were made about the "promise" of stem-cell research. Millions of Americans were literally shocked and awed into believing the federal government should use tax dollars to fund clone-to-kill embryonic stem cell projects. It was an extraordinary campaign of propaganda. And it worked.

Nowhere has this formula been on clearer display in recent years, though, than in the deliberate campaign to desensitize mainstream opinion about homosexuality. In our lifetimes, homosexuality has gone from a cultural and social taboo to Most Favored Lifestyle, complete with protected legal status, a wholly enthusiastic entertainment industry microphone, and a national press corps dedicated to positioning its advance as the next civil rights frontier.

The shock of this campaign was established as far back as 1948 when Dr. Alfred Kinsey released his book *Sexual Behavior in the Human Male*, in which Kinsey asserted that 10 percent of the male population in America had engaged in homosexual activity. Kinsey's study has been discredited as unreliable (his highly self-selecting "random" sample included many children who had been sexually abused and a disproportionate number of male convicts who had been raped in prison). But that didn't stop Hollywood from joining in the lionization of Kinsey with the Oscar-nominated eponymous film.

Since Kinsey's time, homosexuals and their political sympathizers have organized a pervasive campaign including court cases, television programs, and celebrity endorsements. Gay Episcopal Bishop Gene Robinson from New Hampshire has even implied publicly that he believes Jesus might have been gay. Now, if a bishop believes Jesus might have been gay, who could be against the homosexual lifestyle?

The history of America's culture war is really the history of the radical Left's assaults on long-standing and long-accepted cultural norms. Let's take a look at when and how many of the major cultural battles have bubbled to the surface:

- 1965: In *Griswold v. Connecticut,* the US Supreme Court invalidated a state law prohibiting the use of contraception by married couples by manufacturing a constitutional "right to privacy."

- 1967: Colorado became the first state to pass a law allowing abortion in cases involving "severe defects," among other things.

- 1968: In *Epperson v. Arkansas,* the US Supreme Court declared unconstitutional any law prohibiting the teaching of evolution.

- 1969: The homosexual rights movement kicked off with riots in New York City.

- 1969: New York passed a law allowing abortion up to the twenty-fourth week of pregnancy. California passed a no-fault divorce law.

- 1973: The US Supreme Court invalidated all state laws banning abortions before the third trimester.

- 1987: In *Edwards v. Aquillard,* the US Supreme Court ruled that the teaching of creationism in schools violated the First Amendment.

- 1993: Pres. Bill Clinton announced his "don't ask, don't tell" policy on gays in the military. Meanwhile, the Hawaii Supreme Court ruled that a law prohibiting same-sex marriage may violate the state's constitution.

- 1999: Vermont passed a law creating a legal recognition for same-sex union.

- 2000: In *Stenberg v. Carhart,* the US Supreme Court invalidated all state bans on partial birth abortion.

- 2003: In *Lawrence v. Texas,* the US Supreme Court ruled that states cannot ban homosexual sodomy. Meanwhile, the Massachusetts Supreme Court decided that homosexuals have a constitutional right to marry.

- 2004: A federal court ruled that Alabama Chief Justice Roy Moore must remove a Ten Commandments monument from state property.

- 2005: A state court ordered the death of Terri Schiavo.

As this timeline demonstrates, every major battle front in the culture war has been fought because of the assertive assault on long-standing cultural and societal norms by the secular Left. The Christian Right has done nothing to force its values on a helpless and unwitting public. The exact opposite is true.

Leftists propagandize the theory that mainstream objections to these secular provocations are merely the result of what Thomas Frank calls "the Great Backlash": ". . . a style of conservatism that first came snarling onto the national stage in response to the partying and protests of the late sixties" and which "mobilizes votes with explosive social issues."[9]

Democrat strategists Jim Carville and Paul Begala elaborated on this theme when they wrote, "Republicans have conducted a decades-long campaign to win over middle-class and lower-middle-class voters with cultural populism. They stoke anger and resentment on cultural issues in order to win votes, then use the power they receive from the votes to hammer these people on economic issues."[10]

But doesn't the assertion that the Religious Right fabricated a "backlash"—an idea I reject in favor of more spontaneous outrage among normal Americans—presuppose that Christian conservatives were reacting to the imposition of leftist values rather than imposing rightwing values? And doesn't it further presuppose that the Left's imposition is offensive in the first place?

I mean, the Religious Right, despite its considerable political strength, could not possibly ignite a backlash against a law that a large majority supported. By furthering the "backlash" theory, the radical Left acknowledges how out-of-step they are with the mainstream and just how aggressive their assault on traditional values really is.

Perhaps recognizing how unpopular their offensive has become, the radical Left now employs linguists and sophisticated marketing gurus to help them impose their values with a force less blunt, but more deceptive, on the Middle American majority.

Saying liberals "must understand the use of language," Democratic National Chairman Howard Dean commends Berkeley linguist George Lakoff as "one of the most influential political thinkers of the progressive movement." Dean claims Lakoff has the techniques to help the Left find its "way out of the morass" by using what Lakoff calls "framing"—verbal word games that come awfully close to Orwellian Newthink.

Lakoff counsels his acolytes to "Always start with values, preferably values all Americans share like security, prosperity, opportunity, freedom, and so on. Pick the values most relevant to the frame you want to shift to. Try to win the argument at the values level. Pick a frame where your position exemplifies a value everyone holds—like fairness."[11]

It seems likely, however, that the only people Lakoff will manage to brainwash are those like Dean who are already inclined to buy this snake oil. Instead of talking about taxes, for example, Lakoff thinks leftwing politicians should talk about "membership fees." Lakoff thinks that instead of asking Americans if they support "gay marriage," pollsters and reporters should ask, "Do you think the government should tell people who they can and can't marry?" (I'd like to find the person who says no to that question and then ask them a follow up question: should the government tell you that you cannot marry, say, a five-year-old?)

This has resulted in Howard Dean sounding like an absolute fool preaching about "a woman's right to make up her own mind on her health care" (abortion) and "issues like whether we respect all citizens or only some of them" (gay marriage).

With verbal ticks and deceptive language such as Dean's, Leftists now hope to convince the vast majority of Middle Americans that they share their values. But they really just leave folks confused and scratching their heads. At least before we knew they simply hated us.

If that doesn't work (and it won't) Ted Nordhaus and Michael Shellenberger have another plan. "Rather than focusing on reframing the Democratic message, as Berkeley linguist and cognitive science Professor George Lakoff has recommended," writes Garence Franke-Ruta in the *American Prospect*, Nordhaus and Shellenberger argue "that the way to move voters on progressive issues is to sometimes set aside policies in favor of values."

Franke-Ruta concludes by writing, "American voters have taken shelter under the various wings of conservative traditionalism because there has been no one on the Democratic side in recent years to defend traditional, sensible, middle-class values against the onslaught of the new nihilistic, macho, libertarian lawlessness. . . ."

Well, duh! The Nordhaus and Shellenberger plan, whether they admit it or not, is for liberals to become more conservative culturally, to stop attacking Middle American values. Isn't that what conservative Christians have been urging them to do for over forty years now?

The culture wars don't just take place in the US Capitol, state houses, and courtrooms. Many of these battles take place in courts of public opinion, in the entertainment world, or even in the realm of market capitalism.

Consider the annual leftwing assault on Christmas. Through fear of being labeled anti-Semitic, many large chain retail outlets have eschewed even the use of the word "Christmas" in favor of "holiday" or "season." Polls routinely show most Americans find this kind of thing stupid, even offensive. And yet more and more stores have erased the word "Christmas" from their annual December sales displays. That is until hundreds of thousands of conservative Christians took action in 2005 and shamed many of them into bringing back "the reason for the season." Under pressure from grassroots activists, Wal-Mart, Target, Walgreens, Lowe's, and Macy's all agreed to bring "Christmas" back. Here again, we find conservative Christians reflecting the view of the vast majority of Americans.

In perhaps the ultimate statement of irony, Jeremy Gunn from the American Civil Liberties Union griped, "Don't they have anything better to do?" The answer might literally be no. While the Christmas wars might seem a trite example, there is nothing more important to the future of this great country than to have radical secular soldiers defeated on the culture war battle field.

10

THE FAKERS, THE SECULARITES, AND THE LEFTWING THEOCRATS

Everyone knows there is one political party in America that abuses religious language to further its agenda, right? One party that abuses "God is on our side" rhetoric.[1] One party that claims divine endorsement for its public policies, while claiming the policies of the other guys are "sinful," right?

Of course, we all know who I'm talking about.

The Democratic Party.

Wait! The Democrats?

You thought, perhaps, I was following the cocktail murmur of the chattering class to say that the Republicans were overselling their relationship to the Guy Upstairs? Well, a quick survey of the recent literature might provide a much-needed shock to your system:

- "God is a liberal," declare Jim Carville and Paul Begala.[2]

- "Jesus is not a Republican," demands Clint Willis. "Jesus is a progressive."[3]

- "When did Jesus become pro-rich?" asks liberal evangelical author and activist Jim Wallis.[4]

- "The role of government is to protect its people and work for the common good. This is not the time for a budget reconciliation process. To do so is not only unjust, it's a sin," screams the leftist National Council of Churches USA.

- Here's how the *Hill* described a Nancy Pelosi floor speech on the budget process in 2005: "In the final Democratic speech before the vote, Minority Leader Nancy Pelosi said a vote in favor of the bill amounted to a 'sin.'"[5]

- "Our moral values are closer to the American people than the Republicans' are," says DNC Chairman Howard Dean (who, by the way, denounced his church in Vermont over a dispute about the placement of a municipal bike path).

- "I think they [Christian conservatives] get the Bible ass-backward, ignoring the most important teachings of Jesus, which place love and compassion above greed and intolerance," argues leftist pundit and author Bill Press.[6]

Since their 2004 drubbing at the hands of approximately thirty million conservative Christians, the American Left has gone way over-the-top to declare itself the true vehicle of God's message. Jim Wallis's best-selling book on the subject of faith in public life is ostentatiously titled *God's Politics*. That's a claim to divine authority that would make the Reverend Robertson blush.

This alone should put to rest the question of how large a role Americans of faith played in the 2004 election. Americans who actually attend church regularly, pray daily, and so forth vote overwhelmingly for Republicans. Liberals have noticed this, and there appears to be a deliberate attempt on their part to reach out to religious voters.

That's good. But are they serious? The answer, sadly, is no.

The rabbi and longtime radical agitator Michael Lerner assembled this new-fangled Religious Left to Berkeley where he hosted a "Conference on Spiritual Activism." The content of the conference, as reported by Mark Tooley in the *Weekly Standard,* was a mix of political smears against Pres. George W. Bush that sounded no different from those of secular critics of the president and wacky chimerical pronouncements bordering on occultism. Seriousness was not the order of the day.

Berkeley professor Michael Nagler, for instance, charged those pro-lifers with hypocrisy who voted for the eleventh-hour stay in the Terri Schiavo case and who also voted for the Iraq War. Or here's David Robinson of Pax Christi on the Bush administration: "They're lying our kids to death in Iraq." According to Reverend Osagyefu Uhuru Sekou of Clergy and Laity Concerned, Arabs are the "new niggers."

And then the speakers got around to sex. Reverend Sekou informed the conference that his grandmother "believes God has a penis." Thus, they should not take on traditional religious teachings head on. And then there was Unitarian minister and sexologist Debra Haffner, who argued that rather than teaching believers to sublimate certain sexual impulses, religions should embrace sexual freedom tout court.[7]

Elsewhere, the World Council of Churches, the flagship organization of Religious Leftism, which claims to represent over 340 ministries in over 100 nations, has spearheaded an effort to urge its members to divest in companies that conduct business with Israel. The Anglican Communion, which includes the Episcopal Church in the United States, along with the Presbyterian Church USA, joined this boycott in order to protest "draconian conditions of the continuing occupation under which so many Palestinians live."[8]

To the extent some Mainline Protestant churches involve

themselves in matters of cultural import, it is typically on the side of the radical Left. The Episcopal Church USA ordained V. Gene Robinson in 2003 as the new bishop of New Hampshire. Bishop Robinson's ascent has nearly torn the Anglican Communion apart, as his ordination is a clear rejection of the Anglican Communion's traditional moral teaching on the matter of homosexuality and restraint. Bishop Robinson is an out-of-the-closet homosexual who lives with his lover and who lives a severe lifestyle that has landed him in alcohol rehab more than once.

But the dramatic blending of leftwing politics and faith has even begun to seep into traditional conservative faith traditions. With the promise that their effort is not political, so-called "Red Letter Christians" have begun to promote aggressively a leftist vision of evangelicalism.

Dr. Tony Campolo wrote a piece for the popular religious website Beliefnet.com about a "new" organization, to which he belongs, one that he swears is not designed to counter the so-called Religious Right. They call themselves "Red Letter Christians" and their agenda should seem surprisingly familiar. "Red Letter Christians," Campolo explained, should "transcend partisan politics" by embracing radical environmentalism, agitating against wars, forcefully advocate more funding for public schools and more foreign aid, and work to bring an end to racism, sexism, homophobia, and poverty.

It was simply the normal run of liberal public policy preferences dressed up in vestments. What's more, the agenda was basically irreligious; it substituted a social gospel for the real deal.

It seems clear that establishing a leftwing evangelical political movement is *exactly* what these "Red Letter Christians" have in mind. And the fact that they are being less than honest about it ought to be troubling to Americans of faith.

Yet another group of evangelicals has weighed in on the global warming debate. On the same week during the winter of 2006 that the Northeast faced its most bitter cold snap in decades, the Evangelical Climate Initiative, a coalition of eighty-six "prominent" evangelicals (some were far less prominent then others, to be sure), publicly launched their campaign to "address global climate change."

Privately, many evangelical leaders I met with in preparation for this book told me they thought the members of the Evangelical Climate Initiative had been bamboozled by radical environmentalists who had been flirting with them for over a year. One extremely prominent evangelical leader even paraphrased a famous retort by an environmental activist: "In an hour I could find eighty-six pastors named Steve who think this thing is bunk."

A huge number of evangelical leaders who had signed an earlier statement of principle regarding man's Christian responsibility to serve as good stewards of God's creation nevertheless refused to sign on to the Evangelical Climate Initiative.

Liberal Catholics in the House of Representatives have also gone to great lengths to try to prove to the God-fearing public that they respect the role that faith plays in public life. On Fat Tuesday 2006, a group of Catholic Democrats in Congress, headed by Rep. Rosa DeLauro (D-CT)—who is virulently pro-abortion—issued a "Catholic Statement of Principles," which ought to concern conservative Catholics for its misrepresentation of Catholic social teaching and ought to concern secular liberals for its unabashed advocacy of theocracy.

Their "Statement" read, in part (typos in the original):

> We are committed to making real the basic principles that are at the heart of Catholic social teaching: helping the poor and disadvantaged, protecting the most vulnerable among us, and ensuring that all Americans of every faith are given

meaningful opportunities to share in the blessings of this great country. That commitment is fulfilled in different ways by legislators but includes: reducing the rising rates of poverty; increasing access to education for all; pressing for increased access to health care; and taking seriously the decision to go to war. Each of these issues challenges our obligations as Catholics to community and helping those in need.

We envision a world in which every child belongs to a loving family and agree with the Catholic Church about the value of human life and the undesirability of abortion B we do not celebrate its practice. Each of us is committed to reducing the number of unwanted pregnancies and creating an environment with policies that encourage pregnancies to be carried to term. We believe this includes promoting alternatives to abortion, such as adoption, and improving access to children's healthcare and child care, as well as policies that encourage paternal and maternal responsibility.

Unfortunately for Representative DeLauro, she has misinterpreted an important principle of Catholic social teaching. "Subsidiarity" holds that the functions of government should be performed at the lowest level if at all possible. Only when local governments prove utterly unable to cope with a localized problem (say, in times of natural disaster), should higher authorities intervene.

The principle of Subsidiarity, as Tom McClusky of the Family Research Council explained in our interview, "is consistent with the conservative idea that local governments under local control are better equipped to address social ills because they are closer to the unique struggles within their own communities."

There are other problems for the Democrat Catholics in

Congress. While it has become a Mainstream Media pastime to label conservative Christians as "theocrats," Rep DeLauro and her coalition have come a lot closer than even the Christian Coalition of the 1990s to giving a single denomination such a powerful voice in the process of determining the public policy of the federal government (typos in original):

> In all these issues, we seek the Church's guidance and assistance but believe also in the primacy of conscience. In recognizing the Church's role in providing moral leadership, we acknowledge and accept the tension that comes with being in disagreement with the Church in some areas. Yet we believe we can speak to the fundamental issues that unite us as Catholics and lend our voices to changing the political debate—a debate that often fails to reflect and encompass the depth and complexity of these issues.

One can't help but wonder how the American Civil Liberties Union and Americans United for Separation of Church and State feel about members of Congress inviting the Vatican to provide "guidance and assistance" on matters of public policy. The silence of those two groups, which are generally very anxious to ridicule conservative Christians, has been very loud indeed.

We should not close the door on the possibility that all this liberal God-talk is window dressing, honeyed words spoken tongue-in-cheek with a wink and a nudge to the separationist "watchdogs." It's not as if "Red Letter Christians" and the Catholic liberals in the House of Representatives have actually changed their positions on any issues. They're just using more nuanced language to try to reposition themselves as servants of God.

In this, they are following the advice of liberal evangelical activist Jim Wallis, who advised them to "reassess their language and style, they way they morally frame public policy issues, and their cultural disconnect with too many Americans including many people of faith."[9] But this renewed effort by liberals to play the "God card" is so obviously affected that the silence of those who feared "theocracy" during the Schiavo tragedy hardly seems surprising at all.

It is entirely likely, indeed probable, that most of them are sincere in their faith commitments. Nevertheless, Democrats and liberals have telegraphed their desire to reach out to so-called "moral values" voters ever since their 2004 election debacle, so it is hardly impolitic for me to assert that this over-the-top conversion story is decidedly political in nature. But there is little unity behind this revamped message strategy.

In fact, the Left has begun to splinter into three distinct and irreconcilable camps in this regard. I call these groups the Fakers, the Secularites, and the Leftwing Theocrats.

SHAME ON ME

During the 2004 Democratic primary campaign, former Vermont Gov. Howard Dean infamously told a reporter that his favorite New Testament book was Job. Why would Dean, who earlier in the primary excoriated Republican politicians for obsessing over issues such as "God, guns and gays," even raise the topic of his favorite piece of Scripture, especially considering he had so obviously not read the book, which appears in the Old Testament.

I believe Howard Dean was trying to pull a fast one over the American people. By that time Dean had developed a reputation for being openly hostile to people of faith. A story about him renouncing his Episcopal faith over a controversy regarding a bike path behind his local church convinced a great many people that Dean was not particularly connected with the Almighty.

Which was a problem for the Dean campaign, because at the time it was beginning to look more and more like he might win the Democratic Party's nomination for president of the United States. And most Americans are uncomfortable with the idea of their leaders being indifferent to higher things. So Dean's campaign made a very public act of contrition by announcing that they would begin to highlight the angry little man from Vermont's spiritual side.

As it turned out, the Christianizing of Dean proved premature. After blurting out "George Bush is not my neighbor!" to a humble farmer in Iowa named Dale Ungerer and his infamous post-Iowa scream debacle, fewer and fewer people came to see the former governor as a man of faith, let alone as presidential timber.

Dean's dubious conversion story (and yes, Republicans play this game, too) is illustrative of how politicians attempt to use professions of Christian belief to placate public opinion. I cannot say if Dean, and the countless other Democrats who have beefed up their Christian bona fides since 2 November 2004, is sincere in his newfound religiosity. It's just that he and those other newly minted Christians so often seem to interpret Scripture and doctrine in such ways as to confirm their already-existing positions on social and fiscal issues. Rarely, if ever, does a change in worldview follow their change in rhetoric.

First Things editor Joseph Bottum points out that this revived spirituality in formerly indifferent polls always manages, somehow, to coexist with traditional leftwing issue positions such as the advocacy of abortion on demand.[10] And somehow, that just doesn't seem to jive.

I call this new politico-religious denomination "the Fakers." The Fakers have almost no record of couching their public policy preferences in religious language or imagery prior to 2 November 2004. Indeed, like Dean, most Fakers specifically avoided mixing religion and politics. Sometimes, they ridiculed the practice.

Who are the Fakers? Dean has to be considered their High Priest. Former V.P. Al Gore is a Faker, too. Prior to the rise of the Religious Right, Gore rarely spoke of faith in public life. And when he did, it didn't come off too well. During a 1997 press conference at the federal Department of Housing and Urban Development, Gore embarrassingly called Mary and Joseph "homeless."[11] At a MoveOn.org summit on judicial nominations, Gore ripped in to "rightwing religious extremists," saying, "Rightwing religious zealotry is a throwback to the intolerance that led to the creation of America in the first place."[12]

Almost a year later, however, a much calmer Gore would quote a Bible passage—"Where there is no vision, the people perish"—in an equally harsh, though perhaps less sweaty, assault on the Bush administration.[13] House Minority Leader Nancy Pelosi is a Faker, too. Representing the notoriously hedonistic city of San Francisco, we can perhaps forgive Pelosi for her historic hostility to faith in public life. As James Taranto has written, "When a conservative politician cites the Bible in support of his views on, say, abortion or homosexuality, people like Pelosi get their backs up about the mingling of church and state."[14] And yet, as we have already seen, Pelosi has called the passage of a Republican budget a "sin," and went on for a bit:

> The gentleman from Washington [state], Mr. McDermott, quoted the prophet Isaiah. And as the Bible teaches us, to minister to the needs of God's creation is an act of worship, to ignore those needs is to dishonor the God who made us. Let us vote no on this budget as an act of worship and for America's children.[15]

Voting against a budget as an *act of worship?* This hyperbolic overreach is characteristic of the newly ordained Fakers. They are so unfamiliar with the role faith has played in public life over the past several decades that they often overcompensate with outrageous statements that, if spoken by Christian conservatives, would evoke howls of "theocracy" from the political Left.

We can safely say that former Pres. Bill Clinton is a Faker. When it was putatively advantageous for him to do so, Clinton bashed conservative Christians heavily during the 1994 campaign. But woe to anyone who stood between Clinton and a minister if cameras were around during his intern sex scandal.

We find a great many Fakers among the fifty-five Democrat Catholics in the House of Representatives who, on 28 February 2006, signed the Catholic "Statement of Principles." Can Rep. Cynthia McKinney (D-GA) really be said to love her neighbor as she does herself?

The Fakers are not doing their erstwhile allies on the genuine Religious Left any favors. Leftwing evangelical activist Jim Wallis parodies this liberal God talk as "I have faith. But don't worry . . . it won't affect anything." Wallis has also ribbed Dean, describing his preaching as "inauthentic."[16]

Fakers began to refine their craft after the 2004 election. To them, achieving success is not an exercise in altering their issue positions to better reflect the values of Middle America, but rather is an exercise in altering their language in order to pretend to reflect those values.

"Yes, Kerry should have spoken—and future Democrats must speak—in moral terms," Robert Reich opined.[17]

Steven Waldman was even more flagrant in his just-use-better-words advice:

When thinking of values, faith, and how to win elections, it's useful to ask, What Would Clinton Do? Bill Clinton always combined economic liberalism with a handful of cultural issues designed to appeal to red-state voters: welfare reform, crime, and national service. He picked these issues carefully, knowing that they would show traditional Americans that he wasn't a morally permissive liberal who didn't understand right from wrong.[18]

The problem with such advice, of course, is that it assumes Americans of faith can be fooled into believing Democrats have truly changed. It is an even more condescending message strategy than the Democrats' previous efforts, which essentially involved them telling conservative Christians that they are wrong and stupid.

In the end, however, the Fakers are destined to fail in their public relations campaign, not merely because they seem so insincere, but because they are so obviously in league with our second group of liberals: the Secularites.

AND NO RELIGION, TOO

Despite the let's-try-and-fool-'em rhetoric of the Fakers and the genuine (though, as we will see, misguided) belief of the Leftwing Theocrats, the political Left is still, by its very essence, godless. That's not just me saying that. Steven Waldman and John C. Green identify "non-religious Americans, or seculars" as the largest "Democratic tribe" of "religious" voters.[19] Waldman and Green also credit Secularites with the "common view that Democrats are less religious than Republicans."[20]

But this is more than a "common view." It is reality.

The nominations and confirmation battles of Chief Justice John Roberts and Associate Justice Sam Alito to the Supreme Court of the United States demonstrated just how tight a chokehold the

Secularites have on the Democratic Party.

Democrats in the Senate came under intense pressure from anti-Christian groups such as People for the American Way, the American Civil Liberties Union, and Americans United to oppose these two obviously well-qualified nominees. Liberals thought they could outrage mainstream Americans by dredging up John Roberts's religious convictions—and the religious convictions of his wife—only to have their assault misfire wildly. In the end, many Secularites concluded that normal Americans simply weren't shocked by the same things that shock them.

Secularites tend to be the same "Wall Worshipers" we met in chapter 2, the theophobes who believe the state needs to be protected from religion, not vice versa.

Secularites also shout the loudest about leftwing cultural issues. They are vehemently pro-abortion, still insisting that unrestricted abortion is a common good for women and America. Secularites are the people who oppose parental notification and consent laws for teenagers to obtain an abortion. They oppose efforts to stop the brutal practice of partial birth abortion. They even opposed efforts in Washington to allow prosecutors to charge murderers who kill pregnant women with two crimes. To Secularites, radical personal autonomy is the driving force on issues of morality.

Whereas some Democrats of faith might struggle with the issue of legalized gay marriage before finally endorsing it, Secularites have no doubts. They don't merely support gay marriage outright, they even claim it would benefit American society. How could anyone oppose such a glorious expression of love between two people? they ask. They reject the notion even that traditional marriage is worth saving. Aren't our current high divorce rates proof that marriage is little more than a convenient sexual and financial arrangement, anyway?

Secularites fight efforts in Washington to promote marriage and they oppose efforts in local school boards to inform parents about the extremities of sometimes-graphic sex education in their children's schools.

To Secularites, any hint that a moral line has been crossed by libertine public policy is the foretaste of theocracy. They see no distinction between jihadists who set ablaze European embassies in the Middle East over tasteless cartoons and conservative Christians in Kansas who organize a political campaign. To Secularites, religious belief is the enemy.

Whereas many liberals see the above controversies not as black-and-white issues, but rather in shades of purple, Secularites agree with conservative Christians that they are mostly black-and-white. Only Secularites scream that black is better than white, often putting them on the business end of the 80/20 issues we discussed in chapter 8. Because Secularites are so numerous within the Democratic Party and scream so loudly, they often end up screaming for the Democratic Party as a whole, much to its electoral detriment.

The great enemy of the Secularites has traditionally been the Religious Right. The Secularites tolerate the rhetoric of the Fakers because they know it is fake. They will gladly work side-by-side with Nancy Pelosi because they know she only quotes the Bible for affect. But should the Secularites ever turn a critical eye to our third group of liberals, the resulting conflict could permanently tear the Democratic Party apart.

GOD TOLD ME TO RAISE TAXES

After the 2004 election and again after conservative Christians objected to the state of Florida's decision to kill Terri Schiavo, it became fashionable among some liberals to refer to those conservative Christians as "theocrats."

"Anyone who invents a Christian government must draw on scraps of religious dogma—and there is no telling which scraps he or she will stress," writes Clint Willis.[21] Of course, Willis was referring to the conservative faithful. But what of those on the political Left—in some cases, the extreme political Left—who are nevertheless true believers in Christ?

A very small but loud (and apparently growing) minority of liberals want to remake America in their own radical interpretation of Jesus's teachings. On a very few issues, these Leftwing Theocrats can find common cause with the Religious Right. But the majority of Leftwing Theocrats are adding the stink of respectability to otherwise long-since debunked approaches to social engineering.

Jim Wallis, editor of *Sojourners* magazine, is among the leaders of this sect of liberals. That Wallis is a true believer is not in question. Such died-in-the-wool rightists as Fr. Richard John Neuhaus and Dr. James Dobson have tipped their hats to the authenticity of Wallis's faith. And it is true that Mr. Wallis offers something different than the standard liberal class warfare and we-know-better-than-you sanctimony.

Wallis inserts a "Fourth Option" into the American approach to governance. Unimpressed with the first three options—traditional conservatism, traditional liberalism, and libertarianism—Wallis advocates a political philosophy that marries traditional moral conservatism and traditional fiscal and social liberalism, which, Wallis claims, "appeals to people who refuse to make the choice between the two."

But Wallis's approach cannot be said to be middle-of-the-road. By his own admission, Wallis's vision of social justice is "radical." His economic policies are nothing short of socialist. In the name of "caring for the poor," Wallis would punish the wealthy in our society with such a vengeance that his policies would almost certainly destroy the American economy as we know it.

In the name of "peace," Wallis supports foreign and military policies that would almost certainly have Americans speaking Arabic and praying five times daily while facing east inside the next decade.

Wallis's vision is far more radical than what any traditional liberal would ever advocate in the public square. But what makes Wallis's prophecy all the more intriguing to some—but, to me, frightening—is that he argues that his vision is shared by Jesus Christ Himself.

I have no doubt that believers such as Wallis are sincere in their belief that Jesus advocated for the same radical public policy that they do. But it is this fact, combined with the fact that Wallis et al. have gained a considerable amount of stature within the political Left in recent years, that ought to concern conservative Christians, mainstream Americans, and even Secularites—for Wallisites have made claims of divine endorsement that would make Pat Robertson blush and Jerry Falwell roll his eyes.

On the two families of issues Wallis professes to care most about—issues of poverty and peace—Wallis deliberately claims the endorsement of Jesus. But I believe Wallis has dangerously misinterpreted Jesus's words, especially as they relate to issues of poverty. And if he succeeds in his mission, he would transform America not into a Christianized utopia but into a theocratic dystopia in which we citizens are more the lepers ministered to by Christ than the apostles who stood by His side. Let me explain.

DON'T EAT THE RICH

Central to Wallis's economic program is Mark 10:25, "It is easier for a camel to go through the eye of a needle than for a rich man to enter the kingdom of God" (NKJV). Leftwing Theocrats believe their job is to ensure that no rich men are available to be turned away from the kingdom.

Indeed, to read or listen to Wallis and co. is an exercise in poverty worship and loathing for those with means. Though their professed goal is to "overcome poverty," they endorse radical economic programs that will only create more poverty. [22] Wallis cites mountains of depressing statistics: thirteen million American children live in poverty; thirty-six million Americans live below the poverty line; forty-five million Americans are without health insurance. And always the fault lies in our greedy corporate-run, free market society.

Likewise, Bill Press charges that "Conservatives have turned Jesus Christ upside down: from a loving Messiah who hung out with the poor and dispossessed, into a coldhearted monster who cares only for the rich and powerful."[23]

Really? In 2005, a devastating hurricane named Katrina flooded the Gulf Coast area, destroying New Orleans. The resultant "poor and dispossessed" provided great marketing material for leftwing activists. "How could George W. Bush and the inept Republicans claim to be Christians when all these people were suffering?!" they demanded.

But an interesting thing happened after the waters had receded and the reporters and television cameras had moved on to other stories. Christians, especially conservative Christians, stayed. And they continued to deliver money, resources, and goods to the caring citizens looking to rebuild that tortured city. Even as late as March, six months after Hurricane Katrina struck, faith-based groups provided "a nearly bottomless well of labor." Southern Baptists alone provided over fourteen million meals.[24]

It bears noting, I suppose, that the Southern Baptists are among the most conservative Protestant denominations in the United States. I mention that not to keep score, but rather to underscore the absurdity of Press's claim that conservative Christians care nothing about the poor. On the contrary, they care so much about the poor they will even help them when the television cameras have gone away.

Similarly, Wallis has expressed "surprise" that conservative Christians, especially those associated with Christian talk radio, also care about the poor. [25] "What I found on conservative Christians radio shows was a deepening concern on the part of both interviewers and callers, for people who are poor," he writes.[26] But while Wallis believes this to be a new phenomenon among conservative Christians, he keeps alive the possibility that maybe it is he who is changing.

What Press and Wallis have discovered is nothing new. Conservative Christians have always cared about poverty. They just don't care so much about poverty that they want everyone to be poor. As Pastor Ted Haggard told me in our interview, "free market capitalism has created more prosperity in the United States and worldwide than any other economic system."

Dr. James Dobson agrees: "The traditional conservative understanding is that liberal politics—and liberal understanding of economics—is what keeps people trapped in the cycle of poverty. In stark contrast, the economic model that rewards initiative and reaches out to the poor by helping them help themselves—part of what has become known as 'compassionate conservatism'—holds the best hope for breaking the cycle of impoverishment."

What both Pastor Ted and Dr. Dobson are too polite to ask rhetorically (though I am not) is: if Leftwing Theocrats want to eradicate poverty so badly, than why do they espouse economic programs that hurt so many people?

One politician that should have learned this lesson is former Pres. Jimmy Carter. Carter, according to one of his own campaign ads in 1980, was "a deeply and clearly religious man" who took "time to pray privately and with Rosalynn each day," seemed determined to enact while president the kinds of economic policies Wallis et al. advocate for today.

The results were disastrous. Carter's economic record was so dismal that economists invented a new word to describe the gruesomeness of the economy's performance under his stewardship: stagflation. We had double-digit inflation and near double-digit unemployment.

Putting into action the same misplaced loathing for the wealthy we see in today's Leftwing Theocrats, Carter kept top tax rates on the wealthy at an unimaginably high 70 percent, which, because our economy is based on a free market system, only served to make everyone poor, not just the hell-bound rich.

Now, almost no one questions President Carter's faith. I certainly don't. But how can we not question his interpretation of Scripture when his policies, based in Scripture, compound the very social ills he hoped to eliminate?

We cannot attribute Carter's economic disaster to Christ's ineptitude as an economist. For, you see, Carter, Wallis et al. have tragically misread Jesus's meaning. Was Jesus really condemning Bill Gates to hell with his camel analogy?

Of course not. Jesus was challenging popular ideas that riches and wealth were signs of God's favor. Jesus was telling His disciples that God loves all creation, even the poor, whose station in life was frequently taken to be a sign that God was unhappy with them.

This is not such a controversial idea today. At the time it was radical, though not in the way the Leftwing Theocrats suppose. Nowhere does Jesus tell His followers that it is Rome's responsibility to eradicate poverty. He tells those who want to follow Him to "go, sell your possessions and give to the poor" (see Matthew 19:21), not "go, sell your possessions and give to the government." Christ was dismissive of the government. He mockingly told the

Pharisees to "render up to Caesar what is Caesar's." He was not telling Jews to pay their taxes like good liberals. He was telling them that those material things were worthless and if Caesar wanted them then let him have them. Who cares?

Leftwing Theocrats take the opposite tack, bestowing on the government almost Christ-like qualities that they in turn deny to the actual Body of Christ, His church.

Carter, for example, writes, "after a lifetime of responsibilities in both religious and political arenas, I reached what was, to me, a surprising and somewhat reluctant conclusion. In efforts to reach out to the poor, alleviate suffering, provide homes for the homeless, eliminate the stigma of poverty or racial discrimination, preserve peace, and rehabilitate prisoners, government officeholders and not the church members were more likely to assume responsibility and be able to fulfill the benevolent missions."[27]

Carter is not alone. Ex-US Senator Gary Hart, who rarely fails to mention his fundamentalist upbringing, says efforts by the church to combat social ills are "blatantly insufficient to meet the needs of many millions of those left behind in our society."[28]

While Jim Wallis has heretofore avoided the kinds of government-worshiping pronouncements of Carter and Hart, his every solution to the shortcomings of our free market system betrays the same disturbing kind of government idolatry.

Rich Republican fat cats will have to answer for their greed when they meet their Maker. That much is for sure. But I'm not sure God will be impressed when these Leftwing Theocrats tell Him they should enter the kingdom of heaven because they agitated for higher taxes. He might be insulted by this kind of money worship.

FOLLOW THAT PLOUGHSHARE

Leftwing Theocrats have attempted to commandeer the issue of national security in the name of Jesus Christ. It is almost beyond arguing that Jesus of Nazareth would have been more tolerant of His enemies than has Pres. George W. Bush, though it is a remarkable stretch to say suggest He would have worn a "Bush Lied, People Died" sandwich board and camped out on the National Mall.

While most evangelical Christians strongly support the war on terror, including the US invasion of Iraq (indeed, as of this writing, evangelicals are among the only voter subgroups left in the country to still support the president's foreign policy), Christian opinion overall varies greatly on the subject. Rather than falling along doctrinal lines, Christians of every stripe seem to hold opinions on this family of issues that reflect their political views, not their religious views. Liberal churches tended to oppose the invasion, conservative Christians tended to support it, and so on down the line.

But in their own opposition to the war in Iraq, America's Leftwing Theocrats would grant a loose coalition of liberal clerical leaders a veritable veto over American foreign policy.

While liberals accuse the Bush administration of instigating a holy war with Islam—"Yes, Virginia, It Is a Holy War," taunts Esther Kaplan[29]—Leftwing Theocrats are swift to point out that a majority of Christian denominations in the United States opposed the war.

Bishop Sharon A. Brown Christopher of the United Methodist Council of Bishops voiced her sect's opposition to the war because "it goes against the very grain of our understanding of the Gospel, our church's teachings and our conscience." The US Episcopal House of Bishops opposed the war on similar grounds. The general secretary of the World Council of Churches called the war "illegal, immoral and unwise."

The message in all of this was not: the United States ought not to invade Iraq; oh and by the way, a bunch of religious leaders think so, too. The message was: the United States ought not to invade Iraq *because* a bunch of religious leaders think so.

In essence, these Leftwing Theocrats conscripted Jesus in a Holy antiwar movement, the rhetoric of which ought to have frightened every Secularite in the Democratic Party. Republicans in Congress were lambasted as theocrats for trying to keep one brain damaged young woman alive. What about these religious leaders who feel empowered to dictate an entire superpower's foreign policy?

This looming fissure between Seculars and Leftwing Theocrats is bound to rip open if the Leftwing Theocrats continue to advance in stature within the Democratic Party. And if the Fakers continue to behave like Seculars but speak like Leftwing Theocrats, the Democrats could have an interesting presidential convention in the next go-round.

If you would like a glimpse at what America's foreign policy would look like under a Leftwing Theocracy, you can, as with the Leftwing Theocrats' economic agenda, look to the presidency of Jimmy Carter. His tenure was the embodiment of Jesus's turn-the-other-cheek pacifism, which He meant for His followers, but not necessarily the state, to employ.

It was during the Carter administration that people began to consider the possibility that the United States might not remain a superpower; that the Soviet Union and its communist governance might be superior after all, and, by the way, is that really so bad?

It was also during the Carter administration that radical Islamic theocrats took over Iran and humiliated the United States during a hostage crisis which, as much as anything, cost Mr. Carter the presidency. This, and Carter's near-ruin of the US economy, is the consequence of interpreting Jesus's teachings to His disciples about the ways they should behave as individual Christians to mean how the government should craft its public policy.

This approach was disastrous during Jimmy Carter's one term as president, and it would be equally disastrous if such an interpretation were to prevail today under Jim Wallis and the Leftwing Theocrats.

GOD'S NEW PARTY?

It is possible that the Secularites are making their last stand as the dominant wing of the Democratic Party, that the Fakers' rhetorical excesses and the Leftwing Theocrats public policy excesses are but embarrassing, though useful, stumbles on their way toward creating a genuine, prophetic Religious Left in America. But that is unlikely.

The Fakers are unlikely to continue their God talk throughout 2006 and 2008. Their voters are not responsive to such talk. Nancy Pelosi represents a congressional district in San Francisco. There, a Republican budget is not unpopular because it is a "sin," but rather because it spends and taxes too little. There, the war in Iraq is unpopular not because a bunch of religious leaders say it offends the gospel, but because George W. Bush is Hitler. At some point, the Fakers will need to pick a political dialect and stick with it. Their natural dialect is liberalese, not God talk.

What's more, there is sufficient evidence that the Leftwing Theocrats are nowhere near as numerous as their powerful political voice might suggest. Jim Wallis's liberal Christian magazine *Sojourners* has a subscription list of twenty-five thousand readers, not an unimpressive number as far as magazine readers go, but neither is it a political movement large enough to overwhelm, say, the highly secular MoveOn.org's 2.5 million. And the pool from which the Leftwing Theocrats can draft their army is shrinking. Liberal denominations in America have bled members for decades, while conservative churches continue to grow.

Finally, the Secularites show no real signs of weakness. During the Supreme Court confirmation battles of John Roberts and Sam Alito, Secularite front groups clearly pulled the strings of liberal senators and set the message agenda for those who were predisposed to reject those two wonderful jurists.

The most likely scenario remains that current trends will continue: the church-going faithful will increasingly vote Republican while the faithless become increasingly liberal, secular, and Democratic.

Some liberals should be commended for reaching out to conservative Christians, such as environmentalists who successfully built a bridge with eighty-six evangelical Christian leaders to form the Evangelical Climate Initiative. In some ways, these secular Earthworshipers treated religious conservatives with more decency and more respect than the conservative pundits who label their role in public life a "myth" and the Republican politicians who rarely keep their promises to them.

But woe unto them who any longer try to win elections by making Christian conservatives into political scapegoats and convenient whipping posts. They are left only to pray for an act of God to alter the political environment to their benefit. And sincerely asking God for guidance is something they are disinclined to do.

NOTES

CHAPTER 1: The New Paranoid Style

1. Peter Slevin, "Classroom Evolution's Grass-Roots Defender," *Washington Post,* 20 July 2005.
2. Martha Rafaele, "School Board Okays Challenges to Evolution," Associated Press, 12 November 2004.
3. "Pennsylvania Parents File First-Ever Challenge to 'Intelligent Design' Instruction in Public Schools," American Civil Liberties Union press release, 12 November 2004.
4. Michelle Goldberg, "The New Monkey Trial," Salon.com, 10 January 2005.
5. Ibid.
6. HB 911, Missouri House of Representatives, 2001.
7. "Judge: Evolution Stickers Unconstitutional," CNN, 14 January 2005.
8. Richard Hofstadter, "The Paranoid Style in American Politics," *Harper's Magazine,* November, 1964, pp. 77–86.
9. Lexington, "The Paranoid Style in American Politics," *Economist,* 5 January 2006.
10. Jeremy Leaming, "Chief Justice Nominee Roberts: He's No John F. Kennedy," The Wall of Separation, official weblog of AU.org, 14 September 2005.
11. Ibid.
12. Patrick Buchanan, Republican National Convention speech, August, 1992.
13. Kevin Mattson, "The Book of Liberal Virtues," *American Prospect,* February 2006.
14. Tom Strode, "ERLC's Land: McCain's Attacks on Christian Leaders 'Despicable,'" Baptist Press, 28 February 2000.

15. William Saletan, "Storming Virginia Beach," *Slate*, 1 March 2000.

16. Warren B. Rudman, *Combat: Twelve Years in the U.S. Senate* (Random House, 1996).

17. Paul Krugman, "What's Going On?" *New York Times*, 29 March 2005.

18. Paul Krugman, "No Surrender," *New York Times*, 4 November 2004.

19. Cal Thomas, "Anti-Christian Bias Characterizes CBS," 25 November 2004.

20. Transcript from 15 February 2005, *Scarborough Country*, MSNBC.

21. Paul Bloom, "Is God an Accident?" *Atlantic Monthly*, December, 2005.

22. Patrick Hynes, "Kathy Sullivan's Comparison of GOP to Taliban Was Far from Funny," *New Hampshire Union Leader*, 23 October 2001.

23. Associated Press, "South Dakota Sen. Tim Johnson Apologizes for Comparing Republicans to 'Taliban,'" 26 May 2004.

24. Greg Pierce, "Democrats to Demonize Christian Conservatives as Being Just Like the Taliban," *Washington Times*, 2 January 2002.

25. Chris Hedges, "The Christian Right and the Rise of American Fascism," Theocracywatch.org, 15 November 2004, http://www.theocracywatch.org/chris_hedges_nov24_04.htm.

26. Colbert I. King, "Hijacking Christianity . . ." *Washington Post*, 23 April 2005.

27. Gregory Paul, "Cross-National Correlations of Quantifiable Societal Health with Popular Religiosity and Secularism in the Prosperous Democracies," *Journal of Religion and Society*, Volume 7, 2005.

28. George Gallup, "Dogma Bites Man," *Touchstone*, December 2005.

29. George Monbiot, "My Heroes Are Driven by God, but I'm Glad My Society Isn't," *Guardian*, 11 October 2005.

30. George Varga, "The Real Deal," *San Diego Union-Tribune*, 15 July 2004.

31. Garry Wills, "Fringe Government," *New York Review of Books*, 6 October 2005.

32. Clint Willis and Nate Hardcastle, eds. *Jesus Is Not a Republican:*

The Religious Right's War on America (Thunder's Mouth Press, 2005).

33. Gary Hart, *God and Caesar in America: An Essay on Religion and Politics* (Fulcrum Publishing, 2005).

34. Hans Bjordahl, "Unhealthy Obsession: The Religious Right's Insatiable Appetite for Hot Gay Porn," *Boulder Weekly*, 20 June 1998.

35. William Fischer, "The Obsession of the Religious Right," *Online Journal*, 3 June 2005.

36. Pete Du Pont, "Gore Carries the Porn Belt," *Opinion Journal*, 10 November 2000.

37. Gary Hart, *God and Caesar in America: An Essay on Religion and Politics* (Fulcrum Publishing, 2005).

38. William Martin, *With God on Our Side* (Broadway, 1996).

CHAPTER 2: In the Beginning

1. "Is America's Faith Really Shifting?" The Barna Update, 24 February 2003.

2. Suzanne Goldenberg, "US Defends Role for Evangelical Christian," *Guardian*, 17 October 2003.

3. Rep. John Conyers, Letter to Defense Secretary Donald Rumsfeld, 17 October 2003.

4. Marty Jezer, "On Anti-Semitism," Common Dreams News Center, 26 April 2002.

5. Chris Mooney, "W's Christian Nation," *American Prospect*, June, 2003.

6. "'Faith-Based' Initiative Threatens Church-State Separation: AU's Lynn Tells Congressional Panel," Americans United for Separation of Church and State press release, 23 March 2004.

7. Bill Press, *How the Republicans Stole Christmas* (Doubleday, 2005).

8. *700 Club* transcript, 22 January 1995.

9. "Religion a Strength and Weakness for Both Parties," PewForum.org, 30 August 2005.

10. "Jefferson's Wall of Separation Letter," The U.S. Constitution Online, http://www.usconstitution.net/jeffwall.html.

11. Thomas Jefferson, "Jefferson's Letter to the Danbury Baptists The Final Letter, as Sent," Library of Congress website,

http://www.loc.gov/loc/lcib/9806/danpre.html.

12. *Wallace v. Jaffree*, 472 US38 (1985), Rehnquist, William dissenting.

13. William Martin, *With God on Our Side* (Broadway, 1996).

14. Bill Press, *How the Republicans Stole Christmas* (Doubleday, 2005).

15. James Hutson, "FBI Helps Restore Jefferson's Obliterated Draft," LC information Bulletin, June, 1998.

16. *McCollum v. Board of Education Dist. 71*, 8 March 1948.

17. *Jefferson's Works*, Vol. 2, p. 217.

18. Kevin Seamus Hasson, *The Right to Be Wrong* (Encounter Books, 2005).

19. Bill Press, *How the Republicans Stole Christmas* (Doubleday, 2005).

20. Michael and Ashley Morrow Novak, "On the Square, February 6, 2006," First Things website, http://www.firstthings.com/onthesquare/?p=172.

21. Joseph Loconte, "James Madison and Religious Liberty," The Heritage Foundation website, www.heritage.org.

22. Kevin Seamus Hasson, *The Right to Be Wrong* (Encounter Books, 2005).

23. Clyde Wilcox, *Onward Christian Soldiers?*, 2nd ed. (Westview Press, 2000).

24. The Pew Research Center for the People & the Press, "Americans Struggle with Religion's Role at Home and Abroad," 20 March 2002.

CHAPTER 3: GOP—God's Own Party?

1. Michelle Goldberg, *Kingdom Coming: The Rise of Christian Nationalism* (W.W. Norton & Company, 2006).

2. *Hinrichs v. Bosma*, 30 November 2005.

3. Rachell Zell, "Alito Would Tip Court to Catholics," Associated Press, 2 November 2005.

4. National Public Radio, "Slate's Jurisprudence: Alito's Hot-Button Issues," 1 November 2005.

5. World Net Daily, "Dean: Democrats 'Going to Use Terri Schiavo,'" 16 April 2005.

6. Bob Burnett, "Republican Morality—Show Me the Money," CommonDreams.org, 30 November 2005.

7. "Religion a Strength and Weakness for Both Parties," Pew-

Forum.org, 30 August 2005.

8. Ezra Stiles Ely, "The Duty of Christian Freeman to Elect Christian Rulers," speech in Philadelphia, 1828.

9. Reuters, "Council of Churches: God Has No Place in U.S. Politics," 4 November 2004.

10. Martin Luther King Sr., "The Most Durable Power," sermon, Montgomery, AL, 6 November 1956.

11. Frederick Douglass, *Narrative of the Life of Frederick Douglass, an American Slave*, Boston, 1845.

12. Frederick Douglass, Letter to William Lloyd Garrison, 27 January 1846.

13. Abraham Lincoln, Second Inaugural Address, 4 March 1865.

14. "Bush God Comments 'Not Literal,'" BBC News, 7 October 2005.

15. Paul Vallely, "Bush's Religious Fanaticism Shaping Our World," *Canberra Times*, October, 2005.

16. Esther Kaplan, *With God on Their Side: How Christian Fundamentalists Trampled Science, Policy, and Democracy in George W. Bush's White House* (The New Press, 2005).

17. Ibid.

CHAPTER 4: 1994

1. Carolyn Lochhead, "Social Security Debate Starts in Earnest Today," *San Francisco Chronicle*, 11 January 2005.

2. Chris Anderson, "Target: Joe Lieberman," Interesting Times blog, 3 February 2005, http://64.233.161.104/search?q=cache:WbuI1tMUnTUJ: interestingtimes.blogspot.com/archives/2005_01_30_interest-ingtimes_archive.html+%22Joe+Lieberman%22+%22Dailykos%22+%22Social+Security%22&hl=en.

3. Susan Page, "Social Security Debate at Stalemate," *USA Today*, 24 April 2005.

4. Guy Teixeira, "Who Deserted the Democrats in 1994?" *American Prospect*, September, 1995.

5. Brian F. Le Beau, "The Political Mobilization of the New Christian Right," The American Religious Experience website, http://are.as.wvu.edu/lebeau1.htm.

6. Joe Conason, "With God as Their Co-Pilot," *Playboy*, March, 1993.

7. Ibid.
8. Ibid.
9. Ibid.
10. Ibid.
11. Greg Goldin, "The 15 Percent Solution: How the Christian Right is Building from Below to Take Over from Above," *Nation*, April, 1993.
12. Ibid.
13. Ibid.
14. Ron Faucheux, "Don Beyer, Mike Farris and the Wizard of Oz," *Campaigns & Elections*, December-January 1993.
15. John C. Green, "The Christian Right and the 1994 Elections," *God at the Grassroots*, eds. Rozell and Wilcox (Rowman & Littlefield Publishers, 1995).
16. Charles S. Bullock and John Christopher Grant, "Georgia: The Christian Right and Grassroots Power," *God at the Grassroots*, eds. Rozell and Wilcox (Rowman & Littlefield Publishers, 1995).
17. Ibid.
18. James Guth, "South Carolina: The Christian Right Wins One," *God at the Grassroots*, eds. Rozell and Wilcox (Rowman & Littlefield Publishers, 1995).
19. Clyde Wilcox, *Onward Christian Soldiers?*, 2nd ed. (Westview Press, 2000).
20. James Zogby, "Democrats and Republicans at War over Religious Right," *Washington Watch*, 18 July 1994.
21. Ibid.
22. Rich Lowry, "Crucifying the Christian Right: Democratic Party Efforts to Combat 1994 Conservative Candidates," *National Review*, 1 August 1994.
23. Esther Kaplan, *With God on Their Side: How Christian Fundamentalists Trampled Science, Policy, and Democracy in George W. Bush's White House* (The New Press, 2005), pp. 270–72.

CHAPTER 5: Janet vs. Mel

1. Linda Chavez, "'Silly' Howard," Townhall.com, 4 February 2004.
2. David Freddoso, "The Leader Is a Liability," *National Review Online*, 8 June 2005.
3. Julia Duin, "'Passion' Critics Retract Reviews," *Washington Times*, 27 February 2004.

4. Leon Weiseltier, "The Worship of Blood," *New Republic*, 26 February 2004.

5. Richard Corliss, "The Goriest Story Ever Told," *Time*, 1 March 2004.

6. World Net Daily, "ADL Director Calls Gibson 'Anti-Semite,'" 19 September 2003.

7. David Edelstein, "Jesus H. Christ," Slate.com, 24 February 2004.

8. "New PTC Study Finds MTV Blatantly Selling Smut to Children," Press release: Parents Television Council, 1 February 2005.

9. Marilyn Brown, "Sex Survey 'Eye Opening' for Parents," *Tampa Tribune*, 11 December 2005.

10. Deborah Orin, "Dirty Trick: Lewd Whoopi Bashes Bush," *New York Post*, 9 July 2004.

11. Ibid.

12. Ibid.

13. Ibid.

14. Edward Helmore, "Kerry's Gold," *Guardian*, 25 January 2004.

15. Maureen Dowd, "Stations of the Crass," *New York Times*, 26 February 2004.

16. Ibid.

17. Ibid.

18. Ibid.

19. Charles Krauthammer, "Gibson's Blood Libel," *Washington Post*, 5 March 2004.

20. Ibid.

21. AndrewSullivan.com, http://www.andrewsullivan.com/index.php?dish_inc=archives/2004_02_22_dish_archive.html

22. "The Politics of Values," *Economist*, 7 October 2004.

23. "Court Dismisses Pledge Case," CNN, 15 June 2004.

24. Charles Lane, "Justices Keep 'Under God' in Pledge," *Washington Post*, 15 June 2004, http://www.washingtonpost.com/wp-dyn/articles/A41802-2004Jun14.html.

25. Ibid.

26. Rob Boston, "One Nation Kept in Suspense," AU.org, http://www.au.org/site/News2?page=NewsArticle&id=6843&abbr=cs_.

27. Ted Olsen (compiler), "Weblog: Supreme Shocker—'Under God'

Stays Because of a Technicality,'" *Christianity Today* website, http://www.christianitytoday.com/ct/2004/124/12.0.html.

28. Bill Mears (contributor), "Court Dismisses Pledge Case," CNN.com, 15 June 2004, http://www.cnn.com/2004/LAW/06/14/scotus.pledge/.

29. Brian Cabell, David Mattingly, and John King (contributors), "Ten Commandments Monument Moved," CNN.com, 4 November 2003, http://www.cnn.com/2003/LAW/08/27/ten.commandments/.

30. Weblog: "Kerry's 'Mainstream' Supporters on Display," AnkleBitingPundits.com, 29 April 2004, http://www.anklebitingpundits.com/index.php?name=News&file=article&sid=621&mode=nested&order=0&thold=0.

31. Esther Kaplan, *With God on Their Side: How Christian Fundamentalists Trampled Science, Policy, and Democracy in George W. Bush's White House* (The New Press, 2005), p. 10.

32. Tom Carver, "Bush Puts God on His Side," BBC News, 6 April 2003, http://news.bbc.co.uk/2/hi/americas/2921345.stm.

33. Rick Perlstein, "The Divine Calm of George W. Bush," VillageVoice.com, 3 May 2004, http://www.villagevoice.com/news/0418,perlstein,53195,1.html.

34. Steven Waldman, "Heaven Sent: Does God Endorse George Bush?" Slate.com, 13 September 2004, http://www.slate.com/id/2106590/.

35. Bill Press, *How the Republicans Stole Christmas* (Doubleday, 2005), p. 14.

36. Rupert Cornwell, "Bush: God Told Me to Invade Iraq," *Independent* Online Edition, 7 October 2005, http://news.independent.co.uk/world/americas/article317805.ece.

37. "Opposition to Gay Marriage Grows," CBSNews.com, 21 December 2003, http://www.cbsnews.com/stories/2003/12/19/opinion/polls/main589551.shtml.

38. "NPR Poll: Gay Marriage Sharply Divides Likely Voters," *Morning Edition,* NPR.org, 26 December 2003, http://www.npr.org/templates/story/story.php?storyId=1567690.

CHAPTER 6: Thirty Million Jesus Freaks Can't Be Wrong

1. "Election Results," CNN.com, 6 April 2004, http://www.cnn.com/ELECTION/2004/pages/results/states/US/P/00/epolls.0.html.

2. Karen Tumulty and Matthew Cooper, "What Does Bush Owe the Religious Right?" *Time*, 7 February 2005.

3. "Moral Values: A Decisive Issue?" CBSNews.com, 3 November 2004, http://www.cbsnews.com/stories/2004/11/03/60II/main653593.shtml.

4. Ibid.

5. Garry Wills, "The Day the Enlightenment Went Out," *The New York Times*, 4 November 2004.

6. Jane Smiley, "The Unteachable Ignorance of the Red States," Slate.com, 4 November 2004.

7. Katha Pollitt, "The Indomitable Question That Plagues Liberals," Slate.com, 5 November 2004.

8. Paul Freedman, "The Gay Marriage Myth," Slate.com, 5 November 2004.

9. Alan I. Abramowitz, "Explaining Bush's Victory in 2004 (It's Terrorism, Stupid!)," *Get This Party Started*, Matthew R. Kerbel, ed. (Rowman & Littlefield, 2006).

10. David Brooks, "The Values-Vote Myth," *New York Times*, 6 November 2004.

11. Jim Wallis, *God's Politics: Why the Right Gets It Wrong and the Left Doesn't Get It* (HarperSanFrancisco, 2005), p. xvi.

12. Charles Krauthammer, "'Moral Values' Myth," *Washington Post*, 12 November 2004.

13. Byron York, *The Vast Left Wing Conspiracy: The Untold Story of How Democratic Operatives, Eccentric Billionaires, Liberal Activists, and Assorted Celebrities Tried to Bring Down a President—and Why They'll Try Even Harder Next Time* (Crown Forum, 2005), pp. 43-44.

14. Anne Schroeder (compiler), "Names and Faces," *Washington Post*, 12 November 2004.

15. New Life Church, Winter/Spring 2006 Small Groups catalogue, p. 104.

16. Ibid., p. 129.

17. Belden, Russonello & Stewart, "The View from Mainstream America: The Catholic Voter in Summer 2004," CatholicVote.net,

July 2004, http://www.catholicvote.net/research_polls/catholic_vote/2004_report/2004_report_full.pdf.

18. Steven Waldman and John C. Green, "Tribal Relations," *Atlantic,* January/February 2006, pp. 136–37.

19. Ibid., pp. 137–38.

20. Glenn Reynolds, Instapundit.com, 9 November 2005, http://instapundit.com/archives/026733.php.

CHAPTER 7: Mere Christians

1. Gene Puskar, "Pat Robertson Calls for Assassination of Hugo Chavez," USAToday.com, 22 August 2005, http://www.usatoday.com/news/nation/2005-08-22-robertson-_x.htm.

2. "Robertson Suggests God Smote Sharon," CNN.com, 6 January 2006, http://www.cnn.com/2006/US/01/05/robertson.sharon/.

3. David R. Francis, "It's True: Churchgoers Are Wealthier," ABC News, 15 November 2005.

4. Anna Greenberg and Jennifer Berktold, Greenberg Quinlan Rosner Research, "Evangelicals in America," p. 2, 5 April 2004, http://www.greenbergresearch.com/articles/1230/757_Evangelicals%20in%20America.pdf.

5. The Barna Group, "Regional Differences," www.barna.org.

6. Ibid.

7. Anna Greenberg and Jennifer Berktold, Greenberg Quinlan Rosner Research, "Evangelicals in America," p. 2, 5 April 2004, http://www.greenbergresearch.com/articles/1230/757_Evangelicals%20in%20America.pdf.

8. Ibid.

9. The Barna Group, "Church Demographics," www.barna.org.

10. Anna Greenberg and Jennifer Berktold, Greenberg Quinlan Rosner Research, "Evangelicals in America," p. 7, 5 April 2004, http://www.greenbergresearch.com/articles/1230/757_Evangelicals%20in%20America.pdf.

11. "Americans Struggle with Religion's Role at Home and Abroad," PewForum.org, March 2002.

12. Ibid.

13. Ibid.

14. Douglas A. Sweeney, *The American Evangelical Story: A History of the Movement* (Baker Academic, 2005), p. 182.

15. The Barna Group, "Church Demographics," www.barna.org.

16. Anna Greenberg and Jennifer Berktold, Greenberg Quinlan Rosner Research, "Evangelicals in America," p. 8, 5 April 2004, http://www.greenbergresearch.com/articles/1230/757_Evangelic als%20in%20America.pdf.

17. The Barna Group, "Church Demographics," www.barna.org.

18. Ibid.

19. David R. Francis, "It's True: Church Goers Are Wealthier," ABC News, 15 November 2005.

20. Anna Greenberg and Jennifer Berktold, Greenberg Quinlan Rosner Research, "Evangelicals in America," p. 10, 25 April 2004.

21. James Zogby, "Washington Watch: McCain and the Debate over the Religious Right," Arab American Institute website, 6 March 2000, http://www.aaiusa.org/wwatch/030600.htm.

22. Bill Berkowitz, "Religious Right on the Ropes," AlterNet.org, 31 October 2001, http://www.alternet.org/story/11840/.

23. Bobby Ross Jr., "Religious Conservatives Lose Ground in Votes," *The Ledger,* 12 November 2005.

CHAPTER 8: I Scream, You Scream, but We Are the Mainstream

1. James R. Edwards Jr., *American Outlook* Magazine website, Summer 2003, http://www.americanoutlook.org/index.cfm?fuse-action=article_detail&id=2995.

2. Dalia Sussman, "Who Goes to Church? Older Southern Women Do; Many Catholic Men Don't," ABCNews.com, 1 March 2002, http://www.abcnews.go.com/sections/us/DailyNews/church_poll 020301.html.

3. Dana Blanton, "More Believe in God Than Heaven," FoxNews.com, 18 June 2004, http://www.foxnews.com/story l/0,2933,99945,00.html.

4. Ibid.

5. Gary Hart, *God and Caesar in America: An Essay on Religion and Politics* (Fulcrum Publishing, 2005), p. 10.

6. Frank Rich, "The God Racket, from DeMille to DeLay," *New York Times,* 27 March 2005.

7. "The politics of values," *Economist,* 7 October 2004.

8. David Kravets, "Newdow Begins His Fight on 'In God We Trust,'" SacUnion.com, 18 November 2005, http://sacunion.com/pages/sacramento/articles/6888.

9. The Barna Group, "How 'Christianized' Do Americans Want Their Country to Be?" www.barna.org, 26 July 2004.

10. *McLean v. Board of Ed. of Arkansas,* US District Court, 5 January 1982, http://www.talkorigins.org/faqs/mclean-v-arkansas.html.

11. *Kitzmiller v. Dover Area School District,* US District Court, 31 December 2005, http://www.talkorigins.org/faqs/dover/kitzmiller_v_dover_decision.html.

12. *Kitzmiller v. Dover Area School District* Trial transcript: Day 7, 6 October 2005, http://www.talkorigins.org/faqs/dover/day7am.html and http://www.talkorigins.org/faqs/dover/day 7am2.html.

13. "Public Divided on Origins of Life," PewForum.org, 30 August 2005.

14. Ibid.

15. Charles Bierbauer (contributor), "Anti Gay Marriage Act Clears Congress," CNN.com, 10 September 1996, http://www.cnn.com/US/9609/10/gay.marriage/.

16. Esther Kaplan, *With God on Their Side: How Christian Fundamentalists Trampled Science, Policy, and Democracy in George W. Bush's White House* (The New Press, 2005), p. 39.

17. "Public Divided on Origins of Life," PewForum.org, 30 August 2005.

18. USA Today/CNN/Gallup poll, CNN.com, 29 September 2003.

19. Andrew Leonard, "This Has Nothing to Do with the Sanctity of Life," Salon.com, 22 March 2005.

20. Bill Press, *How the Republicans Stole Christmas* (Doubleday, 2005).

21. Religious Institute on Sexual Morality, Justice, and Healing, "An Open Letter to Religious Leaders on Abortion as a Moral Decision," 18 January 2005, http://www.religiousinstitute.org/Abortion_OpenLetter.pdf#search='Religious%20Institute%20on%20Sexual%20Morality%2C%20Justice%2C%20and%20Healing%2C%20An%20Open%20Letter%20to%20Religious%20Leaders%20on%20Abortion%20as%20a%20Moral%20Decision'.

22. Transcript, "A Question of Tolerance," PBS.org., 7 August 1996, http://www.pbs.org/newshour/bb/election/august96/abortion_warner_8-7.html.

23. "American Values Poll," Zogby International, 26 August 1999.

24. Ibid.

25. CNN/USA today/Gallup poll, CNN.com, July 1999.

26. James Carville and Paul Begala, *Take It Back: Our Party, Our Country, Our Future* (Simon & Schuster, 2006).

27. Celinda Lake, "The Polls Speak: Americans Support Abortion," *Ms. Magazine* website, Summer 2005, http://www.msmagazine.com/summer2005/polls.asp.

28. Tom Owens, "Veep Candidate Edwards Visits Newton," *Times-Republican* online, http://www.timesrepublican.com/news/story/1012202004_newnews.asp.

29. "GOP the Religion-Friendly Party, but Stem Cell Issue May Help Democrats," PewForum.org, 24 August 2004, http://pewforum.org/docs/index.php?DocID=51.

30. Dalia Sussman, "Majority Opposes Human Cloning Similar Response to Animal and Therapeutic Uses," ABCNews.com, 16 August 2001, http://abcnews.go.com/sections/scitech/DailyNews/poll010816_cloning.html.

31. Bo-Mi Lim, "All Stem Cells Faked in Study," Associated Press, 30 December 2005.

32. "Dean: Democrats 'Going to Use Terri Schiavo,'" *WorldNetDaily*, 16 April 2005, http://www.worldnetdaily.com/news/article.asp?ARTICLE_ID=43840.

33. Frank Rich, "The God Racket, from DeMille to DeLay," *New York Times*, 27 March 2005.

34. Andrew Leonard, "This Has Nothing to Do with the Sanctity of Life," Salon.com, 22 March 2005.

35. Adam Nagourney, "GOP Right Is Split on Schiavo Intervention," *New York Times*, 23 March 2005.

36. Gary Langer, "Poll: No Role for Government in Schiavo Case," ABC News, 21 March 2005.

37. Zogby International, "80%: Non-Terminal Patients Should Not Be Denied Food, Water; Three-to-One: Feeding Tube Should Stay in Place When Wishes Unknown; Americans Divided on Intervention by Elected Officials, Christian Defense Coalition / Zogby Poll of Likely Voters Reveals," Zogby.com, 6 April 2005, http://www.zogby.com/search/ReadNews.dbm?ID=982.

38. Charles Colson, "Evangelical Drift," *Christianity Today*, 29 March 2004.

CHAPTER 9: Onward, Secular Soldiers

1. Decriminalize Private Adult Sexwork Coalition website, www.sexwork.com/coalition.

2. Jimmy Carter, *Our Endangered Values* (Simon & Schuster, 2005), p. 4.

3. Melissa Farley, "Unequal," Coalition Against Trafficking in Women, 30 August 2005.

4. Kevin Mattson, "The Book of Liberal Virtues," *The American Prospect*, February 2006.

5. E.J. Dionne Jr., "Why the Culture War Is the Wrong War," *Atlantic*, January/February 2006.

6. Matthew Wells, "'Religious Bullying' at U.S. Academy," BBC News website, 17 June 2005, http://news.bbc.co.uk/2/hi/americas/4091956.stm.

7. A.O. Scott, "3 People Seduced by the Bloody Allure of the Ring," *New York Times*, 15 December 2004.

8. Frederick and Mary Anne Brussat, "Million Dollar Baby," *Spirituality & Practice*, 9 December 2004, http://www.spiritualityandpractice.com/films/films.php?id=9393.

9. Thomas Frank, *What's the Matter with Kansas?* (Henry Holt, 2004), p. 5.

10. James Carville and Paul Begala, *Take It Back: Our Party, Our Country, Our Future* (Simon & Schuster, 2006), p. 34.

11. George Lakoff, et al., *Don't Think of an Elephant* (Chelsea Green Publishing Company), p. 116.

CHAPTER 10: The Fakers, the Secularites, and the Leftwing Theocrats

1. Tom Krattenmaker, "Playing the 'God' Card," USAToday.com, 29 January 2006, http://www.usatoday.com/news/opinion/editorials/2006-01-29-god-card_x.htm.

2. James Carville and Paul Begala, *Take It Back: Our Party, Our Country, Our Future* (Simon & Schuster, 2006), p. 31.

3. Clint Willis and Nate Hardcastle, eds., *Jesus Is Not a Republican: The Religious Right's War on America* (Thunder's Mouth Press, 2005).

4. Jim Wallis, *God's Politics: Why the Right Gets It Wrong and the Left Doesn't Get It* (HarperSanFrancisco, 2005).

5. Patrick O'Connor, "House GOP Approves Sweeping Spending

Reductions," HillNews.com, 18 November 2005,http://www.hill-news.com/thehill/export/TheHill/News/Frontpage/111705/new-budget.html.

6. Bill Press, *How the Republicans Stole Christmas* (Doubleday, 2005), p. 2.

7. Mark D. Tooley, "Back Down Memory Lane at Berkeley," *Weekly Standard* online edition, 11 October 2005.

8. "Episcopal Church Next to Shun Israel?" WorldNetDaily.com, 24 September 2004, http://www.worldnetdaily.com/news/article.asp?ARTICLE_ID=40603.

9. Jim Wallis, *God's Politics: Why the Right Gets It Wrong and the Left Doesn't Get It* (HarperSanFrancisco, 2005), p. 11.

10. Joseph Bottum, "On the Square," www.firstthings.com, 6 March 2006.

11. George Will, George Will column, *Washington Post,* 17 May 1998.

12. John F. Harris, "Gore Cautions Ending Filibuster," *Washington Post,* 28 April 2005.

13. Stephanie Murphy, "Gore: Country Straying from Principles," *Palm Beach Daily News,* 13 March 2006.

14. James Taranto, "Best of the Web Today," *Opinion Journal* online, 20 December 2005, http://www.opinionjournal.com/best/?id=110007705.

15. Ibid.

16. Deborah White, "Jim Wallis, Evangelical Christian Who Needles Both Democrats & Republicans," About.com, 5 February 2006, http://usliberals.about.com/od/faithinpubliclife/a/JimWallis1.htm.

17. Robert Reich, "Gotta Have Faith," *Why Americans Hate Democrats—A Dialogue* (series), Slate.com, 4 November 2004, http://www.slate.com/id/2109190/.

18. Steven Waldman, "Let's Talk about Faith," *Why Americans Hate Democrats—A Dialogue* (series), Slate.com, 4 November 2004, http://www.slate.com/id/2109267/.

19. Steven Waldman and John C. Green, "Tribal Relations," *Atlantic,* January/February 2006.

20. Ibid.

21. Clint Willis and Nate Hardcastle, eds., *Jesus Is Not a Republican: The Religious Right's War on America* (Thunder's Mouth Press, 2005).

22. Wallis, p. 240.
23. Press, p. 33.
24. Michael Kunzelman, "Religious Groups Pick Up the Slack," Associated Press, 2 March 2006.
25. Wallis, p. 225.
26. Wallis, p. 226.
27. Jimmy Carter, *Our Endangered Values* (Simon & Schuster, 2005), p. 57.
28. Gary Hart, *God and Caesar in America: An Essay on Religion and Politics* (Fulcrum Publishing, 2005), p. 53.
29. Esther Kaplan, *With God on Their Side: How Christian Fundamentalists Trampled Science, Policy, and Democracy in George W. Bush's White House* (The New Press, 2005).

INDEX

1960s, 8, 168–69, 172, 174, 203,206, 210
1970s, 1, 159, 172
1980s, 97, 173, 232
1990s, 104, 107, 159, 170, 174, 221
1994 Election, 27, 81–108, 132,153, 170, 225
2004 Election, 137, 165
   campaign, 50, 82, 108–9, 123, 126, 224
   Catholic vote, 143–44, 159
   Congress, 27
   conservatives/Republicans/Right, 79, 116, 132–33, 137, 142, 152, 154, 162, 216, 228
   exit polls, 79, 126, 129, 132, 150–52
   gay marriage, 125, 152, 185–86
   impact of moral values voters, xi, 5, 72, 126, 129–31, 133, 140, 145, 149, 151, 216, 222, 228
   liberals/Democrats/Left, 8, 10, 17, 116, 125, 132, 135, 140, 144, 185, 192–93, 216, 222–27
   post-election analysis, 127, 129, 132, 137, 146–47, 150–52, 158, 225, 228
   pre-election analysis, 134–35
   pre-election polls, 120
   reactions to, 8, 10, 13, 129
   Ten Commandments, 119
2005 off-year Election, 153–156, 175
60 Minutes, 13

ABC, 18, 180, 196
abortion
advocates, 18, 45, 91, 120, 188–91, 212, 219, 223, 227
and the Bible/Scripture, xiv, 188, 224
and conservative Christians, the Right, x, 12, 95, 102, 153, 188–91, 220, 224
laws, 91, 155, 190, 209–10, 227
and the Left/liberals, xiii, 190, 192–93, 197, 204, 214, 221, 225
drug, Mifepristone, 91
polls/studies regarding, 16, 190
Abramowitz, Alan, 129
Academy of Motion Picture Arts and Sciences, 207
Adams, John, 32
Air America Radio, 88, 136
Alito, Sam, 65–66, 226, 238
al-Qaeda, 121
American Civil Liberties Union (ACLU), 4, 6, 64, 76, 91, 213, 221, 227
American culture, 94, 114, 205
American Prospect, 212
American Society of Newspaper Editors, 178
American Whig Party, 73, 78
Americans Coming Together, 135
Americans United for Separation of Church and State, 4–5, 33, 55, 64, 76, 118–19, 221
Anglican Communion, The, 217–18
"angry white males," 83, 88, 90, 165, 170
Atlantic, 13, 146, 204

Bakker, Jim and Tammy Faye, 173
Barna Group, The, 163, 167, 181
Barone, Michael, 95
Begala, Paul, 190, 210, 215
Berktold, Jennifer, 143, 162, 164, 166–67, 169
Bible, xii, 15, 29, 43, 52, 60, 70, 94, 122, 140, 158–63, 166–67, 188, 216, 224, 228
Bill of Rights, 32, 156
bin Laden, Osama, 14, 30, 123, 126
Black, Hugo, 35, 40–41, 47

Boston, Rob, 187
Bottum, Joseph, 223
Boulder Weekly, 22
Boykin, Lieutenant General, 30
Bradford, William, 50, 57
Braun, Senator Carol Mosley, 186
Bright, Bill, 168
Brokaw, Tom, 161
Brooks, David, 80, 129, 131–32, 147, 150–52
Bullock III, Charles S., 100–1
Bush, George H.W., 10, 103, 191
Bush, George W.
    2000 election, 10, 23, 135, 150
    2004 reelection, 1, 5, 72, 80, 108, 125, 128–30, 132–34, 137–38,
    140–45, 150–53, 223
    and Christians/faith/religion, 13, 18, 20, 24, 32–33, 58, 72, 75–79,
    97–98, 101, 116, 120–24, 127, 130, 133, 138, 143–48, 153, 157,
    159, 175, 187, 203, 231, 235, 237
    governor, 101, 121
    gay marriage, 125, 152–53
    Judge John E. Jones, 184
    the Left/liberals, 8, 75–76, 78, 113, 120–21, 134–37, 149, 196, 217,
    223–24 popularity, 26–27
    Social Security, 84–86, 156
    stem-cell research, 126, 192, 194
    Supreme Court nominations, 65, 189
    theocracy, 18, 21, 187
    War in Iraq, 235, 237

Campolo, Dr. Tony, 218
Campus Crusade for Christ, 168
Carter, Jimmy, 58, 173, 189, 202, 232–34, 236–37
Carville, Jim, 190, 210, 215
Catholic/Catholics
    abortion, 190, 221–22
    anti-, 18, 115, 180–81
    Democrats/liberals, 58, 78, 143, 145, 149, 187, 219–21, 225
    eighteenth century, 53, 55

evolution/natural selection, 178–80, 182–83, 185

"gang of four," 20

John Kerry, 143

John F. Kennedy, 65

John Roberts, 9, 65

President Bush, 120–21, 123, 143–44

priests, ix

Religious Right, 27, 123–24, 133, 144, 146

Samuel Alito, 64–66

social teaching, 219–20

The Da Vinci Code, 19

voting, 124, 130, 133, 143–45, 146, 159, 175

"Catholic Statement of Principles," 219, 225

CBS, 112, 124, 128

Chavez, Hugo, 158

Cheney, Richard, 125

Chicago Tribune, 174

Cho, Margaret, 136

Christian Coalition, x, 95–98, 100–1, 105, 158–59, 174, 221

Christian nation, 29–31, 43, 54, 58, 60–61

Christian radio, 107, 156

Christian Right, 16, 97–98, 100, 102–4, 107, 154, 175, 196, 203, 210

Christianity Today, 106

Christmas, 34, 64, 95, 213

Church of England, 44–45, 54–56, 63

Clergy and Laity Concerned, 217

Clinton cabinet, 89–90, 92, 96

Clinton, Bill, 10, 43, 60, 86–87, 89–96, 98–99, 105, 134, 174, 186, 189, 209, 225

Clinton, Hillary, 26, 191

Cloning, 188, 192–94, 196, 207-08

CNN, 118–19, 186

Colson, Chuck, xii, 201–2

Conason, Joe, 97–99, 103

Constitution, 22, 32–37, 39–40, 42, 44, 46–49, 51–53, 55–56, 66, 77, 98, 118–19, 124, 152, 181, 184, 186

Contract with America, 88, 92–93

D'Onofrio, Vincent, 136

Danbury Baptist Association, 35, 37, 40–41

Darwin, Charles/Darwinian evolution, 2–4, 178–79, 182–84

Dawkins, Richard, 183

Dean, Howard, 26, 66, 79, 81, 83, 110, 113, 153, 195, 211–12, 216, 222

Declaration of Independence, 32–33, 51, 56

Decriminalize Private Adult Sexwork Coalition, 202

Deists/Deism, 41, 51, 53–54, 69

Democratic National Committee (DNC), 105, 216

Dionne Jr., E.J., 204–05

Dixie Chicks, 134, 136

Dobson, Dr. James, x, xii, 35, 45, 118, 147, 157, 160, 162, 184, 229, 232

Dominion Theology, 198

Douglass, Fredrick, 74

Dowd, Maureen, 114–15

Economist, 8, 19, 116

Edwards v. Aquillard, 209

Eisenhower, Dwight, 123

Elders, Joycelyn, 89–91, 105

Ely, Ezra Stiles, 70

embryonic stem-cell research, 126, 192–96, 207–08

Epperson v. Arkansas, 209

Era of Good Feeling, 68

Evangelical Climate Initiative, 219, 238

evangelicals, xiii, 12–14, 20, 24, 27, 31, 55, 78, 95–96, 101, 103, 107, 120–24, 128, 130, 133, 138–43, 145–47, 150–52, 155–56, 159, 162–69, 171–72, 175, 177, 184, 187, 201, 204, 206–7, 217, 220–21, 223, 227, 237–38

National Association of, x, xii

"Evangelicals in America," 162

exit polls, 80, 102, 126, 129, 132, 150–51, 153, 177, 182, 187–88

Fahrenheit 9/11, 116, 134

Fakers, 26, 215, 222–226, 228, 236–37

Falwell, Jerry, x, xii, 11, 13, 105, 157, 159–61, 173, 198, 230

Family Research Council, xii, 26–27, 198, 220
Farley, Melissa, 202
Federal Marriage Amendment, 81, 131, 152
Feinstein, Dianne, 9, 65–66
Fisk, Kyle, xii, 157, 199
Focus on the Family, x, xii, 71, 78, 96, 160–62, 165, 198
Fonda, Jane, 19, 91
Founding Fathers, 30, 32–33, 35, 41, 44, 51
Frank, Thomas, 13, 169, 210
Franken, Al, 88, 142
Franke-Ruta, Garence, 212
Freedman, Paul, 129
Frist, Bill, 81

Gallup Jr., George H., 16
Gallup poll, 16, 118–19
Garofalo, Janeane, 136
gay marriage/same-sex marriage, xiii–xiv, 80, 124–25, 131, 152, 155, 185–86, 202, 206, 209, 211–12, 227
Gibson, Mel, 110–11, 114, 116
Gingrich, Newt, 86–88, 93
Ginsberg, Ruth Bader, 91
God, 16, 233–34
    believers in, 8, 54, 116, 162, 166, 172, 178, 180, 183, 187, 198
    creation, 219, 224, 233
    Democrats/Left/liberals, 216–18, 219, 221–23, 225, 234, 237–38
    God's children, xv
    GOP, 63, 72, 82
    the name of, 17, 118
    playing God, 194
    role in early American history, 29, 36–38, 43, 48–49, 52, 57–58, 75–78
    role in modern government, 29, 50, 59–60, 71–72, 74–78, 121–23, 128, 160, 183–84 Son of, xii
    "under God," 22, 60, 117–19, 124, 180–82
    Word of, xii, 140, 198
God's Politics, 129, 216
GoDaddy.com, 109
Goldberg, Michelle, 5, 198

Goldberg, Whoopi, 113
Goldin, Greg, 98, 99, 103
Goldwater, Barry, 168
Gore, Al, 23, 143, 224
Graham, Billy, 172
Gramm, Phil, 186
Grant, John Christopher, 100–1
"Great Backlash, The," 210
Green, John C., 100, 144–52, 226
Greenberg, Anna, 142, 160, 162, 164–65, 167
Griswold v. Connecticut, 209
Gruber, Jonathan, 170
Guth, James L., 102

Haffner, Debra, 219
Haggard, Ted, x, xii, 142, 160–61, 163, 204, 232
Hannity, Sean, 88
Hart, Senator Gary, 16, 21, 23–24, 179–80, 205, 234
Hasson, Kevin Seamus, 43, 56
Hill, 216
Hitler, Adolph, 15, 21, 136–37, 237
Hoffman, Abbie, 172
Hofstadter, Richard, 7, 8
Hollywood, 8, 17, 89, 94–95, 104, 113, 135, 195, 206–08
Holy Spirit, the, 73–74
Hussein, Saddam, 21, 121, 128
Hutson, James, 40

"In God We Trust," 29, 50, 180–82
Intelligent Design, 2–6, 19, 183–84, 188
Interfaith Alliance, 15
InterVarsity Fellowship, 169
Iraq, 2, 27, 76–77, 79, 121, 123, 126–28, 138, 161, 190, 219, 237–39
Israel, Rep. Steve, 205

Jackson, Janet, 109, 111–14, 116, 119
Jefferson, Thomas, 33, 35, 37–46, 48–53, 55–56, 63, 67–71, 81
Jesus, xii, 18–19, 21, 31, 33, 42, 64, 70, 73, 105–6, 111, 114, 127, 140,

163, 170–71, 179, 205, 208, 215–16, 229–31, 233, 235–36
jihad, 14, 128, 196, 228
Job, 222
Johnson, Senator Tim, 14–15
Journal of Religion and Society, 16

Kaine, Tim, 156
Kaplan, Esther, 77, 107, 121, 187, 235
Kennedy, Pres. John F., 9, 65–66
Kerry, Senator John, 1, 79–80, 108, 110, 113–14, 122, 125, 128, 133,
    138, 143–45, 147–50, 152, 157, 191, 193, 225
Kerry, Teresa Heinz, 114
Kerry-Edwards campaign 1, 113–14
King, Martin Luther, 58, 72, 173
Kinsey, Dr. Alfred, 208
Kinsley, Michael, 31, 128
Kitzmiller, et al. v. Dover Area School District, 4
Knight Ridder, 175
Krauthammer, Charles, 80, 115, 130–32, 147, 152
Kristof, Nicholas, 178–79
Krugman, Paul, 12–13

Lake, Celinda, 191
Lakoff, George, 211–12
Lawrence v. Texas, 210
Leftwing Theocrats, 215, 222, 226, 239–30, 232–37
Lerner, Michael, 217
Limbaugh, Rush, 18, 88, 98
Lincoln, Abraham, 11, 60, 75–78, 81
Lowman, Leon, 161–62
Lowman, Venezia, 161–62
Lynn, Rev. Barry, 4, 33–34, 118–19

Madison, James, 33, 44–47, 49–52, 55–56, 63, 68–69, 81
Mantilla, Yuri, 162
"March for Women's Lives, The," 120
Martin, William, 25, 39
Massachusetts Supreme Court, 124–25, 131, 210

Mattson, Kevin, 10, 203
Mayflower Compact, 57,
McCain, Senator John, 10–12
McClusky, Tom, 220
McCollum v. Board of Education, 40–41
McKinney, Rep. Cynthia, 225
megachurch phenomenon, x, xiii, 139, 164, 167
Meier, Dr. Bill, 198
"Memorial and Remonstrance against Religious Assessments, A," 45
Message Group, the, 2, 6–8, 19, 24, 25, 63
Miers, Harriet, 65, 187
Million Dollar Baby, 207
Monroe, James, 68–69
Moore, Michael, 116, 134
Moore, Chief Justice Roy, 119, 210
Moral Majority, x, 158–59
Moral Values
    Democrats, 67, 71, 130, 145, 216, 222
    decline in, 106
    emphasis on, 69, 71
    myth, xi, 27, 129–30, 151, 180
    Republican, 26, 84
    vote/voters, 5, 13, 27, 80, 126–32, 145, 151, 180
MoveOn.org, 77, 134–36, 138, 142, 146, 224, 237
Moyers, Bill, 198
MTV, 111–12

Nagler, Michael, 217
Nation, 77, 98
National Association of Evangelicals (NAE), x, xii, 157, 160, 163, 199, 204–05
National Bureau of Economic Research, 162, 170
National Council of Churches, 216
National Public Radio, 50, 65, 125
National Review, 17
National Right to Life Committee, 11
NBC, 17–19, 136, 161
"neoconservatives," 80

Neuhaus, Fr. Richard John, 20–21, 229
New Life Church, xii, 140, 142, 161, 167, 204
New Republic, 22, 110
New Testament, 69, 222
New York Times, 9, 12, 15, 18, 21, 50, 80, 114, 124, 129, 131, 178–79, 207
Newdow, Michael, 60, 64, 117–18, 181–82
Newsweek, 15, 19
NFL, 112
Ninth US Circuit Court of Appeals, 117–18, 181–82, 206
Nordhaus, Ted, 212
North, Col. Oliver, 102

O'Beirne, Kate, 143
Old Testament, 222

Parents Television Council, 112
Passion of the Christ, The, 110–11, 114–16, 119, 207
Paul, Pope John II, 143
Pax Christi, 217
Pelosi, Nancy, 83, 85–6, 216, 224, 228, 237
People for the American Way, 106, 227
Peter D. Hart Research, 106
Pew Forum on Religion & Public Life (Pew Research Center), 60, 67, 120, 150–51, 185, 187, 193–94, 199
Pfaff, Jim, 71, 78, 96
Phelps, Fred, 159–60
Planned Parenthood, 201
Pledge of Allegiance, 15, 29, 60, 117–18, 181–82
Pollitt, Katha, 128, 138
Pope Joan, 18
praying/prayer, xiv, 14, 19, 38, 42, 50–51, 53, 60, 69, 76, 121–23, 138–39, 142–43, 146–47, 166–67, 173, 205, 216, 230, 233, 238
premillennial dispensationalism, 198–99
Presbyterian Church USA, 217
Press, Bill, 34, 39, 44, 122, 188, 216, 231–32
Promise Keepers, 106, 174
Prostitution, Trafficking and Traumatic Stress, 202

Quayle, Marilyn, 180

Reagan, Ronald, 11, 96–97, 102, 111, 133–34, 159, 168
"Red Letter Christians," 218, 221
Reed, Ralph, 105
Reich, Robert, 89, 128, 225
Religion News Service, 154
Religious Institute on Sexual Morality, Justice and Healing, 188
Republican National Committee, 114
Republican Revolution, 170
Reynolds, Glenn, 154, 156
Rich, Frank, 16, 179–80, 196
Roberts, John, 9, 65–66, 226–27, 238
Robertson, Pat, xii, 11–13, 18, 34, 95, 97–98, 157–61, 173–74, 198, 230
Robinson, Gene, 208, 218
Rolling Stone, 114
Ronstadt, Linda, 17
Roosevelt, Pres. Franklin, 58, 60
Rove, Karl, 20, 138
Rudman, Warren, 12

Saletan, William, 11
Salon, 5, 187, 196, 198
Schiavo, Terri, xiv, 12, 66, 154, 195–97, 207, 210, 217, 228
Schlafly, Phyllis, 173
Schwarzenegger, Arnold, 153
Scott, A.O., 207
Scripture, xi, xiv, 42, 120, 140, 144, 146–47, 222–23, 233
Second Great Awakening, 68–69, 73, 81
Secularites, 215, 222, 226–28, 230, 237–38
Sekou, Osagyefu Uhuru, 217
separation of church and state, 9, 22, 33, 45, 55, 66
September 11 (9/11), 14, 123
Sexual Behavior in the Human Male, 208
Shaath, Nabil, 76–77
Shalala, Donna, 89, 91
Sharon, Ariel, 158

Shays, Rep. Chris, 196
Shellenberger, Michael, 212
Slate, 11, 111, 122, 128
slavery, 68, 71–76, 78–79
small groups, 139–42, 148
Snowe, Senator Olympia, 189
Social Security, 2, 80, 84–87, 156
socialized healthcare, 86
Sojourners, 229, 237
Soros, George, 134–35, 142
Spirituality & Practice, 207
Sprigg, Peter, xii, 198
state constitutions, 32, 48, 58, 125, 186
Stenberg v. Carhart, 209
Subsidiarity, 220
Sullivan, Kathy, 14
Super Bowl, 109–11
Supreme Court, The, 22, 29, 35, 40, 50, 65–66, 91, 117–18, 124–25,
    131, 181, 183, 187, 207, 209–10, 226, 238
Swaggart, Jimmy, 173

Take It Back, 191
Taliban, 14
Taranto, James, 224
Teixiera, Ruy, 92
Ten Commandments, 50, 95, 119, 124, 180–82, 210
Terrorism, 127–28, 131
theocracy, xi, 18–21, 25, 63, 66–67, 143, 189, 198, 200, 221, 224, 227,
    230, 238
theocrats, xiv, 9, 15, 21, 45, 186, 217, 223–24, 228, 230–39
theophobes, 32–34, 40, 42, 44–45, 49–53, 55, 60, 72, 81, 118–19, 229
Timberlake, Justin, 109
Time, 111, 127
Tooley, Mark, 217
Truman, Harry, 58

"under God," 22, 60, 117–19, 124, 180–82
Ungerer, Dale, 223

US Air Force Academy, 205

Village Voice, 121
Virginia Bill on Religious Freedom, 44–45
Virginia Mafia, 67–68
Vote for Change Tour, 134

Waldman, Steven, 122, 146–47, 149, 225–26
Wall Street Journal, 23
Wallis, Jim, 129, 131–32, 147, 158–59, 215–16, 222, 225, 229–34, 237
Washington, George, 53–55, 58, 67
Washington Post, 1, 13, 15, 117, 136, 170
Washington Times, 19
Weekly Standard, 217
Weisskopf, Michael, 13, 170
What's the Matter with Kansas?, 13, 169
Wilcox, Clyde, 59, 103
Will, George, 179
Willis, Clint, 21, 215, 229
Wills, Garry, 20, 128
Wolfe, Alan, 154, 156, 175, 199
Woo-suk, Hwang, 192–94
World Can't Wait, 18
World Council of Churches, 71, 216–17, 235

York, Byron, 134–35
Youth for Christ, 169

Zogby, Dr. James, 104, 174
Zogby, John, 120, 197